# The Education
# of Mrs. Henry Adams

"Who shall set a limit to
the influence of a human being?"
Ralph Waldo Emerson

# The Education
# of Mrs. Henry Adams

*Eugenia Kaledin*

University of Massachusetts Press
Amherst

*For Catherine Oster*
*&*
*Elizabeth Kaledin*

Originally published by Temple University Press, 1981
The University of Massachusetts Press paperback edition published 1994
Copyright © 1981 by Temple University
Preface to the University of Massachusetts Press paperback edition
copyright © 1994 by Eugenia Kaledin
All rights reserved
Printed in the United States of America
ISBN 0–87023–913–9
LC 93–44278

Library of Congress Cataloging-in-Publication Data
Kaledin, Eugenia.
    The education of Mrs. Henry Adams / Eugenia Kaledin.
    p.  cm.
    Previously published: Philadelphia : Temple University Press,
1981.
    Includes bibliographical references and index.
    ISBN 0–87023–913–9 (alk. paper)
    1. Adams, Marian, 1843–1885.  2. Adams, Henry, 1838–1918.
3. Historians' spouses—United States—Biography.  4. Historians—
United States—Biography.  I. Title.
CT275.A34K34   1994
973'.07202—dc20
[B]                                                             93–44278
                                                                  CIP
British Library Cataloguing in Publication data are available.

This book is published with the support and cooperation of the University of
Massachusetts at Boston.

# Contents

# Photographs

# Acknowledgments

This manuscript was first read by John Malcolm Brinnin, whose many suggestions strengthened it considerably. Millicent Bell and Norman Pettit of the Boston University English department contributed valuable critical reactions and encouragement. Eugene Goodheart added a number of wise and useful observations. The editorial staff working on the Henry Adams letters at the University of Virginia—Ernest and Jayne Samuels, J. C. Levenson, Charles Vandersee, and Viola Winner—immeasurably enriched the background of my work and helped me to augment and authenticate many details.

The Adams family papers of the Adams Manuscript Trust, specifically microfilm reels 590 through 599, were courteously provided by the staff at Lamont Library, Harvard University, and were a prime source of material on all members of the Adams family.

Miscellaneous Adams papers, including Clover Adams' letters still in the process of being microfilmed, as well as all her photographs still in family albums, were made available by Stephen Riley and, later, by Louis L. Tucker and the helpful staff at the Massachusetts Historical Society: Winifred Collins, Aimee Bligh, Gertrude Fischer, and Molly Collingwood. Prints of Clover's photographs were supplied by Ross Urquhart and Stephen J. Kovacik. The Massachusetts Historical Society also generously provided the Dwight, Shattuck, and Gilman Papers mentioned in this study.

Various letters were culled from the E. L. Godkin, Samuel Gray Ward, and Henry James Collections at

Houghton Library, Harvard University. Here, I examined the work of Louisa Catherine Adams, which was copied and edited by Henry Adams. Permission to quote from the letters of Henry James was generously granted by Leon Edel.

Alumni records and obituaries were helpfully provided by the staff at the Harvard Archives.

Material on the founding of Radcliffe College was made available at both the Schlesinger Library at Radcliffe, and the Massachusetts Historical Society.

The published *Letters of Mrs. Henry Adams*, which were edited by Ward Thoron with great diligence, provided clarifying references to the personalities and political issues touching the Adamses. They should be read by all scholars seeking to know the day-to-day details of the Adamses' life together. Of particular interest are the appendices the Thorons added, which present contemporary issues as Henry Adams' circle of friends saw them.

Family papers of Edward (Ned) Hooper's daughters, which include many of the unpublished poems and letters of Ellen Sturgis Hooper and a large number of letters from her Aunt Caroline Sturgis, are the foundation of this book. These materials were conscientiously gathered and organized over the years by Louisa Hooper Thoron, the unofficial historian of Henry Adams. Mrs. Thoron kept many family treasures as well, including Clover Adams' library, one of her Worth dresses, and some of the Hooper art collection. Her memoir of her Uncle Henry, at the Massachusetts Historical Society, remains a valuable personal tribute to his involvement in their family affairs.

Clover's childhood correspondence is also included in these family papers. Faith Thoron Knapp and Mary Potter Swann generously made all this material available without restrictions. The interpretations that appear here, however, should not be considered representative of family opinion.

Ellen Sturgis Hooper's privately published volume of

poetry was provided by the Treasure Room of the Boston Public Library.

The unpublished letters of Ellen Emerson concerning the Agassiz School were graciously offered for my perusal by Edith W. Gregg.

Bennett Simon's class in Psychoanalytic Theory for the Social Scientist at the Boston Psychoanalytic Institute supplied ideas and useful bibliographies, as did the late William Binstock's more advanced class, Psychoanalysis and the Human Sciences, taught with Jean Elshtain. Dr. Edmund C. Payne, also of the Institute, read some of my manuscript and shared his insights with me.

The unpublished doctoral dissertation of Sister M. Aquinas Healy, "A Study of Non-Rational Elements in the Works of Henry Adams as Centralized in his Attitude Toward Women," which provided a thorough catalog and analysis of all of Henry Adams' references to women, was invaluable to me.

The scholars of Henry Adams' life and works, specifically Edward Chalfant, Ernest Samuels, and Charles Vandersee, have been most helpful with suggestions and advice about materials. I have felt myself fortunate to be able to profit from their much greater knowledge and experience of the Adamses.

It goes without saying that any work that mentions Henry Adams must be indebted to the lucid and painstaking three-volume biography by Ernest Samuels. Without this solid foundation of necessary scholarly detail, I would have had to write a much narrower study. Perhaps the same debt should be acknowledged to Leon Edel for any work that even mentions Henry James. The enormously comprehensive biographies these men have written have made it possible for different kinds of scholars to pursue more specialized ideas with the security of knowing that there are nets of fact to fall back on when daring fails. If the act of writing biography ends up—for even the best of us—as "somehow practically thinning," it is not, in the case of Clover Adams, because there has been a scarcity of excellent background material.

I owe much to a number of encouraging individuals: to David Hall, who invited me back into the world of ideas; to Nicholas and Jonathan Kaledin, who cheered me on; to my friends Claire Sherman and Mona Harrington, who became scholarly examples; and to Grace Clark, who always provided more than perfect typing. Without the constant support—in every sense—of Arthur Kaledin, this book could not have been written.

My debt to many women—students and teachers, librarians and editors, poets and scholars, and more militant feminists—I cannot begin to measure by listing names. I consider myself fortunate to be part of a moment in history that encouraged women to examine their own lives.

# Preface

In a letter to her father, Marian Adams (always called "Clover" by the people closest to her) included a newspaper clipping on a new novel by Alphonse Daudet. The novel was distinguished, the journalist wrote, for providing "the history of those who would otherwise have no history." When I started this book, it was to provide Clover Adams with such a history.

That her husband, Henry Adams, had written the story of his life without mentioning his marriage seemed unjust to me. For marriage, even if unsuccessful (which the Adams marriage was not), must contribute some dimension to any human being struggling to define education in a more complex way. Many critics simply ignore the omission, or attempt to account for it on the level of Victorian conventions. But Henry Adams strongly resists conventional classifications; his individuality continually challenges biographers to fathom his special complexity. He seems to force readers to adopt his own kind of circumspection in order to detect the powerful reality of his wife, the woman who provided him, he said, with the twelve richest years of his life. Once we discover Clover Adams' outlines, however, she continues to look out at us from Henry Adams' thought—like the puzzle drawings of hidden faces in treetops. We cannot stop seeing her; her presence dominates all of his later work.

I have tried to clarify the ideas that she represented by showing to what extent her world and her experiences growing up were quite different from Henry's. I have tried to underline the importance of her connections with the Transcendental community that encouraged the idealism that Henry Adams, while he pretended to be scientific, could never bring himself entirely to reject. When he later wrote, in the story of his own education, that he had once approached the Transcendental world of Concord "in much the same spirit as he would have entered a Gothic Cathedral," he seemed to outline precisely the form his personal spiritual search had taken; the Gothic cathedral came to represent for him that unobtainable Utopian vision connected with an entire community's awareness of non-rational values. After knowing more about Clover Adams' own intellectual background, no reader of *The Education of Henry Adams* should approach the book without seeing how much her own connections must have shaped Henry's changing vision of the world he had once uncritically accepted.

Although I have attempted to make Clover a "representative" woman of her time and place, just as she attempted to make many of her own contemporaries "representative" with her camera, I have found, paradoxically, that her most representative quality is her eccentricity. Clover Adams does not fit any more neatly into the patterns of conventional genteel behavior after the Civil War than Henry Adams does. She is never—if she can help it—submissive, pious, domestic, or partisan, in any conventional sense. She deliberately disavowed a ladies magazine definition of womanhood, no matter how extensively she may have been aware of genteel proprieties, or how much she was torn by her own ambivalence toward them. The irreverent spirit of Transcendentalism permeated her soul leaving her rootless and unaffiliated, intellectually free and committed to uncommitment. Like the nineteenth-century characters Edmund Wilson wrote about in connection with the Civil War, her individual voice remains so intense that we can almost hear her speak as we read the weekly letters she wrote from Washington or Europe to her father in Boston. Hers was a deliberately defiant personality that managed to enjoy the richness of the life she and Henry Adams were

wealthy enough to choose; yet she never forgot the standards of the Boston reformers she knew as a child. The
New England tradition of self-criticism first grew more
deeply in Clover than it did in Henry.

If Clover's life is to be valuable as a metaphor, it must
be as a metaphor beyond her own time and place. It must
suggest a number of the paradoxes that continue to
haunt American civilization: that the failure of status and
wealth to provide personal fulfillment remains as much a
part of our heritage as the dream of success; that the freedom of spirit we cherish may finally become enslavement
to lack of commitment; that an individual's concern for
seeking out and cultivating the *best* in American life can
end up alienating the most passionate democrat from his
political roots, and, ultimately, from society as a whole.
In Clover Adams' story, opportunities and limitations,
satisfactions and disillusionments often appear to be balanced. Her experiences provide few occasions, if any, to
draw simple conclusions about the meaning of her life.

That her close friend Henry James saw Clover not
as a representative woman, nor as a representative
nineteenth-century figure, but as a representative American, must give us reason to go on thinking about the
necessary complexity involved in restoring the life of
"Mrs. Henry Adams" to history, not only as a living individual but also as a moving symbol of the ambiguities of
our culture.

# Preface to Paperback Edition

**W**hat Clover Hooper did to liberate the imagination of Henry Adams, a number of new historians and culture critics are now doing to enrich our vision of America. During the decade since this book first appeared a new generation of thinkers has entered the historical establishment. An intellectual world once overwhelmingly committed to European roots and linear descriptions of political and military events as the only subjects worth serious study, now listens to the voices of Native Americans and to strangers from other shores. And it now includes the vitality of women as a shaping force in our history. Many imaginative culture historians now "reinvent" lives previously defined only by white male definitions of power and by traditional choices of documentary materials. Investigators with broad vision have begun to establish myths and oral sources as well as journals and personal letters as being as important as legal treaties and battle maps in helping clarify the rich texture of the American past. And new interpretations of American lives have even begun to validate honest discussion of human passions.

Because of the brave speculations of a number of serious women thinkers whose theories have often been scorned as too far-fetched, new angles of vision are opening to extend the narrow records of our past. Many previously invisible personalities and unrecorded events are emerging from the shadows to force us all to ask important new questions about American values.

Although the decade from 1980 to 1990 was liberating for

different historical viewpoints, where the Adams family is concerned, conflicts of vision existed from the beginning. Mercy Otis Warren's 1805 history of the American Revolution* was immediately attacked by John Adams for misrepresentation. A good friend of Abigail Adams, Warren did not hesitate to publish criticism of her friend's husband for pride and pomposity; John retaliated with assertions of inaccuracy. He thought it outrageous that a woman should dare to write history at all and he accused her of presumption of talent for putting pen to paper "with so imperfect information" and "so little impartiality." Mercy Warren was properly silenced; her comments on Adams' arrogance wiped out. How many Americans today know that a contemporary woman's history of the American revolution ever existed? In a society committed to the open discussion of ideas, silence remains the ultimate weapon.

Since the 1970s many elegant books have described different ways writers may be silenced and people wiped out of history. Restoration has begun. Some invisible women like Sally Hemings, Jefferson's slave, have been seen for the first time from a woman's point of view; some, like the midwife Martha Ballard, have finally been interpreted seriously; and one pioneer gender theorist, Mary Beard—perhaps now considered the equal of her husband—has had her earlier work re-issued. Not reviewing books and letting them go out of print, as Mary Beard's had, are especially effective ways to silence differences. As more and more books disappear into underground storage so that libraries have room on their shelves for what is momentarily deemed important, we must be more conscious of which records we want to see survive into the technological future. Interpretations of history not only characterize the past, they also shape the future versions of American civilization. The power to describe the world, Adrienne Rich once suggested, may be the ultimate power.

Because the Adams men have clearly been part of the political power structure, their wives have commanded

---

*History of the Rise, Progress, and Termination of the American Revolution (3 vols.)

historical attention. The letters of Mercy Warren's friend Abigail Adams have been considered a valuable record of the American past, yet these letters were not taken any more seriously as feminist documents by historians than they were by her husband. Abigail's concerns for women's rights were treated as mere banter. When the family published the first edition of Abigail's letters they also silenced her in a different way, they deleted passages reflecting signs of her depressions. Many past historians have had difficulty interpreting women as they are, not as these interpreters wanted them to be. Honest historical models of complex individual women are still not plentiful.

Until quite recently most women have assented to the history male historians wanted told. How could they not? Who trained them? Who defined their social roles? The Adams women, even when their despair has been acknowledged, tend to be stereotyped like characters in romance: the uppity bright ones, the neurotic complainers, the malingerers, the contented domestics, or the sharp-tongued shrews. A dominant idea in much of the writing about these women is the glory of connection with powerful men. Perhaps the nature of recording history—itself vicarious power—has made the satisfactions of such connections particularly important. Certainly many women would still value them highly; the colossal achievements of Eleanor Roosevelt remain testimony to how creative connections can become. But a new group of scholars has taken over the interpretation of our past. Looking more deeply at what women want, we have begun to consider the complexity of women as individuals on their own terms. And we are also using more varied materials to do so.

Clover Adams is such a complex woman. Left out of her husband's life story, she will not be found amid the bills for hay and the banquet menus preserved for posterity on the great collection of Adams microfilms. Of course, what the Adams family thought of her is there, along with many of her letters. But these items reveal only a partial record of who she was. Writers of biography need, as Leon Edel has urged, to look for the figure under the carpet as well as the obvious pattern on top. To know who Clover was, we need to read the political speeches of her China-trader grandfather William Sturgis and the poetry of her mother Ellen Hooper published in the Transcendental magazine *The Dial*, next to Margaret Fuller's first version of "Woman in the Nineteenth Century." We need to know the impassioned letters her Aunt Carrie Sturgis wrote to Ralph Waldo Emerson about women's rights and women's education. And we need to know the ideas of Emerson, "the apostle" of Clover Hooper's youth. To understand the rich texture of Clover's background we should also visit the Boston Museum of Fine Arts to look at the dazzling Japanese prints her Buddhist cousin donated to the museum and we should note how many distinguished American paintings in that institution were also given to the public by her brother. American historians—like American politicians—have tended to ignore altogether the importance of the arts as a shaping force. It is all too easy for outsiders again to dismiss or exaggerate differences between complicated social groups. How many biographers of the Washington society lives of Clover and Henry Adams have also considered the serious impact on Clover of her reformer cousin, Josephine ("Effie") Lowell?

Josephine Shaw Lowell, one of America's great philanthropists, was one attachment Clover tried to keep. Lowell, the first woman appointed to the state board of charities in New York, had been, like Clover's father and brother, involved in the Freedmen's Bureau helping slaves get established after the Civil War. She went on to found the New York Consumers' League, The Women's Municipal League, and the Civil Service Reform Association. Her busy schedule left her little time to be part of Clover's life. But although Henry Adams did not like reformers he did not criticize war-widow-cousin Effie, as he had Transcendental Aunt Carrie. Effie Lowell remained a sporadic presence in Clover's correspondence. Did she make Clover wonder about what options would have been available for her own life under less confining circumstances?

What I was trying to discover when I wrote this book was how an intelligent woman found expression in a world of simultaneous freedom and social confinement. What John Adams would have said of a woman's presumption in trying to write an intellectual biography of another woman we can imagine. I saw the hostess part Clover played so well, not primarily as a social role but as an educational one; and I never found her "sharp tongue" as nasty as the words of the Adams men. Yet there is no doubt that she was a critical thinker. Writing about Effie Lowell who translated social concerns into actions would have been easier than trying to understand the tensions Clover faced in her world of influence, but I thought it more important to try to articulate a serious woman's struggle to make use of her mind. Few biographical models of American women as social or cultural critics were available when I began writing; Henry Adams' historical contempt for "bluestockings" remained very much alive.

Clover's attachment to her reformer cousin suggests that she well understood the power of active commitment, but more like her intensely intellectual husband, she valued uncommitted analysis. Like Abigail Adams, Clover Adams made her letters a social and intellectual critique of her Washington and European worlds. Writing to her father regularly, she was claiming the right to define culture on her own terms as Emerson had urged all Americans to do. Hardly frivolous, Clover appeared happiest when Henry allowed her to help with his translations or research. I hoped my emphasis on her education and intellect would tempt teachers of gender history and psychology to make comparisons of her experiences with the proprietary life her husband complained about in *The Education of Henry Adams*.

In a country beset by anti-intellectualism, it may be true that thinking men have also found it hard to take themselves seriously as culture critics, but *The Education of Henry Adams* remains in most college curriculums. Many readers still react strongly to Henry's descriptions of himself and his friends, "the best and brightest," as failures in the contest of American life. We cannot ignore the reality that these friends, and Adams himself, were all given serious educations and professional skills. And every social institution encouraged them all to use their training and intellects. By contrast, the education that most women received was not focused in any way. It gave with one hand and took away with the other. Clover Adams might well have protested, as Margaret Fuller, her Aunt Carrie's close friend, had a generation before, that middle-class women were educated like men but denied ways to use their educations purposefully. Not having to earn a living was a disadvantage for Clover whose husband disapproved of so many kinds of activities. But like Fuller she did manage to use some of her talents. The modest collection of her own photography work Clover Adams assembled in the years before her suicide remains a testimony to her artistry and her sense of history. And, again, like Margaret Fuller, her influence was vast.

Influence, as opposed to power, remains one of the most difficult areas for computerized historians to assess with intelligence. Henry Adams' refusal to mention Clover in the story of his life would seem to deny her very existence; yet careful study of his work reveals the powerful impact she had on his imagination. Even as he wrote, his value system turned away from the narrowing political historical world of his fathers toward the cultural worlds of his wife. Ironically, her influence may well have turned into his power to describe the world, the ultimate power.

We need to continue to encourage scholars of all ages and backgrounds to look for the invisible and value the unconventional. Like Clover Adams they may end up helping us all redefine and enrich American civilization. I am happy to see this book reprinted as part of a movement to restore complexity to American women.

Lexington, Massachusetts

# The Education
# of Mrs. Henry Adams

# 1

# The Importance
# of Marriage

*We learn nothing rightly until we learn the symbolical
character of life.*
Ralph Waldo Emerson, "Education"

The American woman of the nineteenth century will live only as the man saw her. . . . This is pure loss to history," wrote Henry Adams, "for the American woman of the nineteenth century was much better company than the American man."[1] That he contributed to this loss in an extreme fashion by neglecting to mention his wife or to refer to the years of his marriage in his autobiography seemed not to trouble him. He enjoyed being enigmatic. Perhaps, as some critics have suggested, such silence was simply the ultimate tribute of an age that tried to romanticize and dramatize death: yet to annihilate all traces of his most intense human relationship, to deny the existence of a companion who had provided him, as he testified, with the most satisfying experience of his life, seems a peculiar tribute from a man who valued literary testimony and who wrote of his marriage that "for twelve years I had everything I most wanted on earth."[2] Perhaps, in the final act of writing his autobiography, Henry Adams saw himself putting aside deep personal relationships in order to join in the nineteenth-century American literary tradition of Cooper, and Thoreau, and Melville, and Mark Twain—a tradition painfully unable to account for the human need for heterosexual love because it seemed compelled to stress the primacy of individual intellectual fulfillment. Defining the pleasures and limitations of "free" human beings was one of the tasks our early writers set themselves. To have made personal sexual emotion a dominant value in any nineteenth-century American life story might have interfered with the more serious philosophical consideration of "self-reliance" that necessarily informed the writing of this age of competition and self-definition. In deliberately describing himself as an "eighteenth-century" man, moreover, Henry Adams underlined the fact that his mind had been shaped in an age of reason. He meant to show that his life was trained for achievement, not pleasure, and that there was little time for any passion in the making of the new civilization that his ancestors helped form.

Adams once wrote with some irony to his lifelong English friend, Charles Milnes Gaskell, about daily activities in Boston: "In this Arcadian society sexual passions seem to be abolished. . . . How they ever reconcile themselves to the brutalities of marriage, I don't know."[3] But whether he was really so different from the Bostonians who thought that "sex was a species of crime" remains a question. He once remarked that "anyone brought up among Puritans knew that sex was sin."[4] He wanted to be different, to be more alive than his rigid New England companions, but he knew well that, in his time, only Walt Whitman, the uninhibited New Yorker, had been able to absorb the vitality of sexual energy into his literary personality:

> Adams began to ponder, asking himself whether he knew of any American artist who had ever insisted on the power of sex, as every classic had always done; but he could only think of Walt Whitman; Bret Harte, as far as the

magazines would let him venture; and one or two painters, for the flesh tones. All the rest had used sex for sentiment, never for force; to them, Eve was a tender flower, and Herodias an unfeminine horror.[5]

The New Englander, no matter how passionate he may have wanted to be, seemed doomed to accept the fact that his education had denied him, and many other nineteenth-century Americans, any choice in the matter. After Clover Adams' death, when Henry Adams and the artist John La Farge lived together as travelers near a waterfall in Japan, La Farge, who was the father of nine children, wrote home comparing their idyllic existence to Huck's and Tom's, making a point of how much they actually "cherished their peculiarly American naiveté about sex."[6] Part of the nineteenth-century American's mythology seemed to insist that men could subdue the fires within themselves as easily as they could tame the wilderness without.

Yet, in writing the story of his education years later, Henry Adams' circumspect mind tried to make the reader aware of the importance of what he was leaving out. We now readily accept the truth that autobiographers are as selective as historians or novelists; much evidence suggests that Adams, toward the end of his life, when he wrote about his own experiences, saw himself as a self-conscious artist with the freedom of imagination to write what he liked. He had given up hope of having any political position, and he consistently denigrated the identity of professional historian, the rational role he had played for many years. In response to a college alumni questionnaire, he listed himself simply as "a man of letters." It seems feasible that he should, on the surface at least, want to be part of a greater American literary tradition that would deny him the use of sexual imagery. "American art," he insisted, "like the American language and American education, was as far as possible sexless." Yet this very sexlessness remained a challenge to his imagination.[7]

The deliberately paradoxical Adams, who had already reminded the reader that every classic had always insisted on the power of sex, may have been alerting his audience to the unspoken role his wife had played in the redefinition of his own identity; he wanted somehow to leave a respectable clue that his own development had been exposed to this overwhelming emotional force. Six years after Clover's death, Adams wrote to his long-standing friend Elizabeth Cameron that he had stopped caring about writing his *History:* "It belongs to the *me* of 1870; a strangely different being from the *me* of 1890."[8] In telling the story of his life, he would suggest, in his own reticent, New England manner, the truly powerful educational value of the years of his marriage (1872–1885)— years he neglected to mention in stressing that his faulty education ended in 1871. What Adams was in reality doing was expanding his definition of education; he had seen the limitations of the eighteenth-century training that shaped his early values, and he now included emotional dimensions of married life that enabled him to create a more complex vision of what society might be. From Clover, he learned to look at the institutional life his family had taken for granted with new critical eyes; the man of letters Henry Adams became had little to do with the politician he started out to be.

After Clover Adams' suicide in 1885, Henry found it necessary to destroy all the historical evidence that related to his wife; he burned every letter that had come to her, along with all his early diaries that might have mentioned her. At the same time, he made a particular, and perhaps unconscious, point of absorbing her "femininity" into the system of values that embodied his real education. This redefinition of self often emerges among mourners. One analyst has trenchantly noted that mourning may not only involve the gradual "piecemeal relinquishment" of the lost "lover," but also "the internalization" and "the appropriation" of aspects of the person who is gone. Such internalization is not by any means uncommon. An explanation of this "introjection" may illuminate the personality of Henry Adams, although described in unfortunate psychoanalytic jargon: "The outcome of mourning can show something like a new intake of objects into the superego structure insofar as elements of the lost object, through the mourning process, become introjected in the form of ego-ideal elements and inner demands and punishment."[9] Such an absorption of the qualities of his dead wife emerges in Henry Adams' later writing, when he is no longer a scientific historian but has become a passionate social critic. The story he recounts of his education becomes a familiar one—a record of personal change: "Typically, these identifications make their presence known not by the actions of the person, though they sometimes spill over into action, but from his report of subjective experience, that is, from his observations of changes in his experience of himself and others: he makes it clear that he felt like, the same as, or merged with, for instance, the hero, the victim, the object of artistic contemplation."[10]

In his artistic contemplation of himself, the twenty years left out of *The Education of Henry Adams*, the years that included his marriage to Clover Hooper, stand out in Henry's life story by the very artistry of omission, like the silences in the music of Beethoven he had slowly learned to appreciate. The twenty years left out of the autobiography especially suggest its quality as literature, rather than as history, by exploiting resonance rather than clear-cut definition as a means of reaching our understanding. No reader of Ernest Samuels' detailed exploration of Adams' life could ever think of *The Education of Henry Adams* as any more literal than *The Autobiography of Benjamin Franklin*, or the *Confessions* of Rousseau.

When the ego of Henry Adams, as he described it in his *Education*, "returned" in 1893 to go on recording his consistent failures and ever-developing consciousness, it demonstrated the conventional capacity for change that almost all confessional writing seems to embody. Imitating yet another American religious and literary tradition, he made marriage a conversion experience. Like St. Augustine's life, which he wanted "to complete," and like the self-discoveries of his countrymen, Thoreau and

Emerson, Henry Adams' education suggested the eternal truth that Erik Erikson has most recently clarified in modern psychoanalytic terms: the human being's ever present ability to change the direction of his ideas. As Adams had reminded Elizabeth Cameron, he was indeed not the same man he had been in 1870; the years of his marriage, along with the experience of his wife's death, had modified most of his conventional beliefs and had enabled him to see his culture and his existence more in terms of the frustrations of all thinking, feeling men, than in terms of the political successes of his forefathers. Although there is truth to the frequent assertion in the autobiography that Adams had always been sensitive to women's superior qualities, it is important to remember that he is not telling his life story as he lived it; he is telling it from the vantage point of age, and he wants to underline that sensitivity as part of a better system of values. Belief in the great importance of feeling was his wife's legacy.

By the time he started to write *Mont-Saint-Michel and Chartres* and *The Education of Henry Adams*, he had long since undergone a complete shift in identity, and the values he wanted to emphasize as a literary artist differed from those that had shaped his early decisions when "his father's character was . . . the larger part of his education."[11] After thirteen years of marriage, the eighteenth-century mind of Henry Adams, which started life with a firm belief in political institutions, in traditional education, and in the strength of the legal establishment, had come not only to accept the kind of twentieth-century anarchical scepticism now often identified with his name, but also to celebrate the renewed glorification of primal feminine force. In so changing, Adams found himself part of the Romantic literary tradition, which glorified nature as opposed to civilization—a tradition that more modern writers like D. H. Lawrence have extended in erotic terms. Adams' shift in interest from history to anthropology, his search for mythological sources of power rather than for chronological explanations, illustrates yet another aspect of his modernity. To be sure, the nineteenth-century New Englander would choose the twelfth-century Virgin Mary as his most powerful female symbol, but his distortions of traditional Catholicism, his interest in the continuity of reproduction as "power," and, finally, his own searching anthropological expeditions to primitive societies attest to his capacity to envision a more realistically influential role for women. All these concerns had been heavily reinforced by the powerful spirit of his wife.

The two novels Henry Adams wrote, *Democracy* and *Esther*, were also conceived and written during the *missing* years of his marriage. They may well be basically autobiographical, but the fact remains that Adams chose to embody his own dilemmas in the lives of heroines—not heroes—whose ideological conflicts about democratic politics and religion showed that certain classes of women had the freedom to reject all institutional compromises. Marriage provided no easy solution to their needs; at the same time, it must be said that the novels also honestly revealed a paucity of any realistic alternatives for the capable, free-thinking, nineteenth-century woman.

Clarence King, the geologist, a close friend of both Adamses, asserted that Henry later regretted having exposed his wife's religious experiences in *Esther*, seeming to make her a chemical subject *vis à vis* religion. In *Democracy*, he had shown their common disillusionment with the compromises in American politics. Details in the novels sometimes correspond to details in Clover's letters to her father, suggesting that she may have actually helped write some of the descriptive passages. More important, however, is the way Clover expanded Henry's understanding of the realistic limitations that confronted upper-class women in defining their own lives. *Esther* focuses on woman as artist and as charity worker, underlining the heroine's inability to be professionally absorbed. Ironically, her great freedom ends not in a sense of intellectual liberation, but in a sense of tragic impasse when she cannot marry either the minister she loves, because she disbelieves in his religion, or the scientist who loves her, because she does not return his passion. When Clarence King wrote that the logical end of the story was for Esther to jump into Niagara Falls,[12] his frightening intuition mirrored Adams' own sensitivity at the conclusion of *Democracy*. No self-sufficient social role was available to these intellectually gifted people; neither love nor work provides them with purpose. In both novels, the independent heroines come to feel that life without a strong companion is not worth living: "Oh how I wish I were dead! How I wish the universe were annihilated!" cries the husbandless Madeleine Lee. The most privileged upper-class women in Henry Adams' novels end up having no more freedom than the poorest working-class heroine of Rebecca Harding Davis has economic choice. Intellectual insight and economic privilege have provided no certain path to the good life; in fact, the awareness of democratic possibility leaves the heroines all the more bereft at the end of the novels, when they can find no social fulfillment whatsoever. Wealth offers only momentary diversion. Going off to Egypt, as Madeleine Lee does at the end of *Democracy*, might distract a fictional heroine from the political problems of democracy, but such a trip might also suggest its limitations. Henry Adams was just beginning to learn from the anthropological work of his good friend Mariette Bey that American society—by contrast even with the ancient Egyptian world—failed to provide realistic equality for talented women. Although most critics of the novels rightly stress Henry's own personal political powerlessness as the theme of both books, it may be necessary to underline his insistence that women are the most sensitive gauges of this state.

Never sympathetic with the masses of working men, Henry Adams found women to be his main source of identity with the powerless in the democracy he was always striving to understand: "The woman's plight was therefore not just more acute, more melodramatic, or more familiar to readers; it was above all more representative. It denoted mankind's."[13] From Clover, who had been a more passionate democrat than he ever was,

Adams learned to translate political beliefs into transcendental terms. He sought to identify with the "cosmic" spirit of Walt Whitman; in his own reticent New England manner, Adams eventually managed to imitate Walt Whitman's bisexuality by using his own self to express the doubts and disillusionment of every man and woman in society, just as Whitman had expressed their hopes. Adams' unusual ability to identify with the many Americans who felt themselves somehow culturally betrayed made *The Education of Henry Adams* a curiously popular book when it first appeared, and, in spite of its difficulty and its querulous tone, it remains widely read.

Through his wife, Adams learned to solidify those feelings about himself that all human beings shared. He ended up describing a life of constant achievement as a "failure," because he had so extended his own human boundaries. For Adams, the mythological literary tradition of self-reliance which gloried in worldly accomplishment finally gave way, as it had for Hawthorne, Melville, and Mark Twain, to become the kind of writing that honored what F. O. Matthiessen called "the lasting bond between the ages in man's capacity for suffering."[14] The balanced eighteenth-century mentality of Henry Adams ultimately turned into the sensibility of a restrained romantic. Eventually, Adams fled to the South Seas and Japan in the process of converting himself into the most intellectual anti-intellectual our modern literature has yet produced.

If Henry Adams learned a great deal about women's dilemmas from his wife, he also learned much about their strengths and satisfactions. The qualities he valued in women and wanted to relate to himself were not solely concerned with their realistic powerlessness. He admired as well feminine vitality, imagination, and adaptability; in his later writings, he attempted to clarify such feminine traits in realistic descriptions of vigorous women like Anna Lodge, or in mythical terms like the inspirational strength he found in Our Lady of Chartres. No scholar would argue that the years Henry and Clover spent together as husband and wife were unhappy; theirs was one of the rare unions of intellectual equals nineteenth-century America produced. Henry James, a frequent visitor to "the Clover Adamses," remarked that it was she who always dominated all their lively conversations: "We never knew how delightful Henry was till he lost her; he was so proud of her that he let her shine as he sat back and enjoyed listening to what she said and what others let her say."[15]

Indeed, Henry Adams himself must have seen Clover's death as another example of the many terrible paradoxes that haunted American existence. It was Clover, after all, who had taught him to appreciate the feelings denigrated by his forefathers, that enriched and expanded his own consciousness. Indeed, from some points of view, Clover Adams' life might have been seen as completely fulfilled. "We honor the rich," wrote Emerson, "because they have externally the freedom, power and grace which we feel to be proper to man, proper to us."[16] Emerson had been careful to use the word "externally," because he was well aware of the amount of psychological suffering the rich experienced simply because they had more freedom. But a society with a clear-cut vision of progress cannot look too deeply at its failures, and Americans, Henry Adams noted more than once, hated examining their own paradoxes. Adams would later force many to re-examine their values, just as surely as Emerson had, while he enjoyed the irony of depicting his life as a successful failure.

The biographer of a suicide has not the luxury of ignoring the circumstances of death, no matter what the quality of the life involved was like. Because there can be no simple biological or psychological explanations of why human beings—of all social classes—resort to such a drastic solution for their problems, we must continue to struggle with its complexity. Clover Adams' life did possess "freedom," and "power," and "grace." Not only did she exert a tremendous liberating influence on the husband who absorbed so much of her personality, but she also, significantly for our literature, left a lasting imprint on the mind of Henry James.

"Clover Adams," James had once declared, "is the in-
carnation of my native land."[17] All the possibilities of
democratic existence seemed to shine from her decent,
privileged, capable life. The absolute freedom of her spirit with its subsequent penchant for disappointment and
self-renunciation became a favorite theme of James', not
only in the stories he wrote specifically about the
Adamses, but also in his general fictional approach to the
behavior of American women. In his notebooks, Henry
James recorded a few disjointed comments about "doing"
the Adamses. Perhaps if he had been able to write about
Clover Adams in greater detail, he would have spelled
out the degree to which she defined the tragedy of the
American aristocrat:

> The life of an American "Princess," a true New
> Englander, not married to a European but to an
> American "Prince."—Generations of achieve-
> ment behind them gave them a sense that they
> too should accomplish a great deal for the
> democracy they both believed in. She tried to
> devote her life to defining what was *best* in her
> country, in a political situation where she often
> found herself among the *worst*.
> The small group of kindred spirits that sur-
> rounded her could not sustain her strong intel-
> lect and emotions. Like her husband, she could
> not commit herself to any profession, or cause,
> or political party. When her father died her
> greatest source of emotional support dis-
> appeared. Intensely intellectual, her husband
> could not cheer her or make her feel his love.
> She who had once given so much, saw herself
> finally as a burden to him and took her own
> life—
> After her death, realizing how much she had
> meant to him, he became a different, more pas-
> sionate man. Her great gift for feeling life mod-
> ified most of the beliefs he had grown up with.
> In an effort to immortalize her spirit, he wrote

the story of his own life—as if he were telling it with her values, from her point of view. The ultimate judgment of *The Education of Henry Adams* is hers.

# 2

# Wealth and Transcendentalism

*The most attractive class of people are those who are powerful obliquely, and not by the direct stroke. . . .*
Margaret Fuller, *Woman in the Nineteenth Century*

The woman who is known only through a man," insisted Henry Adams, "is known wrong."[1] Clover Adams (christened Marian Hooper) was descended from an extraordinary community of successful bankers, China merchants, railroad tycoons, and Congressmen; also among her ancestors was an iconoclastic Hooper "punished for reading at public worship, for absence from prayers, and for improper attitude at public worship" who was finally suspended from Harvard for breaking into the Harvard Hall kitchen.[2] The mixed strains of iconoclasm and respectability in Clover Hooper's family background, neglected in the published genealogy, need more careful attention. As so often happens in New England families, a radical reform tradition overlaps with a conservative commercial spirit, and public service takes on a variety of dimensions.

One of Clover's ancestors, Robert Hooper of Marblehead, was actually called *King* Hooper by his neighbors (we cannot be sure whether this was because of his Tory sympathies or because of his superior vigor and prosperity). A 1790 letter to a grandchild reveals that Robert Hooper possessed warmth and a zest for life; it also reveals that he lacked the beleaguered conscience of his Puritan ancestors.[3] We do know that Hooper had a well-developed social conscience, for, in spite of his loyalty to England, he refused a British appointment because he thought to accept it would be unjust to his fellow colonists. Moreover, this "king" outlived four wives, worked for the General Court, supported a school for poor children, and had his portrait painted by John Singleton Copley. Another set of Clover's ancestors, William and Hannah Reed, were also prosperous enough to patronize the best portraitist of their day, Gilbert Stuart.

The Hoopers had always been known for their good taste: "They built beautiful houses and filled them with beautiful things; they came to have a distinction of manner, a 'delicacy' all their own."[4]

Concern for the importance of art, not merely as historical record but as esthetic experience, always surrounded the growing Hooper children. Clover's older brother Ned—with taste more catholic than most Bostonians dared to show—became one of Boston's most distinguished art collectors. In his collection were Blakes and Turners, as well as Chinese bronzes, gorgeous Winslow Homer watercolors, and a statue by Rodin. He was also one of the trustees who helped buy the original collections at the Boston Museum of Fine Arts, just as his father had helped establish the art collections at the Boston Athenaeum.

One of Clover's many cousins was the Civil War hero Robert Gould Shaw, who became the subject of another remarkable work of art, Augustus Saint-Gaudens' bronze memorial at the edge of the Boston Common. Shaw's parents requested that the artist not place Shaw above his Negro men like a European equestrian monument, but rather emphasize by structural organization that the white leader and the black troops had all died together. Although the Confederate commander of the attack on Fort Wagner that killed all the Northerners refused to accord Shaw the honorable burial appropriate to his rank, thinking it more humiliating to bury him in a common grave with his "niggers," the New Englanders were proud of his death and thankful that he was with his "brave" men. Booker T. Washington shared the podium with William James at the monument's dedication. A sense of democratic idealism emerged as well through Saint-Gaudens' insistence on placing a seemingly incongruous angel over the otherwise realistic representation. Whether the spirit symbolizes death or victory is irrelevant; what is important is the nineteenth-century affirmation that transcendental forces impinged on historical events. The monument effectively embodies the myth of heroic democratic idealism; it "sticks like a fishbone in the city's throat," Robert Lowell wrote, emphasizing how troublesome such sincere symbolic gestures remain in a world of frequent corruption. In our mythology, it still remains important to believe that black men and white men are willing to die together for the ideal of equality. Four American poets, James Russell Lowell, William Vaughn Moody, Robert Lowell, and John Berryman, have written about the Shaw monument as an important moral landmark in American life—a tribute to the moment when the ideal was the reality.

Clover Adams later remarked how glad she was that Augustus Saint-Gaudens (a New York shoemaker's son) was sculpting the monument to her cousin rather than the less gifted New England Brahmin, William Wetmore Story. Her allegiance would always be stronger to the discovery of democratic talent than to her own class. While Saint-Gaudens was working on the sculpture, Ned Hooper sent Shaw's saddle to him along with useful photographs of his own black regimental associates; and Clover managed to visit the artist's studio in New York before the final cast was finished. The Civil War remained the sole unifying democratic event Clover would know. She played a modest role in the Sanitary Commission helping prepare bandages for Northern troops, and the war stimulated her imagination also. Although she wrote no poetry, Clover Adams tried to record with her camera some of the Civil War's heroes, as well as their simple graves.

Another close cousin was William Sturgis Bigelow, who (like George Santayana's fictional Peter Alden in *The Last Puritan*) rejected his medical profession, along with his elegant wine cellar, and his precious collection of Chinese porcelains, bronzes, and tapestries, to join a Buddhist monastery in Japan, convinced, like many other disillusioned materialists, that the sages of the East possessed peace of mind that the Western world neglected. Henry Adams would visit him there after Clover's death; at that time, Adams formulated his own literary comment on the ideas of the East in "Buddha and Brahma," a long philosophical poem inspired by his half-mocking meditation under the Bo tree, where he hoped to find Nirvana. Acknowledging the special power of Eastern religious thought was part of Henry Adams' acceptance of the non-rational. Orientalism was nothing new to the Transcendental minds that shaped so much nineteenth-century American thought; yet it was new to the "eighteenth-century mind" of Henry Adams, who had earlier criticized his Transcendental neighbors for being too detached from practical reality. By the time he landed in Japan in July 1886, however, Adams' sense of what mattered most had changed.

If most of the Sturgises came to be identified with successful mercantilism, they nevertheless retained a strong unconventional strain as well. Clover's Grandfather Sturgis, who took a special interest in her childhood, captained a China trade vessel at the age of nineteen, and later became commissioner of the Sandwich Islands. Sturgis was famous for his response to a mocking opponent in the legislature who meant to ridicule his lack of education by launching a political attack on him in Latin; Sturgis responded in the dialect of the Northwest Indians. William Sturgis' liberalism and wit embellish all his letters. He answered one historian who criticized the Indians for bad faith and deceitfulness with his own account that the bad faith and deceitfulness of the white man was more at fault. He also gave demonstrations of Indian

dances and appeared proud of his ability to cope with a
great variety of cultures beyond the Boston scene. A letter from Sturgis dated July 16, 1845, to George Bancroft,
his relative by marriage, craftily sends thanks for a eulogy
on General Jackson: "No one else could have said so
much in his favor and kept so near the truth." There can
be little doubt that this powerful personality, a "merchant
prince" who refused all pretensions, in spite of the doors
opened to him through his civic generosity, made a lasting impact on Clover. During her mother's trip south for
her tuberculosis, Grandfather Sturgis took care of Clover,
who was then four years old. He wrote enthusiastically
of the little girl's health and good nature, concluding,
"She and I have become so intimate that you may find it
somewhat difficult to get her from me—she is certainly
the best child in the world."[5]

Although the Hoopers and the Sturgises, the two families that formed Clover Hooper's immediate background,
did not play a strong political role in shaping the country
as the Adamses did, Clover would have had little reason
before her marriage to feel inferior to Henry Adams. In
fact, certain kinds of political involvement would have
been questionable as part of her family's system of
values. The lively women in Clover's immediate family,
unlike the Adams ladies, did not see themselves serving
the power of great men; they saw themselves struggling
instead for self-fulfillment as many women do today.
One of her aunts, Anne Hooper, was later active in the
women's rights movement, and her cousin Alice Hooper
was on the executive board of the newly formed American Social Science Association, which was committed to
helping women find productive individual careers. Clover's mother, Ellen Sturgis Hooper, and her aunt, Caroline Sturgis Tappan, were involved in a conscious effort
to make themselves interesting intellectuals. They took
drawing lessons, learned new languages, participated
in Margaret Fuller's "Conversations" and Eliza Follen's
classes for women, and wrote and wrote. Clover's Grandmother Sturgis chose an independent life fairly early in
her marriage, ostensibly to seek personal spiritual fulfill-

ment away from her husband. Although family letters are deliberately vague about the reasons for this separation, the letters themselves, which were written from a Boston husband to his Cape Cod wife, are a testimony to its reality.

Although their affiliations are not mentioned next to the bankers in the published genealogy, and although Clover herself, after her marriage, rarely referred to her mother, who died when she was five years old, or to her Aunt Carrie, who clearly annoyed Henry Adams, these assertive women left behind many written records of their values. The next generation of women could never have ignored their influence. Among the family papers, in fact, remains an unusual note from Clover's mother asserting the educational value of reading family documents. Knowing that she would die of tuberculosis before her daughters matured, Ellen Hooper wanted them to know more about her beliefs from the documents she left behind. Curiously, she did not mention the need to communicate with her son: "As I think some of these letters may have an interest for Nella [Clover's sister, Ellen] and Clover, I should like them kept for them—if they do not wish the trouble of looking them over, they can burn them unread."[6] Many letters still exist. There can be little doubt that reading the correspondence of these strong feminine spirits touched the two little girls, who both grew up with the desire to make something better out of the world they lived in.

There is also evidence that both Clover and Ellen were thoroughly acquainted with their mother's poetry. Noting a reference to one of her mother's poems, which was published anonymously in *Longman's Magazine* in 1883, Clover sent the author "that loose sheet and one other and gave her the name" of the poet; this gesture suggests her own familiarity with her mother's work, which was by then privately printed on unbound sheets. We know too that Ellen Hooper Gurney found spiritual sustenance years after her mother's death in quoting lines from the poetry to a friend. Although it is hard to tell exactly when the family gathered together the loose poems they wanted to keep, the watermark on the privately printed edition of Ellen Sturgis Hooper's work says 1871—a date after all three children had grown up—which suggests how much their mother's literary efforts had meant to them during their childhood. Ellen Sturgis Hooper's writings remained a source of spiritual contact between Ellen Hooper and her children throughout their lives. As late as April 12, 1883, in a letter to her father, Clover was still thinking of her mother as "our lady of Emersonian thought and sentiment." Ellen's and Carrie's letters provided the girls with examples of a positive kind of free-thinking feminist inspiration.

The airiness of contemporary philosophical definition as well as the certain evidence of personal association allow us to connect both Sturgis sisters with the Transcendentalists, a far different category indeed from the prosperous bankers who surround them in the published genealogy. (Emerson once suggested that the view taken of Transcendentalism in State Street was that it threatened to invalidate contracts.)[7] Here, the rational ancestors of Henry Adams and the direct forebears of Clover Hooper were in agreement, for State Street, the successful commercial society, provided neither group with answers in their search for the good life. Yet the Sturgises' wealth, more readily than the Adamses' political philosophy, liberated the creativity of their children. Clover's mother had proudly published eight of her poems in *The Dial*, the voice of Transcendentalism. *The Dial*'s editor, Margaret Fuller, wrote admiringly, "I have seen in Europe no woman more gifted by nature than she."[8] Caroline Sturgis also found sympathetic listeners for her unsigned work among the readers of *The Dial*, who shared both sisters' distress at the materialism and emotional aridity that seemed to characterize New England in the 1840s. The first version of Fuller's *Woman in the Nineteenth Century*, "The Great Lawsuit: Man vs. Men, Woman vs. Women," which remains a revolutionary assertion of women's possibilities, actually appeared next to Ellen Sturgis Hooper's poems in the July 1843 issue of *The Dial*.

Aunt Carrie Sturgis, who once asked Henry James, Sr., why he did not imitate Walt Whitman and raise his "barbaric yawp over the roofs of all the houses," and who described Henry Adams as one who "sets himself before himself as the universe," became a passionate "sisterly" correspondent of Emerson.[9] She also remained one of Margaret Fuller's closest friends: "With her, I can talk of anything," wrote the notorious Fuller. "She is like me. She is able to look facts in the face."[10]

When Horace Greeley offered Margaret Fuller a job as a critic on the *New York Tribune*, Carrie Sturgis knew it was right for her friend to leave New England. Later, not wanting her little boy to be raised by a woman "limited in mind" (her husband Ossoli's sister), Margaret Fuller asked Carrie Sturgis to agree to take responsibility for the child if anything should happen to her or to Ossoli; this was certainly the highest compliment she could pay a friend, and the clearest illustration of their intellectual kinship. Like Caroline Sturgis, Fuller "stood for the heart even though so terribly endowed with brains."[11] The intellectual women of this generation found it essential— like the European Romantics they were all reading—to incorporate their feelings into their liberation. Clover Hooper may not have known that it was Carrie Sturgis' copy of Fourier that passed from hand to hand at Brook Farm—inspiration for the new industrial world the Utopians there dreamed of—but she would have absorbed the intense idealism they all shared about the possibilities of a better life.

In the Transcendental Club, for the first time in America, women were considered the intellectual equals of men. The Conversation groups, which Margaret Fuller had founded earlier, provided still another chance for the two gifted Sturgis sisters to develop their intellects in debate over the great issues of living as well as in discussion of classical literature. Fuller had designed her "conversations" specifically to help women "ascertain what pursuits are best suited to us, in our time and state of society, and how we may make best use of our means for building up the life of thought upon the life of action."[12] We can be certain that Clover Adams knew all the stimulating details concerning these "conversations," for Mrs. George Bancroft, one of the original members whom Henry Adams, not lavish with compliments, called "the most intelligent woman in Washington," remained close to Clover throughout her life.[13]

Such group activities were not meant to be primarily social affairs. "To the intellectual New Englanders of the forties, conversation was indispensable and a weighty matter. Conversation was the method of Transcendentalism, the animating spirit of the age."[14] Emerson had called the Transcendentalists "the talkers who talk the sun and moon away"; we can easily imagine Clover later defining the worth of her own Washington salon in similar terms.[15] In the writings of all three Hoopers, Clover, Ellen, and Ned, and ultimately in the work of Henry Adams himself, we find comments in the Romantic tradition that disparage the written word. The degree to which people of the nineteenth century perceived conversation as a source of power and influence, and a broader means of communication, seems hard to imagine now. Perhaps the idea of good talk may have also fulfilled the Adamses' need to communicate on a more general democratic level, for speech could reach people untouched by writing. George Bancroft, a committed democrat and historian, whose wife was a second cousin of Clover's, had felt great sympathy with the Transcendentalists, perhaps primarily because of his wife's involvement with the group. But also, as Arthur Schlesinger, Jr., declared, "Both democrat and transcendentalist agreed in asserting the rights of the free mind against the pretensions of institutions. Both shared a living faith in the integrity and perfectibility of man."[16] Bancroft had urged the Transcendentalists to use their moral intensity for "progress and reform—not merely self-culture." However, his essay, "Reasons Why the Natural Association of Men of Letters Is with the Democracy," expressed the quality of Transcendentalism that became least popular; ultimately, this was the issue that caused the movement to split into active reformers and idealist thinkers.

Some of Ellen Hooper's poems reflected the need for an active reform spirit in a "world of dull cares, hot words, and hard work."[17] The volume of her poetry now in the Boston Public Library once belonged to Elizabeth Palmer Peabody and was given to the library by Ednah Dow Cheney, both vigorous servants of the Boston reform community. One of Ellen Hooper's efforts to make readers aware of human suffering described in Blakean terms the life of a chimney sweep: "He is young but soon will know how to bear both word and blow." More often, however, she saw the poet commenting on every human being's anguish through the expression of her or his own personal suffering:

> . . . *their woes were hallowed by his woe,*
> *Humanity, half cold and dead*
> *Had been revived in Genius' glow.*
>
> The Poet

Like Emerson and Whitman, Ellen Hooper felt that expressive individuality—freedom from past conventions and current dogmas—could be a unifying spiritual force. Her struggle to define the individual soul against the environment that shaped it could as well shape every man's and every woman's. In a typically Emersonian letter to *The Bell,* an Abolitionist magazine that had solicited a poetic contribution from her, Ellen Hooper rejected wholehearted commitment even to a cause she believed in:

> I am sorry to decline. . . . If I should wish to give voice to any feelings on the subject of slavery, I should prefer a different channel, believing that a mite given by the wayside is often more moving than if it were received through the appointed treasury. In saying this, I do not

mean to disparage the *results* of Abolition Societies, for these I am not competent to judge. I honor their zeal and devotion but cannot enter the ranks as a fellow laborer.[18]

Although in one of her poems Ellen Hooper bemoaned the fact that she had chosen to shun the strife, her preoccupation with self-exploration—though surely a New England pleasure-torment inherited from the Puritans—identified her most closely with Emerson's own attitudes toward reform:

He had his own panacea—the development of each individual; and he was impatient of any other. He did not believe in association. The very idea of it involved a surrender by the individual of some portion of his identity, and of course all the reformers worked through their associations. With their general aims, he sympathized. . . . But with the methods of the reformers he had no sympathy: "He who aims at progress should aim at an infinite, not at a special benefit."[19]

Emerson, who was a lifelong friend, would have clearly understood Ellen Hooper's reluctance to become a "fellow laborer" in spite of her general sympathy with the Abolitionists; so too would Clover and Henry Adams, who later had similar feelings about party loyalty and open involvement in political reform movements. Yet the anarchic individualism of Emerson represented no panacea for Henry Adams or for Clover Adams. It is almost too easy to see the intellectual alienation of later generations of democratic thinkers growing out of the individual integrity that Emerson insisted on. He knew well "the self-accusation, the faint heart, the frequent uncertainty and loss of time, which are the nettles and tangling vines in the way of the self-relying and self-directed," as well as "the state of virtual hostility in which he seems to stand to society."[20] Ultimately, social isolation could be rationalized as the final price for honesty; in the future there would remain only the search for spiritual community.

One of Ellen Hooper's most popular lyrics (reprinted in Perry Miller's Transcendentalist anthology) suggested her naturally rebellious attitude toward the work ethic: "I slept and dreamed that life was Beauty. / I woke, and found that life was Duty. / Toil on, sad heart." To Ellen Hooper, the idea of Duty, often a source of comfort to her more conventional "sisters," appeared to be an assault on individual freedom; the fact that this poem was her most popular suggests that she may have been articulating a common disillusionment. Her distress at materialism, a common theme among idealists, found expression in a poem called "The Gift Where Gold Made Yellow Pale." Unlike most of her female contemporaries, she did not relish building a cozy nest; by contrasting the hearth with the natural excitement of the wild wood fire, Ellen Hooper identified domesticity with a "compact utilitarian heap." In her less conventional poems, she managed to capture the intensity of personal emotion that the Transcendentalists were always striving to convey—the quality that John Jay Chapman celebrated as "an elevation of feeling which through them qualified the next generation, and can be traced in the life of New England today."[21] That such passions were usually repressed in the social climate of her youth is an idea her work also emphasized. In its recoil from self-righteousness, Hooper's poem on the New England spirit struggling in her soul seems worth quoting in full:

> *Better a sin which purposed wrong to none*
> *Than this still wintry coldness at the heart*
> *A penance might be borne for evil done*
> *And tear of grief and love might ease the smart.*
>
> *But this self-satisfied and cold respect*
> *To virtue which must be its own reward,*
> *Heaven keep us through this danger still alive,*
> *Lead us not into greatness, heart-abhorred—*

*Oh God, who framed this stern New England land*
  *Its clear cold waters, and its clear cold soul,*
*Thou givest tropic climes and youthful hearts*
  *Thou weighest spirits and dost all control—*

*Teach me to wait for all to bear thy fault*
  *That most I hate because it is my own,*
*And if I fail through foul conceit of good,*
  *Let me sin deep so I may cast no stone.*

At its best, in the philosophical tradition of Thoreau and Emerson, her poetry reveals sharp emotional perceptions and intellectual authenticity. If Ellen Hooper had not given the bulk of her waning energy to rearing her three children, it is likely that her achievements would have been more remarkable.

The poem she wrote about Emerson celebrated his intellect yet qualified the coolness that differentiated him from his band of admiring, passionate "sisters," the same dryness that Henry Adams also commented on in a letter to Oliver Wendell Holmes, Jr.: "In obtaining extreme sublimation or tenuity of intelligence," he wrote about Emerson, "I infer that sensuousness must be omitted."[22] The detached intellectuality that John Jay Chapman also examined in some detail, Ellen Hooper honored in her poem:

## To R.W.E.

*Dry lighted soul, the ray that shines in thee,*
  *Shot without reflex from primeval sun,*
*We twine the laurel for the victories*
  *Which thou on thought's broad, bloodless field hast won.*

*Thou art the mountain where we climb to see*
  *The land our feet have trod this many a year.*
*Thou art the deep and crystal sky,*
  *Where noiseless, one by one, bright stars appear.*

*It may be Bacchus, at thy birth, forgot*
  *That drop from out the purple grape to press*
*Which is his gift to man, and so thy blood*
  *Doth miss the heat which ofttimes breeds excess.*

*But all more surely do we turn to thee*
  *When the day's heat and blinding dust are o'er*
*And cool our souls in thy refreshing air,*
  *And find the peace which we had lost before.*

The high idealism and calm integrity that Emerson represented were only parts of the heritage Ellen Hooper wanted to leave her children. Feeling guilty for not fulfilling her own promise as an example of achievement, and aware that she was dying of consumption, Ellen made a special effort to include her children in her suffering:

*I give thee all, my darling, darling child*
  *. . . I lay my page of life*
*Unrolled with bitter shame before thine eyes*
  *That thou mayest shun or better share the strife—*
*All this is thine—and prayers to speed thee on,*
  *And patience, which would wait th'appointed hour,*
*But oh, my child, example ask thou not,—*
  *Thy mother's life shows not the ripened flower—*

The mother's failure to become a "ripened flower" should somehow touch her family. In a poem that addressed itself to the sacrifices a mother makes, putting "on and off herself as need may be," she stressed the common idea that her own frustrated hopes might flower finally through her children:

*Cast seed into the daily furrow line*
  *Thy hoarded hope, thy childhood's cherished plan,*
*Cast these into it too, and make no sign.*

*Then stand and watch*
  *And if no harvests wave—*
*For thee and for thy child*
  *There is beyond the grave.*

Always, "there is beyond the grave"; eternity, a nineteenth-century comfort to the dying, might finally make a mockery of any worldly achievement. Like most of the other Transcendentalists, Ellen Hooper attended no worldly church. Although her husband owned a pew at the Unitarian King's Chapel there is more evidence that Ellen Hooper found her religious identity outside of organized religion (Emerson had once remarked that they were all religious but "hated" churches). Her deep concern for the reality of emotions would have allied her with those fellow Transcendentalists who rejected the pale negations of Unitarian thought; her God was personal, not institutional. And both her daughters, unlike most of their more conventionally ritualistic contemporaries, would follow her religious example.

That she had not been able to create more of the beauty that was so important in her life was a source of lasting grief, but her sense of eternal life consoled her. In the idea of the infinite, a mother separated from her children would find them again. Of a mother dying in childbirth, she wrote,

*One look the mother cast upon her child*
  *As entered he one portal low of time*
*While she the other passed through—*
  *A first look and last—never to greet him more*
*Till on Eternity's calm distant shore—*

Still, she knew it had to be the strength of her love on earth that stayed with her children during their lives. "Love," Emerson insisted, was, to the Transcendentalist, "the last and highest gift of nature."[23] Through her poems and family letters, and in fragmented descriptions of her affection written by her daughter Ellen, we discover that Ellen Hooper was a loving, attentive mother. She wanted to help her children benefit from her own struggles: "The treasure I so dearly won, And spent my life to seek," the poet-mother wrote, "I long to pour out on some needy son of time."

In a prose passage included among the poems, the dying woman tried to console herself by recording her influence on her son, Ned: "Sometimes do I take refuge from my knowledge in his faith, and feel a happiness in the belief that the tedious realities of my working day are ministering spirits, though I see them not save as forms of flesh and blood." Purporting to respond to those self-contained New Englanders who advised restraint against loving, she protested:

### Answer to "Love Not"

Love thou—for though the thing thou lovst must die,
   Must perish from the earth and from the sky,
Its memory until thy dying hour
   Shall be to thee a spell of love and power.

It seems most unlikely that five-year-old Clover would ever forget the mother who left such lines as part of her children's education.

The intensity of "life's hoarded store" of feelings, the "keen transport" that identified Ellen Sturgis Hooper's short life with "wine" rather than "water," remained in the sensibilities of all the Hooper children. In her brief career as a mother, she managed to turn the "prose articles" of her house into "mysterious and admirable" poetry for her children. The "tedious realities" of her working day did become "ministering spirits" for the young Hoopers, who all three reflected their mother's awareness of the need for social reform, along with her intense esthetic sensibility. Above all, the children seemed to have retained her emotional integrity, the strong individualism that communicates itself through the "deep or vivid response" that R. P. Blackmur found so characteristic of Clover Adams' letters.[24] Henry Adams would later define this response as pleasingly "eccentric."

In a biographical description of Clover's sister, Henry Lee Higginson, a founder of the Boston Symphony and close friend of the Hoopers, captured the kind of heightened sensibility that was characteristic of both girls:

> Ellen was, he wrote, "a beautiful flower" of such peculiar quality that she baffled description. . .—full of intelligence and mischief and waywardness as a small girl . . . running over with fun and bright thoughts—as a grown woman intent on the ideas of clever men and women whom she daily saw, full of interest for the new aspects of life, and full of fire for the cause of the Union in our great Civil War. . . . She loved books and sought the occupation and solace of them. Once, in talking with Mr. Emerson, who was the beloved apostle of our youth, and who had known her parents, he said: "Miss Hooper, reading is a matter of race with you." She replied, "Yes, I do read very fast." . . . She loved the sea and the skies, and delighted in walking and riding on horseback in the woods. . . . She was a wonderful woman, gifted with the love of poetry, nature, books, talk, wit, humor, and most of all, love of men and women. . . . She could not express fully what she thought and felt, because she was running over with thought and feelings, and yet shy. . . . Her brilliant kindly wit, her frank truthfulness, her exquisite ways and her charming manners all remain in the memories of her lovers.[25]

The description might have fit Clover exactly.

There can be no doubt that the ideas of Emerson shaped the young Hoopers' minds. The great American scholar's concern for individuality as opposed to institutions, and his belief in idealism and feeling as opposed to materialism and pedantry remained significant values to Clover Hooper Adams throughout her life. When her husband noted that the Adamses had "little or no affinity" for the "eccentric offshoots" of Concord, he knew the same could never have been written of the Hoopers.[26]

It was Robert William Hooper, their father, who actually reared the children after his wife's death. Trained in Paris after his graduation from Harvard to be an eye doctor, R. W. Hooper was economically secure enough to be able to put aside his professional standing in order to spend a good deal of time with his motherless family. Although this decision was not a gesture against society's vocational values it nevertheless marked the choice of a personal option over a professional one, a rare decision for a man in striving nineteenth-century America. Perhaps the lingering power of his wife's personality persuaded him to value the world of feeling above the world of achievement, in much the same manner that Clover Hooper's values would later influence Henry Adams. Dr. Hooper did not entirely abandon his medical practice, however; he put his knowledge to use for charitable causes, serving the tradition of reform that meant so much to many Transcendentalists.

As might be expected, Robert Hooper was an indulgent father. Henry Adams, commenting on the irregularity of his being permitted to live with his in-laws for a full month before his marriage, remarked that his father-in-law-to-be was a "good deal of a slave to his two daughters"; no evidence exists to contradict his statement.[27] Compensating for the loss of their mother, Dr. Hooper—in competition with Grandfather Sturgis, a number of loving aunts, and a devoted housekeeper—lavished affection on all his children, but Clover, the youngest, was his favorite.

Robert Hooper also set an example of a community-involved intellectual life for his family. He was part of a lively, organized intellectual circle that included such remarkable thinkers as Emerson and Oliver Wendell Holmes. Holmes, in fact, wrote a note to the Adams family before Henry's marriage to Clover in praise of their daughter-in-law-to-be. For over thirty years a trustee of the Athenaeum, the distinguished Boston library and art gallery, Robert Hooper was characterized in one obituary as "a man of scholarly tastes and habits, far wider than his professional training would lead us to expect."[28] Yet this very professional training added to the richness of his life by enabling him to express a deeper concern for human suffering, a concern that included active work to help "contraband" freed slaves, as well as volunteer services in a number of local hospitals.

He frequently treated the patients at the Worcester Asylum for the mentally ill, and what seems most remarkable about these visits is that he took his daughters with him. In an effort to share with the inmates there the esthetic bounty he valued as much as his wife did, he donated Washington Allston's painting *St. Peter and the Angel in Prison* to the Asylum. A Worcester newspaper noted that this occasion was "but one of many on which the inmates of that institution have had cause gratefully to remember the kind heart and generous hand of Robert W. Hooper." A letter from the hospital found among the family papers thanked him for his long-term "sympathy with the unfortunate persons in our care," and for attempting "to lighten the sorrows of those who, insofar as power of thought and expression is theirs, must always think of you with gratitude and bless your name."[29] Because of these visits, an awareness of deep irrationality and instability remained a lasting part of the Hooper children's education (as it must also have been for Emerson, whose brother spent much time in asylums, and for Whitman, whose brother was retarded). This was a dimension of human consciousness that the Adams family, which stressed the power of human rationality to order life, rarely acknowledged, in spite of the aberrations in their own family. A typical Adams attitude may be perceived in Charles Francis' comments on the death of a neighbor's daughter in her twenties: that the girl was "deficient in the brain," he wrote, "materially impaired feelings of sympathy at her death." When his brother

George Washington Adams committed suicide, ostensibly because he had got a girl pregnant, Charles Francis noted that, although the death was an "unpleasant conclusion," it was not "untimely." He added that George's desire to give money to the girl he had seduced was "a foolish effusion of a thoughtless moment."[30] Compassion was to be feared, not cultivated.

After her father died, Ellen Gurney made at least one effort to continue his charity toward the mentally ill. *The Boston Daily Advertiser* reported in 1886 that "through the kind interest of Mrs. E. W. Gurney of Cambridge who contributed a sum sufficient for the purchase of a dozen wheels and an ample supply of wool, spinning has been introduced at the Worcester Lunatic Asylum."[31] Ellen Gurney's concern for work as therapy in the year following Clover's death may reflect convention as well as her own desperate sense of need. The year after her mother died, nine-year-old Ellen embroidered a sampler with the motto, "Constant occupation prevents temptation."[32] Ellen Gurney too would commit suicide within the year after making her generous gift, feeling despair and worthlessness after her gentle husband Ephraim Whitman Gurney died. The death of loved ones often challenges the self-esteem of women who feel ambivalent about their independent worth.

Clover Adams received an education concerning mental instability and suffering that may have conditioned many of her attitudes toward the society in which she lived. If she had examined the family papers while she was still young, she would have realized that her own mother had also experienced periods of deep depression and that her grandmother's isolation often amounted to withdrawal from all society. That, as a child, she apparently witnessed the arsenic suicide of Sturgis Bigelow's mother would have made, as Charles Francis Adams, Jr., noted, "a dangerous impression on her mind."[33] When Clover later remarked to her father that "the insane asylum seems to be the goal of every good and conscientious Bostonian," she may have been thoughtlessly jesting, as Ernest Samuels suggested; but perhaps she was also cultivating her bravado, trying to come to terms with the reality of her own fears.[34] Her sister, Ellen, also worried about her own stability, for she acknowledged in a letter to Charles Eliot Norton, "The one thing I couldn't bear was that I should go mad, become imbecile as I did."[35]

It probably did not occur to Clover that madness may have been another way of "coming out of civilization" as the Brook Farm Transcendentalists had attempted to do in their socialist experiment because establishment life offered little sense of purpose for many individuals. But that the fear of madness remained among several of the women closest to Clover is indisputable. One of the cousins most frequently mentioned in her letters, Adeline Bigelow, has been (as all references to Clover were later deleted from Henry Adams' records) totally expunged from the genealogical tables in the early edition of letters. She was indeed admitted to Somerville Asylum. The *Letters of Mrs. Henry Adams* would remind us of George Santayana's indictment that "a genteel tradition forbids people to confess that they are unhappy."[36] But earlier generations were more willing to share their pain. Clover herself and Adie, as we learn of her from the manuscript letters, were not so genteel that they denied their feelings and fears; their relationship was intense and honest. There was a genuine degree of heroism in their efforts to challenge the genetic forces they both believed shaped their lives. And Clover's early jesting about which insane asylum each girl would prefer to be in, surely reflected, as much as any kind of insensitivity, the black humor of the doomed.

If awareness of the mental instability of different social groups was a real part of Clover Adams' education, so too was her exposure to the solid virtues of the working class—transmitted through Betsy Wilder, the Hooper family's housekeeper. Even before Ellen Hooper's death, Betsy was a regular part of the family. Clover's fondness for her emerges in many of her letters. She made things for Betsy and took the trouble to send her such souvenirs as a bouquet of flowers from Mrs. Rutherford B. Hayes, an exchange for Betsy's gift of six-leaf clovers. When she returned home for the last time to take care of her father, the forty-three-year-old Clover continued to share Henry Adams' letters with her ancient nurse. Although none of Betsy's letters remain, scholars need only consider the references to servants in the Adams family papers to realize how different Betsy's status was. Clover always saw her as a loving and supportive human being—as part of the family. She immortalized Betsy Wilder in one of her most eloquent photographs.

Even a cursory glance at the letters that remain among Clover's family papers reveals a good deal of passion and warmth. The Hoopers were noted for "good feeling and attachment to each other."[37] If there were serious problems of instability, there was also deep concern for the people who were suffering. The openness of such a group, particularly the Sturgises, must have been a revelation to Henry Adams, whose own family may have had "more wintry coldness at the heart" than he had ever been willing to admit.

# 3

# A Woman's Schooling

*Tell all the Truth but tell it slant—*
*Success in Circuit lies.*
Emily Dickinson

**I** only wish I were a little girl and were to be sent to Mrs. Agassiz," wrote George Ticknor, "in time I should amount to something."[1] That George Ticknor, the Brahmin intellectual who helped found the Boston Public Library, appreciated the quality of instruction offered by the Agassiz family to New England's daughters at their new school for girls is certain. How he envisioned "amounting to something" remains a more complex issue.

Both Clover and Ellen Hooper attended the Agassiz School, as did several of their cousins, Ralph Waldo Emerson's daughter, and many well-to-do outsiders who often boarded in Boston so that they might take the daily horse-drawn bus to their Cambridge instruction. Contrary to Ticknor's statement, the school was not for little girls; it seems to have included the variety of ages now found among the students in a community college.

In 1859, when Clover was seventeen, her Grandfather Sturgis wrote of her education:

> Clover Hooper still attends the school of Mr.
> Agassiz at Cambridge and will I trust continue

to do so at least a year longer, for it is an excellent place to acquire valuable and useful knowledge. Clover is a good scholar and excels too in
all domestic and household matters. . . . Everybody must try to be useful in this world.[2]

There is no doubt that Clover was being exposed to some
of the liveliest minds in Cambridge at that time, but how
much "useful" knowledge she was getting must be questioned.

The elementary school preparation available to the
girls who later attended the Agassiz School would have
necessarily been rigorous enough to provide them with
tools to do fairly sophisticated work. We know that James
Russell Lowell's mother had taken him as a small child to
Miss Dana's School for Girls, where such preparatory
training was available; he began Latin and French at age
seven and was reading Sir Walter Scott by the age of
nine. If girls attended elementary school (which was not
compulsory), we may conclude that their early education
was not at all inferior to, or different from, their
brothers'. Clover Adams attended Miss Houghton's, a
similar school, with the daughters of both abolitionists
and cotton merchants.

In 1855, when the Agassiz family founded their school
there were few opportunities for girls to receive advanced
training in any field. The Harvard corporation had recently refused to grant permission to female normal
school students who wanted to sit in on Louis Agassiz's
zoology lectures as "inexpedient." A public high school
for girls had met with such opposition in Boston that it
had to be closed; it was, in fact, *too* popular. The hunger
for women's higher education was enormous. When the
Agassiz family opened their private school for women so
many girls enrolled that the large attic classrooms turned
out to be inadequate. Ellen Emerson later wrote to Mrs.
Agassiz how vividly she recalled "with joy that beloved
day . . . when your school began."[3]

What we know of the school conveys the impression
that learning was no less serious than in a similar institu-

tion for boys. "I myself superintend the methods of instruction," wrote Louis Agassiz, who lectured the girls on physical geography, natural history, and botany, "and while maintaining that regularity and precision in studies so important to mental training, I shall endeavor to prevent the necessary discipline from falling into a lifeless routine."[4]

It is worth noting that Louis Agassiz, a well-known opponent of the discoveries of Charles Darwin, became one of the few Harvard Professors able to reach the imagination of the young Henry Adams. In recalling his own education at Harvard fifty years later, Henry cited Agassiz's course, The Glacial Period and Palaeontology, as having "more influence on his curiosity than the rest of the college instruction altogether."[5] Agassiz, as Ernest Samuels points out, "maintained toward science the anti-rationalist point of view" that would ruin the validity of Adams' future study of scientific thought. "The point is crucial," Samuels concludes, "because, though religion disappeared from his early life . . . it was not replaced by a philosophy of naturalism or scientific materialism"; Henry Adams continued "to adhere almost desperately to a philosophy of quasi-idealism."[6] So also did Clover Adams. Agassiz's philosophy would have been easy to reconcile with Clover's mother's Transcendentalism. Telling his life story many years after his wife's death, Henry would unconsciously identify his personal idealism with the Hooper family's interest in the supernatural forces rather than with his own family's concern for the rational ordering of reality.

Young Alex Agassiz, a distinguished scientist who was to become a friend of both Clover and Henry, taught mathematics at his parents' school. A student described the curriculum:

> Alex . . . had the classes in geometry, trigonometry and chemistry, lectures on astronomy, and on chemistry with experiments. Miss Helen Clapp [afterwards head of the well-known school in Boston] taught Latin, botany with

Gray's textbooks, and arithmetic. . . . Miss Le Clere, an admirable teacher, had the French classes and lectures in French literature. Professor Schmidt of Harvard had the German classes; Professor Luigi Monti of Harvard, the Italian. Mr. Gurney, later Dean of Harvard University, taught Greek. Professor J. R. Lowell and Professor Child of Harvard lectured to the School, and there were lectures on art by William J. Stillman.[7]

Professor Felton, later president of Harvard, also helped teach Latin and Greek, Benjamin Pierce, a Harvard mathematician, provided "mathematical puzzles," and Mrs. Agassiz herself taught English and music. In encouraging the elective system, in which students determined their own courses of study, the school was somewhat in advance of Harvard—perhaps the only mark of its frivolity. "Some of the studies may be made elective," Agassiz wrote, "as I disapprove of binding every mind to the same kind of training and should prefer to adapt the education, as far as may be consistent with the order of a school, to individual character."[8] The idea of educating each individual to fulfill himself or herself, rather than to fit into a social mold, reinforced the Emersonian individualism the Hoopers knew so well. Ellen Hooper's husband, Whitman Gurney, an instructor at the Agassiz School who would become dean of Harvard, would later be one of President Eliot's chief allies in championing the elective system against the many conservative faculty members who resisted bringing it to Harvard.

Not only did the Agassiz family, with the help of the Harvard staff, relay much of the conventional university curriculum to the young ladies of the school at the same time as they stressed individualism, but they also improved upon Boston provinciality and Harvard traditionalism by emphasizing the "musical, artistic, and literary" interests of a more cosmopolitan culture. Whitman Gurney would later urge the establishment of the Harvard Fine Arts chair (which Charles Eliot Norton filled) arguing that "the study of history should be recognized to have other sides than the political and legal, from which sides alone it is now approached in the college."[9] The Agassiz School consistently attempted to inculcate its students with the high culture they were to be responsible for maintaining. Music was an especially important part of any young lady's education; it remained a lifelong interest of Clover Adams, who would later ask her father to mail her collection of piano scores to Washington and who would attend as many concerts as she could. The upper middle-class daughters enrolled in the school also devised homemade theatricals and elaborate parties for themselves and were urged to learn to dance at the famous Papanti dancing school. Their brothers went with them but were more reluctant to speak of it in writing; Clover's letters, however, would lead us to believe that Henry was eventually the more enthusiastic dancer. As she grew older, the serious intellectuality absorbed in her home and school environments did not adapt itself easily to pure frivolity.

The Agassiz girls were spared the physical class warfare that Henry Adams described as part of his own education on the Boston Common, but whether their behavior was more genteel than the boys' fighting remains a question. They had a lot of freedom and there was a good deal of unsupervised horseplay in their lives. Descriptions of the bus rides from Boston to the Agassiz School suggest that they were as uncivilized as similar school bus rides would be today; one of the students, Clover's cousin Alice Hooper,

> who rode without seeming to know there is anybody else in the world, now varies her old way of getting ugly and tormenting her neighbors for room, on which occasions she and they begin to fight and roar, and all around her are stirred up and enjoy it immensely.

Another student, Anna Russell, "puts her feet on the seats, wants her own way, throws her muff into everybody's face. Then she snatches somebody else's muff and sends it to the other end of the omnibus, gets people's luncheons and pretends to throw them out of the window . . . but, in all this, she never does a single thing that isn't just too ladylike."[10] Being "ladylike" in nineteenth-century Boston had a wide range of connotations. What is important to realize, however, is how few restraints shaped the characters of these girls. The evidence, including the descriptions of rowdiness, suggests that the Agassiz School was a liberating experience for the young ladies lucky enough to attend it. This group of students was not compelled to believe that conventional decorum and respectable domesticity were goals in life; in fact, one Agassiz graduate went on to develop an unconventional, socialistic, domestic scheme to save women work by using communal kitchens.[11]

For Clover Hooper, the school experience may have been even broader; not only did she profit intellectually from her work at the Agassiz School, but she also gained a friend in her teacher Catherine Howard, who played a motherly role in Clover's life at a time when the young woman's need for intimacy was strong. Catherine Howard's sister described "one friendship which Kate made while teaching in Mr. Agassiz's School—with Clover Hooper, who, though much younger than Kate, formed a strong attachment to her. She visited us several times and always showed a great desire to help Kate regain her health."[12] Perhaps the memory of her mother's consumption—enforced by the many poems and letters left behind that spoke of Ellen Sturgis Hooper's confrontation with death—made Clover all the more anxious to help her ailing teacher. The compassionate Clover wished to help her teacher fulfill an impossible dream; she divulged a scheme, a plan she had long cherished—to give Kate enough money to spend at least a year in Europe.

In the memorial volume to Catherine Howard prepared by her sister in 1882, Clover's letters urging the acceptance of the gift were published. "I am not making any sacrifice, nor entailing any degree of self-denial on myself," she wrote, "Three years ago I made a will and left you five thousand dollars—but you see, I don't die but only 'wax fat and kick,' and so not wishing to be balked by destiny in my lawful pleasures, I told my brother the other day that I meant to ask you to take it now [1869] when I might have the pleasure of seeing you get some fun of it."[13] Clover's jocular, indifferent tone finally persuaded the impecunious teacher to accept the ample gift. Sensitive to attitudes toward money that were necessarily different from those of her own class, Clover remarked, "Knowing Kate as well as I do, I would not for worlds ask her to go to Europe and let me pay her expenses. She would squeeze and economize to the last degree. Now she knows just what she has and can use it as she pleases."[14] Perhaps aware of this story of his wife's youthful generosity, Henry Adams would later subsidize John La Farge's trips to Japan.

The Clover Adams later "improved" by Henry into worrying about her appearance and wearing Worth gowns because her husband jestingly insisted, "people who study Greek must take pains with their dress,"[15] was a far cry from the free-spirited student who advised her teacher on how to dress in Europe: "I believe in few dresses and mostly short; people seem to me to be delightfully shabby in traveling. I was advised to take a curtain for my stateroom and all sorts of bags and nonsense, and took nothing, and was very happy and untrammeled."[16] Eventually, Kate Howard spent a week with the Adamses in Washington, suggesting Clover's reluctance to give up that part of her education which meant the establishment of a lasting emotional tie as well as the training of the mind. At this time, however, the two women did not share many activities; in fact, Clover sought companionship for Kate when she and Henry went out together. How Henry felt about Clover's close relationship with her former teacher is not articulated, but after her marriage, all of Clover's earlier women friends seemed to disappear from her life.

How a girl who attended the Agassiz School "amounted to something," in George Ticknor's terms, is worth considering. Women of Clover's class were exposed to almost the same knowledge that men were exposed to, but the expectations of what they were to do with it were quite different. We know that Ellen Emerson, who had been writing fairly complex papers about glaciers and the Arctic regions, went on to an apprenticeship in housekeeping and after that to begin her career as superintendent of the house.[17] Perhaps this description from a letter home, an early example of a vocabulary of professionalized domesticity, simply enhanced her sense of domestic necessity; to go on studying geology in depth would have been out of the question. The Agassiz School, in spite of its associations with intellectual quality, did not really intend to prepare women for any social or professional role outside the home. Ellen Emerson wrote that she had the famous Professor Felton of Harvard for her Greek teacher, but in spite of his eminence Greek flourished but poorly, because the students had a recitation only once a week. Society expected no more; for women, as guardians of culture, were to remain in the home. We might finally conclude that Margaret Fuller's plaintive description of women's education remained applicable to the education offered by the Agassiz family a generation later:

> Women are now taught at school all that men are. They run over superficially even *more* studies, without being really taught anything. But with this difference: men are called on from a very early period to reproduce all that they learn. Their college exercises, their political duties, their professional studies, the first actions of life in any direction, call on them to put to use what they have learned. But women learn without any attempt to reproduce. Their only reproduction is for purposes of display. . . .[18]

Fuller did not use "reproduce" with any sense of its more ironical meaning for women. There is no question that her own Conversation classes were meant to reinforce the legitimacy of female intellectual activity; indeed they provided some impetus for the founding of a number of new women's colleges. In similar fashion, the seriousness of the Agassiz School provided the necessary background for the beginning of Radcliffe College in 1879, which was a more deliberate attempt to equate women's education with men's. Clover's sister Ellen remained in Cambridge and played a role in shaping the new institution for educating women.

In a letter from Washington, Clover would write: "To my sister, hand in glove with Mrs. Agassiz in the founding of Radcliffe College," revealing her pride and her vicarious pleasure in Ellen's involvement with the new college for women.[19] Some letters mentioned the money Clover was sending to support the Harvard Annex; others bemoaned the fact that "Washington nabobs" could not be counted on to contribute—"No one here cares for higher education—for women or men either."[20] New Englanders, on the other hand, with a tradition of intellectual achievement reaching back to the Puritans would not be so boorish. The story of the founding of Radcliffe College, or the Harvard Annex as it was then called, may illustrate better than many overtly hostile gestures toward women's equality, however, the ambiguity the nineteenth century felt about women's roles—an ambiguity that caused all but the most stalwart feminist to feel hesitant or insecure about the pursuit of her own intellectuality. On the one hand, most enlightened people in New England, believed that education for women was important and was somehow related to their roles as trustees of morality. The more aggressive suffragists felt education essential to any kind of sophisticated voting. Even *Godey's Ladies' Magazine*, which consistently avoided controversy, always supported all levels of education for women. On the other hand, members of powerful male institutions made clear their reluctance to provide educational resources for a group of intellectually suspect individuals, they did not concur with the idea that all intelligent human beings, regardless of sex, deserved to be educated—a sentiment eloquently expressed in Margaret Fuller's *Woman in the Nineteenth Century*.

President Eliot's 1869 Harvard inaugural speech bravely acknowledged the need to discuss wider educational opportunities for women: "America is the natural arena for these debates; for here the female sex has a better past and a better present than elsewhere. Americans as a rule hate disabilities of all sorts, whether religious, political or social."[21] Whether Eliot considered woman's disability to be her female sexuality or her lack of education seemed quite consciously ambiguous. "As in the case of certain ethnic minorities," says Hugh Hawkins in his biography of Eliot, "inclusion of women at Harvard was regarded by portions of its constituency as a sign of institutional decay."[22] Eliot forthrightly concluded that, after all, "the world knows next to nothing about the natural mental capacities of the female sex." Women living in such an environment of hesitation could not help being shaped by these innuendoes of incompetence.

Although Clover's sister Ellen seemed to question Eliot's opinions of women's intellectual abilities, her letters, which showed concern for the new students' housing and health, indicate her awareness of the common fear that women were often too weak to withstand the pressures of rigorous mental activity. Unlike most women of her age and class, however, Ellen Gurney was willing to experiment with serious learning. Harvard Classics Professor Goodwin remembered her "toiling up the long staircase of Harvard Hall . . . with her Greek books to hear a comedy of Aristophanes," and, he continued, "Her coming to Cambridge made an era in our intellectual life. She brought into it a fresh vitality which I shall never forget. I never undertook any important work in connection with my professorship without consulting her as well as her husband, and I never failed to receive the best advice."[23] "She became at once most devoted to the new women's college," Goodwin continued, "and Mrs. Agassiz always depended upon her in every forward step which was taken. She was one of a class of ladies who one year entered their names as students of the 'Annex,' paid their fees, and read Greek poetry with me in my study." He might have added that her involvement with the college was so intense that the first commencement of four graduates took place in the Gurneys' private library.

Whitman Gurney, who was encouraged by his wife to share an "unabated interest in the education of women," planned to offer the Annex the same three-year course in the development of political institutions that he was then teaching at Harvard. Remarking that two of his students ("one could not have more satisfactory pupils") had somehow been misled on the schedule of the program, he complained, "I should wish the Annex more scrupulous in fulfilling all reasonable anticipation founded on its statements."[24] The mix-up seemed typical of the obstacles facing serious women students, but at that time no woman would have dared to protest.

Indeed, President Eliot lectured the ladies, not on Chemistry—his field of scholarship—but on good manners. Women had to be reminded of their place. Elizabeth Cary Agassiz's letters continually reflect her awareness that being "aggressive" might ruin the whole enterprise. She never dared assert that bright women deserved to have a good education; rather she would continue to express gratitude to Harvard for allowing her "little craft" to be "moored safely . . . against the great body of instruction which represents the scholarship and teaching force of our old university."[25] Should a woman student complain about suffocation in an overcrowded classroom, her tone would be rebuked as "anything but courteous."[26]

But even Elizabeth Agassiz would occasionally lose patience with Harvard when a student's use of the Harvard Yard and library was in question. She once managed to complain to Eliot:

> It seemed to me absurd that the student should lose a privilege which was already hers as a resident of Cambridge—As far as I can remember the little I said at our meeting was to recom-

mend that the College Yard should not be used as a thorough-fare by our pupils however convenient it might be in that way—as shortening distance, etc. This rule I told them should be observed but did not apply to a special purpose like that of a visit to the library.

What do you say about this matter? I am inclined to believe that we may allow things to go as they are and that if here and there some of our pupils go to the library to consult some book they cannot reach otherwise it will be allowed to pass without adverse criticism.[27]

When Justin Winsor, the Harvard librarian, qualified his answer to one Annex student's request by adding, "I fear this lady fancies the relations of the Annex to her being are other than those of sufferance," he was probably conveying exactly the mixed feelings most members of the Harvard establishment had about women's education. Rather than encouraging women to learn, Harvard was setting up all sorts of subtle difficulties to discourage them from seeing themselves as worthy of the attention of serious scholarly minds.

Whatever the strengths of the Hooper daughters' education, it did not provide them with any depth of self-assurance. The general ambiguity of the intellectual establishment, which wanted woman to be a good influence on man rather than an individual in her own right, took its toll. Giving with one hand, yet taking away with the other, America's most secure university reinforced the anxiety women invariably have about competition with men. Harvard's doubts about women underlined women's eternal doubts about themselves. For example, Ellen Gurney had intended to give all of Whitman Gurney's library, 7,750 volumes, to the Annex; but after his death, her own uncertain belief in women's judgment, reinforced by such confrontations as Mrs. Agassiz's, finally caused her to write Justin Winsor that the Annex should have any of Mr. Gurney's books "which you can spare or duplicate."[28]

Outsiders making inquiries (in the hundreds) into the nature of the Annex's provisions for education, often seemed to sense its inadequacies. "Is Harvard," wrote Vandalia Varnum in 1880, from Cornellsville, New York, "with all its antagonistic bearing toward women the best place for me to secure the best results?" One father, who was touchingly concerned for his daughter's future, in 1879 noted, "I find on comparing, that the 'Preliminary Examinations for Women' are, on the average, considerably more difficult than those for entrance into the [Harvard] Freshman class." A mother from Cleveland wondered,

> Will you also tell me if young ladies are treated
> by the professors and students in a manner to
> make a sensible girl feel such self-respect as
> would render her comfortable if she came a
> stranger and alone to Cambridge as a student.
> Does the certificate given at the end of a full
> and satisfactory course of study state *explicitly*
> that the course would entitle the holder to the
> degree of A.B. if she was a man student. . . .[29]

Other institutions perceived Harvard's hesitant commitment to women's education. "We may create an Annex of our own," wrote the president of Columbia, "which will be, what Harvard Annex is not, a regular branch of our college." In a letter to Thomas Wentworth Higginson, which is included in the papers of Radcliffe's Treasurer, C. C. Thackford at Cornell noted, "Co-education was established here without consulting the Faculty, and many of them having Harvard and Yale notions have from the first been opposed to it."[30] That President Eliot, as Hugh Hawkins points out, "could firmly deny both that Harvard deprived women of intellectual rights and that it had embarked on so perilous a course as 'what is called co-education,'"[31] must have thoroughly confused the women involved in its programs. Indeed, "during the first decade of Mr. Eliot's presidency, Harvard showed no intention of admitting women to any of its professional schools or to candidacy for a Harvard degree."[32]

Ned Hooper, the loyal treasurer of Harvard University, sometimes encouraged his sisters' pursuit of education, but more often shared the ambivalence of the institution he represented. Unable to make any connection between his sisters' involvement in women's education and the need for Harvard's commitment, he peevishly wrote to Elizabeth Cary Agassiz in 1893: "I have no prejudice in the matter of education of women and am quite willing to see Yale or Columbia take any risks they like, but I feel bound to protect Harvard College from what seems to me to be a risky experiment."[33] To be sure, neither Clover Adams nor Ellen Gurney was able to participate fully in the "risky experiment." Ellen was in her late thirties, considered "old," when she helped form the Collegiate Institute that would become Radcliffe, and Clover had already moved to Washington. Yet their spiritual involvement in the founding of the college was nonetheless real; they were aware of an important need as much as they were victims of cultural restraint. What they saw finally as the limitations of their own educations, training that enabled them to perceive the quality of their intellects but neglected to develop their potential, might be profitably compared with Henry Adams' symbolic sense of the limitation of his own training.

For nowhere are the sardonic exaggerations of *The Education of Henry Adams* "more misleading than in the brilliant chapter on Harvard College."[34] If we consider his general picture of a life ill-trained to cope with modern science and politics and drained of feeling by narrow parochial tradition, we can understand why Henry has chosen to show Harvard as a "negative force"; yet, as Ernest Samuels illustrated in detail, "Nothing could have been farther from the fact. The four years at that maligned institution touched Adams' mind at so many points and so pervasively that even had he been a willing debtor he could hardly have listed his full obligation." Not only was his intellectual ability, particularly his writing skill, recognized and encouraged during those years that "he took to the pen," but his mind was also trained to take such work seriously. The ability to write out tensions became a self-preserving strength to Henry Adams; he recognized his literary skill as "a sort of blind man's dog to keep him from falling into the gutters."[35]

Adams, moreover, learned to feel, as few men did and no woman ever could, a "proprietary interest" in the college: "His father, his grandfather, and his great-grandfather were only the more distinguished members of a lineage which had made the mental scale of Harvard its own."[36] If the experience at Harvard failed to *educate* him, in the sense that Adams struggled with the word in the story of his life, if he clearly understood that the Harvard graduate's worst weakness would be "self-criticism and self-consciousness," Adams nonetheless asserted that that same graduate would also have had high ambitions, and "nearly always led a life more or less worth living." His attitude towards Harvard as "worthless" became part of a literary pose suggestive of Emerson's ambiguous definition of "The American Scholar." Adams would acknowledge that Harvard also provided him with a sense of "calm": "Self-possession was the strongest part of Harvard College, which certainly taught men to stand alone."[37] The self-possession and self-confidence as well as the skills and knowledge acquired at Harvard would remain with Adams in spite of his pose of failure. When, as a professor, he would write to Justin Winsor requesting the Harvard carpenter to build special wooden boxes for the purpose of sending old *Boston Advertisers* back and forth to Beverly Farms, we cannot imagine for a moment that Winsor would question his rights to special privilege.

"Self-possession" and the ability "to stand alone" seemed to be precisely what even the most spirited middle-class women could not find in the educational atmosphere of Harvard; their intellectual resources were not being trained to give them independent strength. For the

Hooper women, particularly, who had developed the capacity for deep emotional attachment that Henry Adams often felt he lacked, self-reliance seemed out of the question. Each sister's inability to cope with the loss of someone deeply loved ultimately drove her to a despair beyond mourning and to her death. We cannot imagine either woman writing, as Adams did to Henry Cabot Lodge after Anna Lodge died, "Try to go on with your daily work. You can probably do it better now than ever. You will work not for the public but for yourself."[38]

With the full onslaught of the Civil War in 1863, the Agassiz School disbanded, but the students, as so often happens in wartime, did not lose their sense of feminine solidarity. They threw themselves into the war effort with intensity and enthusiasm, if not with the greatest efficiency: "Mrs. Agassiz's girls had the mortification of having their work [they were sewing bandages] returned as not done well enough."[39] Both Clover and Ellen continued to work for the Sanitary Commission in Massachusetts, an organization that functioned somewhat like the Red Cross in more recent wars. Most women working for the "Sanitary" made bandages or raised money, while the more truly independent, like Louisa May Alcott, went off to nurse soldiers. The war gave them what their education did not, a tremendous sense of their own worth:

> The part which the women of America took in the recent war was proof of the virtue of the system of our democratic society. The days for the flattery of women, like the days of chivalry, have gone by; but never did women, as a portion of the community, show themselves more worthy of respect and admiration, than during these years in which they bore so heavy and bitter a portion of the sacrifices, so essential a portion of the labors, which the country required from her children. The main work of the supply of the necessities of the Sanitary Commission was performed by them; and to every

demand made upon them, whether for such work as only they would do or for work in which they shared with men, they showed themselves sufficient. Whatever women have done in other countries and in past times for soldiers whom they loved, or for a cause to which they were devoted, was more than matched by what our women did. The story of the war is a story of what was done by the combined efforts of men and women; and the history of the Sanitary Commission is a record of their common zeal, devotion, and labor.[40]

After the war, Clover and Ellen both traveled to Washington to watch the Grand Review parade of the armies of Grant and Sherman, an adventure they each recorded in letters to cousins. Because their indulgent father could not then accompany his daughters, they "rushed out into the street in the rain for a *man*," wrote Ellen, and "Clover foamed at the mouth and swore," she was so determined to go. Having finally persuaded the father of one of their "Sanitary" friends to accompany them, they set out without any room reservations: "I only tell you all this to show you what fun we had in meeting one obstacle after another and knocking them over as fast as they came up," noted Clover, whose bravado clearly impressed Ellen, who wrote, "Clover's courage rather oozed."[41]

Once in Washington, they visited hospitals, talked to ex-slaves, and rode out to Sherman's encampment. They attended the trial of the conspirators against Lincoln. "It's crowded; but we squeeze in and get some reporters' chairs. . . . Being a woman has its advantages on this occasion" Clover remarked (suggesting that she was well aware of other occasions when it did not). While in the Capital, they went to look at Lincoln's bloody pillow—"a painful sight, and yet we wanted to see it, as it is an historical fact and makes it so vivid to be in the place where such a tragedy has been enacted." Her insistent honesty, like Henry Adams', would always remain one of Clover's most appealing strengths. Both sisters, however, retained the sensibility that enabled them to balance emotions: "It was a strange feeling to be so intensely happy and triumphant, and yet to feel like crying . . . dear old 2nd Massachusetts Infantry," Clover wrote, "not an officer in it now that we know."[41] "You felt," remarked Ellen, "as if there were another army—larger and finer—marching above them." Of the ex-slaves they encountered, Ellen believed that "their fervid faith and strange power of imagination and sympathy made them see what a colder, more critical race could not. . . ."[42] Although both women exploited their romantic sensibilities and admired spiritual power, they never gave up wanting the better education that the colder, more critical race offered its sons as a means to political power and intellectual fulfillment.

"I never had such an interesting evening in my life," wrote Clover to her cousin, Lou Shaw, summarizing the enthusiasm of her involvement on the Washington trip. Not once in an eight-page letter did she describe herself as unequal to the task of writing about her experiences. Although she commented that it was "absurd to try and describe such a week,"[43] she had no qualms about attempting it. After her marriage to Henry Adams, Clover would express many doubts about her ability to write.

# 4

# Becoming an Adams

*So much is said of woman being better educated*
*that they may be better companions and mothers of men! . . .*
*The intellect, no more than the sense of hearing,*
*is to be cultivated, that she may be a more valuable companion*
*to man, but because the Power who gave a power by*
*its mere existence signifies that it must be brought out*
*towards perfection.*
Margaret Fuller, *Woman in the Nineteenth Century*

Oh for the pen of Abigail Adams,"[1] wrote Clover to her father from her wedding trip in 1872, suggesting that along with the desire for fluency, she may have consciously felt herself drawn into the great epistolary tradition of the Adams family. Charles Francis Adams had praised the letters of his grandmother Abigail as exemplary in their honesty: "There is not so much room for the doctrines of expediency and the promptings of private interest, to compromise the force of public example." He added:

> The expression of feelings by women in the heart of a community, at a moment of extraordinary trial, recorded in a shape evidently designed to be secret and confidential, this would seem to present the surest and most unfailing index to its general character.[2]

Henry Adams would later write. to his English friend Gaskell that—except for Franklin—the best letter writers of the American Revolutionary era were his own ancestors: "In the way of letters there is nothing but my old great-grandmother Abigail Adams's that are worth reading."[3]

To the Adamses, letters were rarely just personal messages; more often, they became a form of recording social history. The eighteenth-century perception of the letter as a serious literary form remained with Henry Adams; he analyzed his own letters as his father had analyzed Abigail's: "I still would like to think that a century or two hence when everything else about it is forgotten, my letters might still be read and quoted as a memorial of manners and habits at the time of the great secession of 1860."[4] The idea of being a "public example" remained real for generations of Adamses. Simply to be an Adams was to be aware that society was looking to see what role you would play and how you would analyze your part. When Emerson later articulated his concern about "representative" men to Clover's contemporaries, he was conceptualizing the trust in a democracy's ability to produce leaders in every field—the kind of men that the Adamses realized they must become. Ernest Samuels poignantly describes Henry and Charles writing nightly in their journals during their Harvard years:

> There is something almost of pathos in the picture of the two brothers in their room at Mrs. Storey's entering each day's epitaph with the sense of a hypercritical posterity—the fate of an Adams—standing at their shoulders. Of Henry's journal nothing survived the impulsive destruction of his papers that followed the suicide of his wife in 1885.[5]

But the contempt or fear he expressed for the written word in 1885 was certainly not a part of Henry Adams' early training; and Clover wanted to share his passion for keeping records. Not only would she help him with the details of his historical work, she would also contribute her own account of their life together in her dutiful, detailed, weekly letters to her home. The letters she wrote her father, flip and personal as they often were, might also become a "memorial of the manners and habits" of the period just after the Civil War. During the one period of her honeymoon when we know she felt depressed, she wrote no letters for two and a half weeks: correspondence was meant to be social criticism not personal therapy. Eventually, the gregarious Dr. Hooper with fatherly pride would read Clover's letters aloud to gathered relatives and friends, making her all the more self-conscious as a writer. Her very own words would sometimes be repeated to her from Boston visitors to Washington, and she would have to urge her father to use discretion concerning special tidbits: "I wouldn't have my gibes come back to hurt feelings," she insisted.[6]

If becoming an Adams meant becoming a social reporter, becoming the wife of an Adams seemed to have more far-reaching consequences. Even the vigorous Abigail, who urged her husband to remember the ladies and be more generous and favorable to them than his ancestors had been, received few rewards beyond cajoling and tolerant affection for her suggestions. In the introduction to his grandmother's letters, Charles Francis Adams noted that he had deleted those letters "too uniformly mournful in their tone to be suitable for insertion in full," and he had cut out private matters "not deemed suitable for publication."[7] The impression of complete fulfillment that Abigail Adams suggested to him, the habits of a vigorous mind "formed in contending with difficulties" represented some degree of distortion. Abigail would have been closer to the women in Clover's family than to the Adams men in her frequent lamentations about women's education: "I regret the trifling, narrow, contracted education of the females of my own country," she wrote in 1778. "In this country, you need not be told how much female education is neglected, nor how fashionable it has been to ridicule female learning." Although she acknowledged her happiness in marriage to be "connected with a person of a more generous mind"—as Clover herself would have done—the fact remained that becoming "learned" was out of the question for a woman, no matter how intellectually capable she was:

> There are so few women who may be really called learned, that I do not wonder they are considered as black swans. It requires such talents and such devotion of time and study, as to exclude the performance of most of the domestic cares and duties which exclusively fall to the lot of most females in this country.

Wanting to be loved perhaps more than she wanted to be admired, Abigail Adams made her letters eloquent and consoled herself for her lack of knowledge with the assurance that most gentlemen, after all, "consider a companion more desirable than a rival."[8] Ultimately, history would acknowledge her as an intellectual force.

Abigail's daughter-in-law Louisa Johnson, John Quincy's wife, may have been less philosophical as well as less vigorous. To her, Abigail wrote an autobiographical letter (similar to one addressed to an interested publisher) illustrating some of the pride in her self-made mind, along with some of the regrets:

> But neither grammar nor orthography or our native language was considered a part of female education and I have through life lamented the deficiency in this respect. . . . As to style I make not any pretensions to it and must trust to the candour of my correspondents to receive the matter as flowing from the heart without regarding the elegance of diction. I might almost say with Gray's hermit
>
> > The little learning I have gained
> > Is all from simple nature drained.
>
> . . . Your style is much more correct and elegant than mine.[9]

Perhaps these final words were meant to cheer up her delicate daughter-in-law, whom Henry Adams would remember as the grandmother with southern sensibilities so out of place in Quincy, Massachusetts.

Henry attributed his heritage of contention and alienation to Louisa Johnson Adams; in her, he found "those rebellions against law and discipline, which marked more than one of her descendants."[10] As a contentious spirit, Clover Hooper might have also identified herself with the eccentric Louisa. It was Louisa's diary, *Adventures of a Nobody*, that Henry carefully copied by hand, augmenting it with some of her letters for publication, just as his father had paid similar homage to Abigail Adams. Criticized by his brother Charles for giving so much attention to this "ancient lady of our house," Henry retorted— "You like roughness and strength; I like taste and dexterity."[11] Yet he dropped the project. Louisa Johnson Adams, nevertheless, was the person he felt closest to. In the *Education*, he wrote of his grandmother, "Try as she might, the Madam could never be Bostonian, and it was her cross in life, but to the boy it was her charm."[12] Her southern blood and her English birth somehow denied her access to New England austerity, and her exotic, emotional, impractical qualities suggested a more poetic world to the young Henry:

> Louisa was charming, like a Romney portrait, but among her many charms that of being a New England woman was not one. The defect was serious. Her future mother-in-law, Abigail, a famous New England woman whose authority over her turbulent husband, the second President, was hardly so great as that which she exercised over her son, the sixth to be, was troubled by the fear that Louisa might not be made of stuff stern enough, or brought up in conditions severe enough to suit a New England climate, or to make an efficient wife for her paragon son, and Abigail was right on that point, as on most others where sound judg-

ment was involved; but sound judgment is sometimes a source of weakness rather than of force, and John Quincy already had reason to think that his mother held sound judgments on the subject of daughters-in-law which human nature, since the fall of Eve, made Adams helpless to realize. Being three thousand miles away from his mother, and equally far in love, he married Louisa in London.[13]

As Abigail had foreseen, Louisa's life, as recorded in the diary Henry assiduously copied, turned out to be "one of severe stress, and little pure satisfaction," including the "four miserable years in the White House"[14] mentioned in Henry's *Education*. Louisa could not make herself share her husband's pride in serving his country, nor could she appreciate his interest in politics: "Mr. Adams had always accustomed me to believe that women had nothing to do with politics, and as he was the glass from which my opinions were reflected, I was convinced of its truth and sought no further." Less charitably, she later wrote, "My husband's time was entirely occupied by his public avocations," and she noted what might be true of many public servants, that political honors "have been purchased at a most bitter expense of duty to my children, personal suffering to myself, loss of health, and freedom of thought."[15]

In a letter written in 1840 to her son, Charles Francis, she spoke with pain of her "want of essential resources." Like her grandson Henry, Louisa Johnson Adams struggled to understand her own sensitivities: "The faults of my character have never been corrected owing to a happy but alas a visionary education, which has made the disgusting realities of a heartless political life, a source of disappointment."[16] The copy of the diary that Henry made often reflected her worries about her "gaucheries" as well as her concern for her children, two of whom she was forced to leave behind when she accompanied her ambassador husband abroad (another child died in Russia). Her observations were often keen as well as innocent, however, and in her writing she maintained the tradition of personal honesty that belonged to all the Adams women apart from their public facades. In 1802, a time when John Quincy was still able to give attention to his family, she wondered if she was too ill-trained to profit from her husband's instruction:

> Our only evening relaxation was when Mr. Adams read to us, who in the fervour of a lately acquired parental duty, our son being eighteen months old, studied all the works on education from Locke to Miss Edgeworth, in which studies I participated orally—I fear without deriving the benefit which ought to have rewarded his increasing exertions in my behalf.[17]

Like most nineteenth-century women of her class, she continued to feel uncertain about how far women's education should go. The "masculine minds" she encountered in certain better-educated women troubled her: "There is generally a want of feminine grace and sweetness in these showy strong-minded women, which produces fear in us lesser lights, and this has always been my first impression on becoming acquainted with them, yet they always appear to me to be what God intended woman to be before she was cowed by her master."[18]

If Louisa could never appreciate politics, she, nevertheless, like Abigail Adams, had absorbed her husband's vocabulary of fundamental human rights to express her feelings about herself. Have Americans of either sex ever readily accepted the idea that anyone should have a "master"? Marriage must always cause suffering in a democratic society unless the partners see their contract as a source of liberation and individual reinforcement rather than as a source of enslavement. Henry Adams, who was interested in the sources of human institutions, would go on to explore the role of women in primitive societies; he would conclude that slavery had never been their natural state. Louisa Johnson's intellectual bequest to her family remains complex, but "in her chafing against the constraints of her husband's New England conscience, she became for her grandson the peculiar intimate connection with his own emotional nature. Her recollected image disclosed to him the antinomies of easy Southern ways at odds with the Northern necessity of unremitting work, and of feminine sensibility in ultimate opposition to a masculine sense of duty."[19] Like Clover— at least as Henry described his grandmother from the vantage point of age—Louisa Catherine relied on her sensibilities for insight into life; she remained, like Clover, dissatisfied with her formal education, but Clover had a great capacity for enjoyment that Louisa Catherine lacked. The letters of Henry's grandmother that characterize her as a restless spirit in search of "repose and contentment, two things utterly and entirely out of my reach," not only reveal her closeness to Henry's own sensitivities but also manage to articulate the kind of *public example* that Charles Francis Adams would hardly have welcomed. The constant difficulty that even prominent women had in clarifying their roles in the nineteenth century emerged in a letter she wrote to her son in 1837:

> The duties of the female sex may generally be expected to be too burdensome to admit of much devotion to pursuits exclusively literary or political, or even to that species of social influence which in other countries has often made women the arbiters of weal or woe to a nation. The position in life of the greater number is determined by the accident of marriage and depends upon the success of exertions made by those who happen to become their partners.[20]

She went on to add a statement that might still baffle many working women, but that would have been understood by those idealized ladies anxious to leap off their pedestals and play some influential role outside of their homes: "Mere wealth is rather an obstacle than an advance to the distinction most coveted." Louisa Catherine concluded with a description of her own life, of leisure hours filled with "the literary tastes which had always predominated," and she boasted that her most satisfying real accomplishment was the large quilt or counterpane, knit entirely by herself, that had been exhibited at the Fair of the Mechanic Association in September 1837. She was pleased to have a woman's skills recognized.

If Charles Francis Adams could not value his mother's keen feelings as much as he admired his grandmother's strength, or could never see the letters she addressed to him as illustrations of an age when "great necessities call out great virtues,"[21] his wife's letters would be even more appalling to him as a record of weakness and failure. That the letters of Abigail Brooks Adams, or the letters about her, survive at all is a tribute to the honesty of a clan whose main measure has been public achievement.

"The condition of my wife 'tis give me constant anxiety, the worst part of which is that I know not what it is best to do for her," wrote the laconic Charles Francis in his diary on June 30, 1873.[22] Had he been less inhibited, he might have included the same entry fairly often during the second half of their life together. To be sure, Mrs. Adams seems to have had many real physical complaints, yet students of nineteenth-century women's ailments will recognize her sudden recoveries and causeless depressions as typical of the neuroses of her class and time. Neurasthenia, caused by frustration, was a common nineteenth-century New England female ailment.[23]

According to Charles Francis Jr.'s report of her reaction to his father's appointment as Ambassador to Britain, Abigail Brooks could be genuinely hysterical: she cried all day, "foreseeing all sorts of evil consequences, and absolutely refusing to be comforted"; "My mother," Charles wrote, "took a constitutional and sincere pleasure in the forecast of evil."[24] Not only would the sensitive Henry come to reflect her frequent pessimism, but his attentiveness would also often help to alleviate her pain. He always had a deep respect for his mother's intellectual capabilities and seemed to be the son most able to empathize and cope with her frequent afflictions.

In one letter to his brother Brooks, Henry mentioned discussions with his mother that had left him "feeling more like a selfish low-minded fool than I ever did before in my life"; another time he wrote Charles Gaskell that his mother was the only member of his family "with anything to talk about."[25] In the story of his education he credited his mother with making the most of the experience as Ambassador's wife she had so dreaded: "Her success and popularity in England exceeded that of her husband—."[26] In her correspondence with her father, Clover Adams summed up the British reaction to the differences in the elder Adamses' personalities: "The Lord Chancellor's wife, Lady Selborne, said, 'Give my love to Mrs. Adams and to Mr. Adams my regards—if he will accept them!'"[27] Charles Francis Adams' disciplined austerity nevertheless enabled him to achieve his great mission to keep the British out of our Civil War; popularity was never considered a virtue worth cultivating by the Adamses. But public service had limitations for women, and Henry Adams often saw his mother restless and in pain.

In 1872, in the months just preceding Henry's marriage, Abigail Brooks Adams grew particularly miserable. She may have felt fears for Henry similar to those the earlier Abigail Adams had intuited about her son's marriage. She could also have felt the pain of losing her most attentive son. Emotionally dependent on Charles Francis, her husband, who was abroad on another diplomatic mission, Abigail Brooks alarmed her children by having a complete breakdown. Mary, the daughter who most often took care of "Mamma," wrote to her father, "I must tell you honestly if Mamma remains as she is I do not think any of us would dare to undertake a voyage with her without you. . . . Her worries have now got quite her control."[28] Henry himself wrote two days later, "The difficulty is merely that her nervous system does not recover its balance readily. She has nothing to discompose her but is simply nervous. . . . Of course we should all be glad to have you return, and I among the gladdest, for the necessity of taking charge of Mamma cuts wofully [sic] into my regular duties." With the authority of someone still in charge, he warned his less sensitive father that "it would be better to put your return on the ground of business entirely, not of Mamma's health. The latter reason would merely give her occasion for more self-reproaches and worry."[29] A week later, Henry wrote again:

> Mamma has her good days, and her bad days, but her best are by no means gay and her worst are very bad. . . . I am tolerably well accustomed to her and all her troubles do not alarm me very much, but to persons who have had no experience with her, the effect is startling, especially as they see her when she is most upset and uncontrollable. When I returned I tried to make her promise not to talk with others while in these nervous moods but she cant help it, and I cant control her. . . . Half society will consider us, you included, as heartless brutes.
>
> She has no real anxieties and nothing new has occurred. Even her neuralgia disappears when she is mentally nervous. . . . A little excitement or novelty that gives her something amusing to think about always quiets her and makes her bright as usual. *Her difficulty is in having nothing to occupy her mind*, to counteract the influence of unpleasant ideas. . . . She is worried about trifles just as much as about serious matters. [Italics mine.]

He concluded with a gesture of sympathy toward his sister Mary, "who has to bear the heaviest part of the work," and a final assertion of his mother's incredible dependence: "She has the one fixed idea that if you were here, or if you were coming, she would be all right."[30] In January, Henry wrote of his mother, "as she has nothing to do, nor any means of distracting her thought, I see no reason to suppose that her condition will materially change for the present."[31] In a subsequent letter to his friend Gaskell, Henry did not mention his mother, but remarked of a mutual friend, "I hope future generations will invent some method of making things smoother for women."[32] The son who "never in his life" caused his father "a moment's anxiety" clearly could not share the older man's stoicism, although he did indeed grow accustomed to his mother's complaints.[33] Five years later he would describe her, in a sadly matter-of-fact way, as "not more depressed than she always was by the various exigencies of life."[34]

When Abigail Brooks Adams, accompanied by her daughter, Mary, went to New York for electrical treatments to ease her sciatica, she bombarded her husband with a series of anxious, critical letters that conditioning, perhaps, enabled him to ignore. "I find you at your old tricks again," she wrote in November, 1876. "Why do I write all this, you will neither attend to it or think of it again?" "You judge me by yourself," she noted a month later, "you ought not, we feel things so utterly unlike. Things that kill me you never think of twice. However, we are too old to change either your nature or mine."[35] In April of 1877, after almost fifty years of marriage, she could still write, "You can't understand my feelings, our natures are so entirely different."[36] Clover's photograph of Henry's parents managed to capture these differences and disappointments with eloquent concern.

We gather from Mrs. Adams' New York letters that Charles Francis would often promise to visit her then not appear, perhaps for perfectly legitimate reasons, yet nevertheless causing great pain to an individual as dependent and as sensitive as she:

> Two days you have said you thought you should come and then came this note. How I cried. . . . I know it bores you, but Oh how I have wanted you. . . . I don't wonder you don't

want to come, only try to recollect how I suffer,
how I lean on you and that the suffering is all
mine. You have not that, nor do you long for
me as I do for you.[37]

An earlier letter had already protested such indifference:
"Three times you have written you was coming and three
times given it up. Why write so if you do not intend it. It
is nothing to you but the disappointment is more than I
can bear."[38] To be sure, Abigail Brooks Adams—Henry
called her "groany"—was often unreasonable. Having so
little to occupy her good mind unquestionably led her to
entertain all sorts of destructive thoughts. Only the
patient Mary, who constantly sacrificed herself to be her
mother's companion, was spared her wrath. "It serves
John and Charles right to suffer as they do," she once
remarked; later she cried, "What are Henry and Brooks to
me?" With clear sarcasm, she wrote from New York that
"Mr. and Mrs. Henry Adams are to arrive [at the Bre-
voort] tonight. Their coming don't matter to us they are
so far off."[39] She had earlier protested that Clover should
not have allowed Charles Francis Adams to leave Henry's
house on a cold night; and she also criticized Clover's
father, Dr. Hooper, one of the few people ever to think of
inviting Mary out, for not including the former ambassador among his Thanksgiving dinner guests.

When Henry remarked that having her portrait
painted by William Morris Hunt would provide no distraction for his mother, because she "was sure to dislike
the portrait," he revealed a realistic understanding of her
temperament.[40] Few people appear sympathetically in her
letters, whether they are servants, doctors, or members
of her own family; what emerges is her own angry, frustrated personality as well as the New England penchant
for sharp and colorful judgment: "As to Mr. Breckett," she
once wrote, "if I was his wife I should be delighted he
was dead. . . . I would break the will and pay myself as
far as I was able for the horror of living with the wicked,
spiteful, nasty little toad."[41] Stories about Clover often

comment on her sharp tongue, but her words were mild compared to those of her Adams relatives. Invective was an almost conventional outlet for the frustrations and moral judgments of New Englanders as different as Mary Moody Emerson, Charles Sumner, and Grace Norton. The language of Henry and Brooks Adams might also have provided particular examples to Clover of her mother-in-law's sharpness. That Henry Adams' mother emerges in letters as an immensely complex and difficult woman, remains indisputable; to see her as a fulfilled helpmeet is to make no allowance for her intensity or her needs.

All through these querulous, critical, anxious, sad letters gleams, as well, the intellectual competence of Abigail Brooks Adams in terms of her concern for her household and staff. In spite of her emotional dependence, it was she who managed the finances of the Adamses' domestic establishment, and, when her husband grew senile, she played an even greater role in the management of the Adams–Quincy estate. The old man, "placid and not unhappy" in the senility he had once dreaded, touchingly continued to pay his respects to the "wretched" woman who had shared the rewards and disappointments of his life: "Although he was oblivious to his surroundings, he somehow never failed to signify his recognition of his wife by rising whenever she entered the room."[42]

Henry Adams would not have expected marriage to be bland or easy; nor would he have readily believed that domestic pursuits afforded adequate fulfillment for women as bright as his grandmother, or his mother, or finally his sister Louisa:

> Luckily for him he had a sister much brighter than he ever was—though he thought himself a rather superior person. . . . She was the first young woman he was ever intimate with— quick, sensitive, willful, or full of will, energetic, sympathetic and intelligent enough to supply a score of men with ideas—and he was de-

lighted to give her the reins. . . . It was his first
experiment in giving the reins to a woman and
he was so much pleased with the results that he
never wanted to take them back. In after life he
made a general law of experience—no woman
had ever driven him wrong; no man had ever
driven him right.[43]

After Clover had liberated his own sensitivities to the
degree that he could insist that women's values were
more important than men's, Henry recalled how little
most men were able to give in exchange. Louisa was the
first woman who prompted him to question deeply the
world of masculine institutions that had done so little for
her. Even Charles Francis Adams was moved to comment on his daughter's frustrated capabilities: "Poor
Louisa!" he wrote Henry, "superabounding as she is in
activity; it is a great pity she could not have had a field
for the wide and legitimate exercise of it: as it is she must
express it in the hazardous personal experiment of doing
nothing."[44] The tragedy of Louisa's early death by lock-
jaw seemed to have allied nature with institutions in an
indifference to talent and grace. Ironically, Henry's
attempt to restructure his life after Louisa's death drove
him back to the male bastion of the university and to the
proximity of his family. Louisa remained alive in his
memory as "one of the most sparkling creatures . . . in a
long and varied existence of bright women"; her bravery
during the painful process of dying sustained his own
cowardice: "She faced death, as women mostly do,
bravely and even gaily, racked slowly to unconsciousness, but yielding only to violence, as a soldier sabred in
battle."[45]

When Clover Hooper became an Adams she was
linked with a family tradition of gifted women who embodied the belief that Louisa Johnson expressed in poetry:
"They breathe truth who breathe their words in pain."[46]
Unlike the Adams men, who also experienced many frustrations, the women, perhaps with the exception of the
first Abigail, often found their lives more limited than

fulfilled; they were all powerless to control their own environments. To be sure, they would experience many moments of pleasure and vicarious achievement through their sons and husbands, but it is their tradition of suffering that Henry chose to identify with in terms of his own failure to achieve power. Neither wealth, nor social position, nor the rational code of his forefathers could deny him an intimate knowledge of human pain. When he finally acknowledged his own membership in the "hearts that ache," he achieved a rare moment of democratic identity that enabled his work to be popularly accepted as the grim aristocratic prophecies of his brother Brooks never could be. Having felt the continued anguish of a mother who could write, "There is an end to everything and someday life with all its complexities and hard trials will be over and rest will come,"[47] Henry would have been conditioned to accept the final suffering of his wife. That he did not call in their neurologist friend, S. Weir Mitchell, during the seven months of Clover's intense depression may seem less surprising in view of the moodiness he had learned to live with in the thirty-four years before his marriage.

The tragic undertone in Henry Adams' later work may well have grown out of his own meditations on the fate of the women in his family. In his own writing, on his own terms, he often seemed to be struggling with the idea that haunted their friend Henry James, of what we *pay* for our civilization? In the Adams family, as in many James stories, Henry recognized that women paid the highest price for the achievements and power attained by men. Even though the men experienced setbacks and hostility, their accomplishments provided them with a fulfillment that motherhood could only temporarily sustain.

Clover Hooper's entry into the Adams family was not greeted with much enthusiasm. Charles Francis (by then united with his wife) was still in Europe working on the Alabama claims when his son's wedding took place in June 1872; there was no question of the old couple's returning for the ceremony. Enthusiasm, in any case, was not an Adams quality. It was Clover's uncle who provided the newlyweds with a seashore cottage until they set sail for a lengthy European honeymoon which was to include research for Henry.

Charles Francis Adams, Jr., later wrote that he had "trod all over Clover, offending her in every way."[48] He could never blame her, he added, for not liking him. To Henry, he had once ignorantly remarked that the Hoopers were "all crazy as coots," and that Clover would probably kill herself just like her aunt.[49] Brooks Adams had tried to persuade Henry not to marry into a family noted for so much instability; Henry had replied, "I know better than anyone the risks I run. But I have weighed them carefully and accept them."[50] We know from Ellen Sturgis Hooper's printed funeral tribute, from Dr. Henry Bigelow's warning to Ned Hooper, and from family letters that "there was in the family a tendency to melancholy," which Ned overcame for most of his life by plunging into a program of intense work. At the time, Henry Adams believed that he would be able to provide adequate and loving distraction to keep Clover from such depression. Whether becoming an Adams also involved any "risk" was an issue neither of them considered.

Why the risks involved in marrying Clover Hooper should have been thought any greater than the risks involved in marrying into many other distinguished New England families seems baffling when one recalls Clover's letter to her father commenting on the number of neighbors who had been led away to the insane asylum. Brooks Adams would later experience some sort of neurasthenic breakdown of his own; at that time, he had no righteous qualms about going to Clover and Henry's to recuperate. Clover wrote a clinical analysis of her patient to her father, "Brooks Adams is still with us and I fancy means to stay through the month. He eats and sleeps like a Viking and is gaining—if he had quiet nerves and peace in his soul he would gain faster."[51]

After their marriage, Henry was invariably made to feel more welcome at Dr. Hooper's than Clover was when she visited the Adamses. A survey of Charles Francis Adams' diary reveals that he hardly ever referred to her as anything but "Henry's wife"; he sometimes remarked that their visits interrupted his plans and once suggested that their standard of living was too luxurious. Although the specific details are veiled, there is clear evidence in Charles Francis' comments about Clover's "indiscreet conversations," which "nettled all the family," that a temporary estrangement took place in 1879. "I pity rather than dislike Henry's wife," the self-righteous old man wrote, "But henceforth I must regard her as a marplot and a subject of commiseration."[52] Clover's reactions are not recorded; she was out when her father-in-law tried to straighten matters with a personal visit. It is easy to imagine, however, that any clan as critical as the Adamses would have found the outspoken Clover spoiled and difficult. Charles Francis also wrongly inferred that Clover was alienating his favorite son from the family, by "driving Henry to exile in Europe." The emotional freedom of her own background would have been impossible for the rigid Charles Francis to cope with. In a remarkable explanation of why he disliked his own father, Charles Francis, Jr., described the old man's nature as "strong not generous, kindly or sympathetic, self-contained, introspective, Puritanic in the English, and virtuous in the Roman sense. It never occurred to him that he might have been wrong," his son claimed, or that he "pursued an unfriendly course to his children."[53]

Mrs. Adams intimidated Clover from the first. On her wedding trip, when Clover and Henry met the entire Adams family in Geneva, Clover noted with some irony to her sister Ellen, "Mrs. Adams is quite disgusted with me for having given up waltzing, but I think it's not my line."[54] Her letters to her father continued to quote Mrs. Adams's opinions and advice on housekeeping, a subject that did not fascinate Clover. By January 1873, Clover was traveling again and she found herself unable to correspond with her new mother-in-law: "I have become utterly demoralized about writing and I know Mrs. Adams and Mary must think it very strange, but I cannot write except to you who are used to my stupidity and

shortcomings."[55] Adams perfection was not easy to
attain, and, by the time they got to Egypt, Clover's self-
confidence was shattered. This is the only period in her
married life, except after her father's death, where evidence suggests that Clover experienced a severe depression—perhaps based on her long separation from her
father—that expressed itself in a deep sense of incompetence and a loss of self-esteem: "I hoped to keep a journal
on the Nile, but have found it so impossible to write a
decent letter that I have not even attempted it."[56] After
the first year of marriage, all attempts to correspond with
her mother-in-law ended, but Mrs. Adams continued to
write to Henry.

James Truslow Adams spoke of one European trip on
which Clover "had been given such flattering letters of
introduction that she felt she could not present them but
would read them over by the fire when she wished to
cheer herself up."[57] That she needed such cheering did
not appear obvious to her husband, who was all too willing to go along with her jests about her faulty education.
He had written to Gaskell before their marriage:

> She desires me to say to you that . . . all I said
> about her accomplishments is a lie. . . . In fact it
> *is* rather droll to examine women's minds. They
> are a queer mixture of odds and ends, poorly
> mastered and utterly unconnected. . . . My
> young female has a very active and quick mind
> and has run over many things, but she really
> knows nothing well, and laughs at the idea of
> being thought a blue [bluestocking, i.e., intel-
> lectual]. She commissions me to tell you that
> she would add a few lines to this letter, but un-
> fortunately she is unable to spell.[58]

Henry would later turn Clover's talent for spontaneous
impressions into a virtue when he wrote *Esther*, but Clover's anxieties reveal that she did not consider the flaws
in her education any more valuable than Abigail Adams
did hers. She often felt that she really needed the im-
provement Henry had offered to give her.

A woman's ambitions as an Adams would have been first for the men she could help or influence. At one point, it seemed realistic for Henry to write Gaskell, "My fiancée like most women, is desperately ambitious and wants to be daughter-in-law to a President."[59] Later, Clover would seek intellectual fulfillment by helping Henry with his scholarly work: "A friend said that she told him she had once stirred Adams into a spasm of activity by telling him how many candles Bancroft had used while writing before breakfast; and on one of their trips to Europe, gathering material for his historical writing in foreign archives, she would make requests that Adams himself was too shy to bring forward."[60]

If becoming an Adams meant subordinating the self, such subordination was often deemed fulfilling for nineteenth-century women. The ambivalence involved in balancing emotional need with intellectual achievement had not been clarified; even the fiercely independent Margaret Fuller had no qualms about declaring that, after all, "woman was born for love."[61]

# 5

# Growing Up
# in New England

*The New Englander is, and always was, narrow, nervous,
self-distrustful often, always introspective, uneasy,
and till lately, intolerant. . . . But among the New Englander's
many weaknesses is one which gives him what character
he has; it is love of, or rather fear of the truth.*
Henry Adams to H. B. Grigsby, October 9, 1877

$F$our days before his marriage to Clover, Henry Adams described his future wife to Charles Gaskell: "She has grown up to look after herself and has a certain vein of personality which approaches eccentricity. This is very attractive to me, but then I am absurdly in love."[1] "Eccentricity" might have been another way of defining an individual consciousness that attempted to explore experience without obvious institutional guidance. If this declaration of passion seemed extreme for an Adams, Henry's appreciation of eccentricity was not, for he had learned to value the unusual women in his family as well as in his New England background. During his stay in Germany, the youthful Henry remarked with contempt that most German girls were conditioned to have no minds of their own. He admired one exceptional "plucky and headstrong" young woman who had what "we call spirit and Europeans call nobility because common citizens don't often have it."[2] To live by one's instinctive reactions rather than by society's institutional mandates had already become a positive value in American mythology. Clover might have reminded Henry of the same kind of honest, intuitive response to life that the American literary imagination had embodied in characters as different as Natty Bumppo and Hester Prynne. In fact, Henry had once written Gaskell to praise the special American quality of Hawthorne's description of Zenobia's suicide; he also remarked that in any lecture on American literature, it would be a pity not to expose British audiences to the poetry of still another eccentric, Walt Whitman. Whether Clover would have seen herself as unconventional in quite the same way that Henry saw her, remains questionable; yet there can be no doubt that she saw herself as an independent spirit. Twenty-eight years old when she finally married, Clover had made her own decisions on many matters over a number of years. To a young friend who was marrying at a similarly late age, Clover wrote, "I do not think you would have agreed to marry anyone if you could possibly have helped it. . . . I think the freedom of an American spinster becomes wearing as she drifts toward the thirties."[3] Marriage, however satisfactory, never entirely diminished her enthusiasm for independence.

Clover Hooper was aware that the cult of "true womanhood," encouraging total self-denial, was beginning to dominate the thinking of middle-class American women; no woman could escape it. Among her childhood books was The Doll and Her Friends, a story "designed to inculcate a few minor morals . . . chiefly the domestic happiness produced by kind tempers and consideration of others."[4] More inflammatory volumes, such as The Legal Rights of Women, Mérite des Femmes, Woman: Her Education and Influence, More's Female Education, and, of course, the works of Margaret Fuller—At Home and Abroad, and Woman in the Nineteenth Century—remain in her grandfather Sturgis' library (which is now reconstructed in the town library at Barnstable, Massachusetts). The books she knew, like the schools she attended, suggest freedom of choice, never adherence to dogma. Efforts to harmonize what was conventional in her upbringing with what stimulated her intense individuality must have certainly provoked tension which she often expressed with wit and ingenuity. By temperament Clover was unrestrained; she seemed to enjoy cultivating her unconventional, independent side. Her serious, yet often flip responses to almost everything, the remarks judged irreverent by more diplomatic individuals like her father-in-law, strike us now as quite self-consciously original. She made an effort to be deliberately different.

Henry James, who knew the Hooper girls at Newport in the late 1860s, years before Clover married Henry Adams, linked her in his imagination with his beloved cousin Minnie Temple, the inspiration for a number of his strong female heroines. Minnie and Clover were restless, free spirits who possessed a "sincerity" and "wonder" that set them apart from more conventional females. Both girls imagined fulfillment in terms of exploring *all* the possibilities of life—not in terms of confining themselves to any narrow social or domestic role. Even at this early period, Henry James insisted that Clover struck him as the "genius of my beloved country"; in a letter to his brother, William, Henry described how dismal English young ladies were by comparison:

> I revolt from their dreary deathly want of—what shall I call it?—Clover Hooper has it—intellectual grace—Minnie Temple has it—moral spontaneity. They [the English] live wholly in the realm of the cut and dried. . . . The English have such a mortal mistrust of anything like criticism or "keen analysis" (which they seem to regard as a kind of maudlin foreign flummery) that I rarely remember to have heard on English lips any other intellectual verdict (no matter under what provocation) than this broad synthesis—"so immensely clever."[5]

The "intellectual grace" and "moral spontaneity," which Henry James' sensitive imagination would dwell on in many of his feminine characters, may well have been deliberately nurtured in the comfortable, permissive world of Minnie and Clover. In America, young women were encouraged to express their opinions. It seems quite likely that the wildflower-name Daisy, which came to represent James' most famous, uncompromising young heroine, Daisy Miller, might have been suggested to him by association with the equally fresh Clover. Later Clover Adams would naturally find herself involved in the debate about whether *Daisy Miller* could possibly be representative of the decent American young lady: "I stoutly defended Henry James and Daisy Miller to stout Mrs. Smith of Chicago," she wrote her father, "and protested that the latter was charming and that the author adored her."[6] That Clover's wholehearted enthusiasm for Daisy Miller was not a typical judgment of her class may be seen by a glance at a contemporary review in *The Nation* which saw Daisy as a moral lesson, "a perfect study of a type not alas! uncommon." In the *North American Review*, also a voice of middle class respectability, Daisy was described as "irredeemably vulgar in her talk and her conduct." Clover's enthusiasm for the defiant American girl was, as usual, proudly and characteristically eccentric.

In 1885 George Willis Cooke wrote an article on the Transcendental poetry of Ellen Sturgis Hooper for the *Journal of Speculative Philosophy*; the critic noted that her poems were "so suffused with private feeling that her family has been reluctant to have anything written about her, and this had had the effect to keep her from the reputation she deserves."[7] Whether or not the poems deserved more attention remains debatable; but the quality of Ellen Sturgis Hooper's "private feeling" is undeniable. On a trip to the south, which was undertaken to arrest her tuberculosis, Ellen wrote warm, concerned notes to her family, sending "kisses for Clover on her eyes & ears & lips & the tip of her little nose." She surely felt the need to compensate her youngest child, her "pet," with words for all the mothering that illness had taken from the little girl. To the four-year-old Clover she added in another letter: "My precious silver grey, You know I love you as much as ever. I hear you are well and good. I see your little stems of legs trotting up and down stairs. . . . Get someone to write a letter for you but tell them what to say yourself." Clover's mother never failed also to include her remembrances to Betsy Wilder, the loyal housekeeper, already a member of the family. Seven months later—Clover was five by then—Ellen Sturgis Hooper was dead.

The letters written to William Sturgis from the south during this final illness reveal not only Clover's mother's passionate nature but also her intense intellectuality. That most famous poem begrudging the necessity of *Duty*, was complemented by the following note:

> I find here a taste of what I have long coveted— the dignity and repose of the vegetable kingdom. Not that part of it which has to keep up to spring expectations and grow daily greener & bigger, but of the humble lichen tribe, the Chinese of the soil. As far as my Yankee nature and education allow I ape these, and think I do well though I bring discredit on that most original & aboriginal of New England teachings, The Busy Bee—of course.[8]

The daughter of the successful China merchant was the first in her family to articulate in this humorous way the symbolic philosophical differences between the contemplative East and the active West that her friend Emerson was also exploring—the differences that her son-in-law Henry Adams would much later struggle to understand on a more profound level. Her mother, Ellen Davis Sturgis, might have been described as still another family member who left conventional Yankee responsibilities in order to explore more mystical concerns. Letters indicate that Clover's eccentric grandmother, who lived apart from her husband and children for much of her life, was consciously seeking a more spiritual reality; after the death of her poet-daughter she believed that Ellen Hooper's ghost appeared to forgive her for not having helped with the nursing at her death.[9] Although Grandmother Sturgis' poignant letters seem rational enough, the common-sensical ship captain she was wedded to often found himself unable to cope with her searching, spiritual nature. The letters she received from her daughters, Ellen Hooper and Carrie Sturgis, however, show a sustained concern for their mother's idiosyncracies. They did not condemn her irrationality, or the fact that she was neglecting them; they understood the anguish of a gifted woman who was struggling to expand the boundaries of her limited reality. Her daughters saw Clover's grandmother as a seeker, a soul in torment whose vision was different from their own, but whose sensitivities they shared.

Inactivity was not, as Ellen Hooper suggested, easy for most Yankees. Her own final decision to choose contemplation over action, to participate in the esthetic and spiritual side of life rather than in the reform tradition of Transcendentalism, may have been imposed on her by her chronic illness, as well as by the influence of her mystical mother. One of her poems, "It Profiteth Thee Nothing," described her own reluctance to retire from the active life:

> Father, well know I
>     I have utmost need
> To tend that hidden fire, both night and day,
>     But who will warm my cold, my hungry feed
> When I retire to weep and watch and pray?[10]

The approach of death made the poet's conscious search for the meaning of the good life particularly intense; and the high seriousness she represented in her poems did not escape her children—in spite of their surface wit and gaiety. The little girl who was encouraged to "tell them what to say yourself," not to let others put words in her mouth, grew up sharing her mother's interest in worth-

while activity more obviously than she shared her contemplative traits. Perhaps there were moments when
Clover imagined that she might be able to fulfill the
promises of her mother's life—the dreams expressed in
the poetry that her own children might redeem her brief
existence. Like Daisy Miller, in any case, Clover Hooper
had freedom to experiment with the variety of activities
her diverse intellectual background and wealth made
available.

Because she spent a great deal of time with such
cousins as the rascally Alice Hooper, who caused all the
commotion on the Agassiz School bus, or the good-
hearted Effie Shaw (sister of the Civil War hero), who
later became one of America's major philanthropists—the
first woman appointed to the New York State Board of
Charities, or with her grandfather William Sturgis, himself a gifted journal writer fluent in a variety of Indian
dialects, Clover had some chance to record her childhood
in letters, or to be mentioned by different writing relatives. The impact of her extended family, as might be
expected, was not specifically or self-consciously defined
in the letters that mention Clover, but we may deduce
much about the quality of her youth from the small pile
of honest letters she left behind.

Ten-year-old Clover who wrote her aunt of the pleasures of getting berry juice all over her dress while picking blackberries, along with her anticipated interest in
taking up the porch boards to look for her lost lava
bracelet, surely felt little fear of any punitive repercus-
sions from her own behavior. We do not get the impression that her relatives restrained her any more than her
father did. Family legends maintain the record of Clover's proud eccentricity. At her uncle Sam Hooper's house
at Cotuit, she was remembered for sitting on the edge of
the pigpen with a book rather than joining in the childish
games.[11] Clover fared less well at conventional girlish
activities; she described her struggles making slippers
and sometimes asked advice about her sewing when she
visited cousins in Newport, Cotuit, or Lenox. We do not
sense, however, that she was ever made to do anything

that she really did not want to do, or that her life ever lacked stimulation. Her letters give the impression that all the people who took care of her were tremendously loving and solicitous; the Hoopers appear indeed to be full of good feeling and attachment to each other. Clover recorded a number of particularly happy summers in a boarding house in the Berkshires near her passionate Transcendental Aunt Caroline Sturgis Tappan, who had married into the New York family of evangelical abolitionists; in letters home Clover usually referred to her without deference as "Carry," or "Carrie."

That the motherless child was not entirely carefree, might have been expected; but her family always showed concern for Clover's feelings. In a letter to Ellen Hooper from Marblehead, one cousin wrote about the behavior of the eleven-year-old:

> Clover is sitting by me reading *Parents Assistant* & she has been very bright and happy since she has been here & not so desirous of a change as she is sometimes when she is with us. She returns to Woburn the last of the week when it is expected Betsy will have finished her visit to Conway. Clover has just requested me to let her write a little verse at the bottom.[12]

The postscript reminded Ellen that she had "a sister in existence" who would be grateful for any "consolatory epistle." This letter suggests just how important was the maternal role of Betsy Wilder, the housekeeper, in Clover's life, as well as the possibility of early moodiness. She was never trained to accept frustrations. When she was fourteen, Clover wrote to her sister from Newport dramatizing her teenage gloom: "The dark clouds which settled on my horizon have not yet lifted & I don't see any prospect of their so doing. . . . I think it is rather nice to feel melancholy. . . . Grace [Norton] is almost frantic she is so homesick."[13]

Yet such descriptions may seem more like typical teenage anguish than early signs of serious depression. In a climate that put much stock in the cultivation of women's feelings (in the fashion of Mark Twain's later unforgettable Emmeline), Clover was clearly in control of herself in enjoying her melancholy; she might have felt herself developing in the richest possible way. Clover never demonstrated a self-pitying or a sentimental temperament. Along with his final tribute to the value of female feeling, Henry Adams would insist that "the woman as I have known her, is by no means the woman of sentiment. She is, if anything, less sentimental than the man."[14] Sentiment, not sentimentality, may be consistent with a teenager's attempts to achieve the reticence of maturity. In one letter, the sixteen-year-old Clover lectured her twenty-one-year-old sister for intruding on the privacy of an adolescent romance: "When you arrive at years of descretion [sic] you will learn I hope that there are feelings too deep to be expressed & words too near & sacred for utterance. Tommy and I had a very tender parting. . . . We can live on the memory of it." Another time she alerted Ellen to her own proudly restrained maturity: "If you think my letters are going to be gushing you will be mistook—clam I have been & clam I must remain." Pleased with her self-containment and her growing independence, she concluded, "I shall be 16 in September & am very precocious at that."[15] At the same time that she was allowing her feelings for others to flower, Clover was also struggling with the Emersonian idea of self-reliance. Her own Aunt Carrie was one of the characters who had helped the apostle of their youth to define love as "the reflection of a man's own worthiness from other men." In his essay in praise of the value of friendship, Emerson concludes, paradoxically "We walk alone in the world."[16]

In spite of her family's warmth we can have no doubt that Clover's overwhelming childhood loss—the death of her mother—made her similarly aware of the complexity of attachment. Her personality nevertheless emerges boldly and happily in the letters of her childhood and adolescence. The fearless, often indiscreet, honesty that appears in Clover's adult letters was also characteristic of her youth. Although she loved to visit Carrie's friends at the Shaker colony at Hancock, Massachusetts, near Lenox, for example, and she continued to admire the simplicity of Shaker esthetic principles, Clover had no qualms at all about recording her disillusionment with the meal at their nearby restaurant: "The dinner was not to my taste and I thought it rather expensive as it included even the fly legs which were profusely scattered on top of my squash pie."[17]

Yet Lenox was always the area Clover loved going to most. A good number of her own eccentric attitudes must have been shaped in the Tanglewood Hills. The Shaker religious commune founded by Anne Lee—with its peculiar stress on celibate living—would have reinforced a belief in the independent strength of women. For many years in the nineteenth century, the Berkshires offered visitors not only great scenic beauty, but a surprisingly stimulating intellectual community as well. Here lived the Sedgwick clan, dominated by Catharine Maria Sedgwick, a novelist so renowned that Alexis de Tocqueville made a point of seeking her out in the western Massachusetts hills. Although her stories were designed to glorify New England morality, there can be little question that Sedgwick also took pride in the peculiarities of local behavior—the eccentricities that particularly endeared Clover to Henry Adams. The Sedgwick family's school for young ladies, like the Agassiz School, was notable for its quality of instruction and its freedom of expression. Henry Adams' gifted "hot-headed" sister Louisa attended the school for a time but left with the same tensions about the possible roles available to educated women that many women of her class shared. Although Louisa's early death ended her personal dilemmas, she too remained in Henry's consciousness as an example of society's failure to use brilliant women.[18]

In the Berkshires also had settled Fanny Kemble, the unconventional actress Herman Melville called "masculine," whose anti-slavery sentiments ennobled her in New England and prompted the Sedgwicks to defend her divorce from a slave-owning husband. In a letter to an equally unconventional English friend, the famous art critic Anna Jameson (also suspiciously separated from her husband), Fanny Kemble tried to describe the precise freedom and charm of living in Lenox:

> You know the sort of life that is lived here: The absence of all form, ceremony, or inconvenient conventionality whatever. We laugh and we talk, sing, play, dance, and discuss; we ride, drive, walk, run, scramble, and saunter, and amuse ourselves extremely with little materials.[19]

Clover's Aunt Carrie, Margaret Fuller's intense friend, was solidly involved in all aspects of this community, which at the time of Clover's visits revolved about the house of the sentimental writer, educator, and prison-reformer, Catharine Sedgwick.

"The Berkshire literary society," suggests Richard Birdsall in an excellent scholarly history of the area, *Berkshire County*, was saved by its unconsciousness, or its simplicity, "from degenerating into sheer bohemianism for its own sake." He sees the group, nevertheless, as liberated from the narrow social codes of the great coastal cities, indifferent to the "fine points of etiquette" and "bourgeois niceties."[20] The atmosphere was, in fact, both intensely stimulating and thoroughly relaxed. The community represented one of the constant efforts of eccentric Americans to form spiritually compatible groups within the larger society where they, as individuals, might feel totally alienated. The Berkshire community, which was dominated significantly by a woman, Catharine Sedgwick, formed a western version of the Concord community, which was dominated by the ever influential Emerson.

In this community Clover enjoyed the companionship of several older women whose ideas were listened to seriously, women who were both independent and accomplished in their own right. No favorable mention of any similar community appears in the diaries or letters of the Adams women, although there were a number of intellectual and reform groups in pre-Civil War Boston that would have welcomed them—particularly Louisa after her "western" education—and a great number of intelligent women who would have valued their friendship. Although she stayed by herself in a farm boarding house, Clover walked to her meals at Carrie Tappan's cottage, the small house at Tanglewood her aunt had once rented to another of her close friends from Transcendental days, Nathaniel Hawthorne. Hawthorne felt himself so close a friend that, at one point, he picked up his wife's pen to put in a personal appeal for Carrie to take care of their house in Concord (she accepted the invitation).[21] To her father Clover would write from Lenox in 1861, "I am perfectly delighted with my quarters up here & see everything *couleur de rose*. . . . Carrie has put off her calls till I came."

Later that same summer, she would describe her first encounter with the self-assertive actress:

> Miss C. Sedgwick introduced me to Mrs. Kemble & sat *me* down by her & we talked off and on nearly an hour. . . . We got on swimmingly, she found I liked rowing as I said as much in an unguarded moment. Whereupon she remarked that she had a boat & would be happy to lend it to me or to have me row her !!! I'm afraid I looked blank, I'm sure I felt so but I won't back down & I'll row her if I perish in the attempt. I hope she has a short memory.[22]

Until the beginning of the Civil War, the kind of challenge Clover was asking for was hard for most proper young ladies to find. We can be sure that if Fanny Kemble had taken up her offer to row, Clover would have been ready ("I won't back down"). During her early adolescence Clover had no sense of personal limitations; her level of expectation for herself remained high. What she did not relish (at least she so protested) were more conventional feminine activities like dances. When the war broke out, Clover tried to discipline herself to lead a more austere existence. In 1862 she wrote her cousin Annie, then a congressman's daughter in Washington:

> Now that April's come I have made an inward vow not to put on a low necked dress again & hope to abide by it. Thursday evening there is to be a large 'German' at Papanti's which I am thankful to say I had the presence of mind to refuse. I went to one on the 10th of March & waltzed nearly six hours and had quite enough of it.[23]

Small wonder that she had grown weary of waltzing by the time she married Henry Adams.

After the war broke out, Clover felt she could no longer be useful enough in Lenox. In a letter from the Berkshires in 1863, Ellen Hooper demanded if her cousin had yet read Louisa May Alcott's *Hospital Sketches*, a realistic account of Alcott's life as a Civil War nurse. Ellen wrote, "Clover and I are restless to get up to town and to try and get to work again."[24] Most of the young men who had waltzed for six hours at Papanti's were by then headed for the battlefields, and the days at Lenox spent "sitting on the piazza . . . laughing & sewing, eating New York candy & shelling peas for dinner," seemed over for good. Even in 1861, Clover confessed from the Berkshires, "I really feel ashamed to be having such a good and jolly time" as she said good-bye to a number of young men who went off with the Second Massachusetts Regiment, which would later be so decimated that she would recognize few of the men returning under its banner at the Grand Review. "I hope there will be a killing amount of work at the Sanitary all winter," she wrote in 1862, anxious to get back to her volunteer job: "I neither knit, sew, read, nor roll bandages here."[25]

The Civil War, as Francis Parkman declared, gave the Boston Brahmin class—reeling from the corruption that seemed to result from Jacksonian democracy—a chance to be patriotic again; they "rejoiced that at last they could serve their country without shame."[26] Oliver Wendell Holmes, Jr., who was close enough to the Hooper sisters to grant his parents permission to show his wartime letters to Ellen, later noted that the war had been for all of them a "national act of enthusiasm and faith," a renewal of belief in the possibilities of democracy.[27] Although Henry Adams, who was serving as his Ambassador-father's secretary in England, did not participate in the exhilarating group experience of this renewed faith in the Union, Clover Hooper did. All the positive aspects of democracy were reflected in the successful voluntarism of the Sanitary Commission, whose work at last gave both Hooper sisters a tremendous sense of purpose in life.

Clover was herself "touched with fire" as she threw her energies into war work with the same enthusiasm that Henry Higginson had recorded in his memoir of her sister Ellen. In one letter to her cousin Annie, which had a picture of the stars and stripes and the motto "Stand by the Flag" printed at the top, Clover's involvement in the war effort appeared total:

> We literally gorge ourselves with newspapers, believe everything we hear & swell visibly at the very name of Marblehead & Massachusetts. We have been cutting out slings & sew slings & pursue a drum and fife without flagging. . . . Aunt Mary took that stocking you left there and finished them thinking the soldiers the better alternative than moths. . . . Don't for mercy's sake make any more *red* flannel shirts. They have been forbidden by our troops as making them a mark for the enemy, bluish gray is the color ordered.[28]

Hardly a moment of the young Bostonian's time was not organized toward helping the North win the war. When her father, who also tended the wounded at Gettysburg, went to Washington on a government mission to plan for the "contraband" free slaves, Clover wrote him proudly, "I have not had a spare moment. . . . Even now I ought to be working at Union Hall." A letter to her brother in Carolina mentioned that there was a "Sanitary bee every Wednesday and Saturday."

The exhilaration of being part of the great concerted effort to save the Union sometimes made Clover surprised at her own stamina: "Yesterday, Alice, Mr. Hooper and I went to Dr. Howe's 'Sanitary' rooms & stamped blankets, towels etc. from 1 o'clock till 4-½. The store was cold & dark & though it was hard work we liked it." She added a final descriptive note suggestive of their community's spirit: "Mr. Beebe has lent the new Sanitary Commission a house in Winthrop Pl. rent free—isn't that nice."[29] She was thriving on a sense of shared purpose as well as on the actual satisfaction of hard work. "I think people are to be envied who die in these times," she wrote her brother Ned, addressing him as Thucydides, "I wish every man in the country would enlist."[30]

Ned Hooper, perhaps honoring the memory of their mother's unfulfilled reform commitment, had volunteered to work without pay at the Port Royal experiment in Beaufort, South Carolina. There, the most sober members of the Boston anti-slavery community joined forces with the New York evangelical abolitionists to try to establish a working example of successful Negro independence. The northerners planned to establish the economic responsibility of the freed slaves by reorganizing agriculture and educating everybody in a systematic manner. Their successes and, ironically, their failures seemed to complement the example of Clover's cousin Robert Gould Shaw's distinguished black regiment, which the Beaufort community cheered on its way to death at Fort Wagner. Just as Shaw's regiment proved decisively that the Negro could shift from "passive submission . . . to the brilliant aggressiveness of the free soldier," the experiment at Port Royal validated the investment of energy and education in the freed man.[31] All the Hoopers continued to believe in the power of education to liberate the human spirit and to prepare individuals for democratic existence. Clover steadily contributed to the New England Freedmen's Aid Society, which her father had helped plan, in amounts ranging upward of five hundred dollars; Ned took over the society's treasury for many years; and Ellen joined the society's committee that selected teachers. If it was fitting that one of the schools at Beaufort was named "Shaw Memorial," it was just as valid to call the other school "Hooper."

During this period of her life, Clover Hooper found time also to teach newsboys—just as her brother was helping to educate freedmen, and as her sister would later concern herself with the training of women. Belief in the importance of education at every level of society in New England may have grown out of a Puritan necessity to read the Bible, but it remained essential to creating the level of civilization Bostonians envisioned in their democratic Utopia. Clover always tried to be honest about her own efforts to teach spelling and writing. Describing the work of one of her pupils, she noted, "After he had written a few lines he observed, 'Teacher, my writing is better than yours,' which was mortifying but true."[32]

The concern that both her mother and father had felt for "alms and work," for serving "this poor humanity" was equally real for Clover Hooper in the years before she met Henry Adams. Working side by side with reformers like the great Dr. Samuel Gridley Howe, Julia Ward's husband, who fought for Greek freedom and who later founded the Perkins School for the Blind, and Ednah Dow Cheney, her mother's friend who was involved in practically every reform movement for women in Boston, Clover was well aware that "Vanity Fair" had different standards. If she did not entirely absorb the reformers' commitment to a life of social involvement, she did not see herself among the useless ornaments of society either.

Although Clover might later be able to laugh at the provinciality of New England morals—which she often shared—and the excesses of the New England reformers, mentioned in Sherwood Bonner's satirical poem on the Radical Club, found among her papers with her identifications written in, she would also have felt compassion for these reformers. And she would also have been able to appreciate the moral elegance that Henry James glimpsed in his literary portrait of Miss Birdseye in

*The Bostonians.* In fact, Ellen Sturgis Hooper's letters testify to Clover's mother's own closeness with Elizabeth Peabody, the somewhat dowdy representative of the spirit of reform in Boston, who William James thought was the living model for Miss Birdseye. Many years later, when Clover found herself weary of shopping for some exact item of the stylish clothing that Henry Adams admired, she seemed to look fondly back on this period of "shabbiness": "I think of Abby May and Ednah Cheney & order something else."[33] Another time, she begged a younger friend not to judge "granitic shoeless Bostonians too severely."[34] Although after her marriage she grew apart from the earnest, often self-righteous communities that played an important part in shaping her youthful self, Clover could never whole-heartedly reject the eccentrics nurtured by the moral intensity and intellectuality of New England. She had witnessed the satisfactions of living for a purpose.

Thomas Wentworth Higginson cited the Radical Club meetings as a particularly zestful example of New England intensity, because they enabled men and women to have vigorous, serious conversations in the tradition of Transcendentalism. The women who experienced this kind of intellectual equality would have been more vigorous conversationalists than the tedious, conventional females that Henry James had complained about in England. New England, after all, had fostered a genuine tradition of female intellectual rebels, such as Anne Hutchinson and Margaret Fuller in real life, and Zenobia and Olive Chancellor in fiction. It is unlikely that Clover could have ignored this tradition, which was often so close to her own family, in defining herself. Instead, she tried to adapt it to her own potentials.

When the war took most of their bright young male companions from Boston, Alice Hooper wrote to complain to her congressman father, "I pine now & then for a good talk—intimate talk with a man—it's an utterly hopeless indulgence. Clover cheers me by making me laugh— by advising me to advertise for one for twice a week. I wonder what we should do if we couldn't joke."[35] Yet even in wartime the stimulation of the older intellectual community was still available to the young women. In a December 1864 letter, Alice Hooper wrote, "Mrs. Tappan [Aunt Carrie] has had Mr. & Mrs. Emerson in to pass Sunday evenings & she has had some people in to meet him after his lecture and a supper—Clover said it was very successful."[36]

Since Clover was accustomed to being included in all important events, she would hate the British custom of separating the sexes after dinner, and later confessed to her father that she would feign headaches or swallow a button anytime to avoid ladies' luncheons, "a style of killing time which I detest."[37] Her early experience always led her to prefer serious discussions about ideas to social chitchat; her training never placed women in a separate intellectual sphere.

It was natural for the young Hooper women to celebrate the end of the Civil War in the Harvard Yard, to pay tribute to the lost lives of many of the young men they had once waltzed with or engaged in sober talk. Although recent statistics may undermine the nineteenth-century Brahmin belief that most Harvard men were willing to give up their lives for the cause of the Union, Oliver Wendell Holmes, Jr., boasted of his class of 1861—"out of its eighty-one members, it had fifty-one under arms." Contrary to Henry Adams' assertion that Harvard College kept men shallow, Holmes thought the college provided his contemporaries with the vital idealism that enabled them to die:

> It has been one merit of Harvard College that it has never quite sunk to believing that its only function was to carry a body of specialists through the first stage of their preparations. About these halls there has always been an aroma of high feeling. . . . It helped men of lofty natures to make good their faculties.[38]

Holmes believed that the "high feeling" that inspired him to fight the ugliest battles provided the moral strength for other heroes—like Robert Gould Shaw—that enabled them "to toss life and hope like a flower before the feet of their country and their cause." After saluting the surviving heroes, sitting through Phillips Brooks' oration and Emerson's praise of "high thought," the young women veterans of the Sanitary Commission listened to James Russell Lowell's "Commemoration Ode," which celebrated the young men who had sacrificed their lives for an ideal beyond self to rescue the Union:

> *Who now shall sneer?*
> *Who dare again to say we trace*
> *Our lives to a plebeian race?*

shouted Lowell to his audience of American aristocrats. "Be proud!" he cried,

> *. . . for she is saved, and all have helped to save her!*
> *She that lights up the manhood of the poor,*
> *She of the open soul and open door,*
> *With room about her hearth for all mankind.*[39]

The sense of democratic national unity at that moment in Cambridge may have been greater than at any other time in American history. For a fleeting minute, even Harvard seemed to be accepting everybody; Alice reported with great satisfaction that both girls were "fed or not as you please at Harvard Hall."

In spite of the dignity of the occasion, and the satisfying pride the young women shared in having participated in reshaping their country, they were not blind to the reality that the world was not entirely composed of heroes. Alice finished her letter to her mother with the reminder that, even in the Harvard Yard, the ideal and the real did not merge—that one had to remain aware of other worlds: "The country is overrun with crimes and plunderers and we all own pistols. . . . Sherman's bummers are not pleasant creatures to think of."[40] Their satisfaction with the working democracy had lasted for a brief moment during the period of greatest stress and was disappearing even as they celebrated it.

In this letter, which Alice asked her mother to keep as a record for her memoirs, Alice mentions the Hoopers' encounter with Mrs. Sam Parkman in the Harvard Yard. Mary Eliot Dwight Parkman, who was married to the great historian's cousin, was still another strong minded woman in the mold of Mrs. George Bancroft and Carrie Tappan who shaped Clover's early life. She remained a close friend and a Beverly Farms neighbor of both Clover and Henry Adams until her own death in 1879. Like the Sedgwicks, whom she also knew and admired, Mrs. Parkman ran a small school after her physician husband's death. And she was also one of two women on the first board of directors of the American Social Science Association (ASSA). Mary Parkman's most notable achievement, however, was as a professional journalist; at one time she assumed control of the *Nation*'s fiction reviews and wrote in competition with Henry James, their foreign correspondent. Her other book notices were generally published anonymously, which, as she suggested in one letter, prevented gossip and enabled her to work more easily. From her deathbed, she wrote a farewell tribute to the integrity of her editor, Edwin L. Godkin, and praised his faithfulness to a policy of accuracy and rectitude—a policy that she believed the country sorely needed. Henry Adams placed Mary Parkman among those most valued women whose opinions and advice had been "weighty . . . in very serious matters."[41] He once wrote flatteringly that Mary Parkman and Mrs. Bancroft, both independent thinkers, were his only readers: "If I shall have no more, but these two are enough to satisfy my ambition."[42]

Although her "cousin" Francis Parkman always confided in Mary and believed that they had "vital aims" in common, he might have expressed some anguish at the committed feminism of the ASSA, which wanted to free women for productive individual careers in a more egalitarian communal society. Mary Dwight Parkman's concern that "no one of the ninety-six members of Boston's School Committee was a woman," might also have troubled him.[43] Francis, a lifelong ardent anti-feminist, would have agreed that the sphere of education was exactly where woman's cultural influence in public life belonged, if anywhere, safe from the corruption of daily politics.

Mary Dwight Parkman was one of the few old friends from Clover's world who remained close to both Adamses. She provided them with lists of foreign acquaintances, different from Henry's family friends, to visit on their trips abroad. At her death, Clover wrote Edwin L. Godkin, the first editor of the newly established *Nation*, which had so valued Mrs. Parkman's intellectual contributions: "We have lost a very dear friend in Mrs. Parkman, to us in Beverly a loss that no one can make good. It reconciles me to not going back next summer which before I much regretted."[44]

There can be little doubt that the young Clover Hooper had known many more free-spirited, adventuresome women than had Henry Adams. Had Henry's sister Louisa been encouraged by her family to emulate such women, the regret that he and his father felt about Louisa's restless unfulfilled life might have been unnecessary. The need to be diplomatic or restrained, encountered so consistently in the families of statesmen and politicians concerned about the public eye, was never a part of the Hooper–Sturgis environment. Instead, Clover had learned to value the high emotional intensity and unconventionality of her own family, even at those moments when she also understood the importance of restraint. To her cousin Annie, the congressman's daughter who had apparently been discreet in the presence of secessionists, Clover protested, "What made you hold your tongue in Gomorrah, I should think spontaneous combustion would have ensued?"[45] The New England tradition that insisted on the forthright denunciation of evil was part of Clover Hooper's heritage. If her sense of right and wrong would sometimes become self-righteous or seem unkind, it was nevertheless based on a valid concern for clarifying one's beliefs and expressing one's principles. Even Emerson had insisted that the doctrine of hatred had to be preached, for judgment was implicit in every free choice. Clover's life with Henry Adams was meant to be a creative way of establishing a world of values. The couple wanted to help their contemporaries define what was truly important, and the Adamses were both able to dismiss the need to compromise for personal or political gain.

A number of books from Clover's adolescence remain in the Hooper–Sturgis family library: a collection of British poetry dated 1856; *The Poems of Wordsworth* marked Christmas 1855; *The Poems of A. H. Clough,* 1866; and Palgrave's *Golden Treasury* inscribed, "Clover Hooper from the same 1863"—the book that awakened Henry Adams' own poetic sensitivity and "helped Adams to more literary education than he ever got from any taste of his own."[46]

Perhaps many books have disappeared, but what seems consistent with our knowledge of Clover's personality is her predominant choice of poetry among the books that remain. If Clover rarely mentioned her mother, if she told the sculptor and undistinguished poet Thomas Woolner that she *never* read poetry, her library nevertheless persuades us of the Transcendental poet's lasting influence on her daughter.

Many foreign language books still in the family reveal Clover's linguistic skills, which were always so helpful to Henry Adams. Not only did she have some knowledge of the French, Spanish, Italian, and Portuguese volumes left in her library, but she also belonged to a German Club. And she was conscientiously studying Greek in Cambridge with her brother-in-law, Whitman Gurney, when she met the marriageable Henry Adams. If Clover was never able to master any of these linguistic disciplines, she continued to demonstrate an aptitude for, and an interest in, the study of many foreign cultures. Like her grandfather Sturgis, she would not be confined to Bostonian provinciality; part of Henry Adams' charm for Clover must have included his internationalism; he had long been a citizen of the world.

The books that Clover Hooper did not think worth keeping, but which are mentioned in her letters, suggest that her taste was much more catholic than any serious young man's; they might also suggest that friends and relatives felt obliged to provide the motherless girl with the kind of "true womanish" stories that provided the necessary examples for any proper young lady's moral upbringing. She faintly praised one such exemplary text, a gift from her aunt called *A Life for a Life*, as a book that would do a great deal of good.

Another time she told her more intellectual sister Ellen that she was "reading a new novel by the author of *Amy Herbert*. . . . I don't know but it will be too commonplace for Mrs. Lowell's scholars."[47] Clover did not attend the Saturday classes given by Mrs. James Russell Lowell to augment the work at the Agassiz School; Ellen, who was five years older, did. Maria Edgeworth's *Parents' Assistant*, the reading that engrossed the ten-year-old Clover, might have been as uplifting as *The Neighbors*, which was read aloud by the boarders in the Lenox parlor where she vacationed in her teens. Perhaps seeing the scholarly John Gray reading Homer on the Lenox piazza later inspired Clover to proceed with her own study of Greek, for she knew her linguistic capabilities were equal to any man's, and she never wholly identified herself with a woman's domestic world.

Although Clover experienced a broader sense of democratic identity in the great variety of her reading (as well as in her war work) than Henry Adams' education ever permitted him, her values always remained individual. The exposure to what was uplifting in popular literature did not shape Clover's taste any more than the exposure to religion made her pious; invariably, her reactions to conventional situations were eccentric. When she wrote from Newport imagining Ellen in church "just singing the hymns before the sermon," Clover felt homesick, but her intense emotion was for her sister, not for the religious experience. In the same letter she remarked that she had not gone to church herself because "Aunt Mary did not feel well enough to go . . . and I didn't care to go with only Mr. Shaw."[48]

Her later choice of Sunday morning as a time to communicate with her father seemed to underline the value she put on personal human communion as opposed to the conventional orthodox ritual. A letter to a childhood friend written on another Sunday morning in 1871 began, "it seems a fitting time for a friendly chat when the gay church bells have rung the good white sheep into their respective folds & left the naughty black ones to outer sunshine and quiet."[49] The pleasure she took in her naughtiness is unmistakable.

Henry would later write with amusement that his wife enjoyed shocking "the prejudices of the wise and good."[50] Clover would never be won to conventional religion by the overwhelming personality of any minister. Like Henry Adams' fictional Esther, she could not rationalize the value of religion for the sake of, or through the mediation of, any human being, no matter how deep her personal attachment. In the previously mentioned letter, she went on to describe "a dinner at Ellen's where I sat between Phillips Brooks & Mr. F. Parkman, & found Mr. Brooks very uncritical and jolly. . . . I think him much nicer out of the pulpit than in. I've heard him preach twice, but each time neither heart nor brain got any food. Tho' I like his earnestness very much." If "neither heart nor brain got any food" from Phillips Brooks, a reaction shockingly out of tune with the enthusiasm of most of her Boston Brahmin contemporaries, Clover's response to Brooks' uncritical demeanor and her respect for his "earnestness" gave strong indications of what her own values were. That Clover had firmly shaped her critical standards before she met Henry Adams was obvious. The personal religious sensibility she expressed seemed to correspond exactly with that of her mother's friends, with the readers of *The Dial* Emerson had described as "religious people who hated ecclesiastical structure and who rejected old manners and mores."[51] Clover's attitude looked toward the "Christian Anarchism" of the group of younger poets that Henry took up with after her death—a group whose own self-definition harmonized closely with the traditions of Transcendentalism. Clover's iconoclastic spirit seemed to be captured in George Cabot Lodge's lines on a prominent member of that group, Trumbull Stickney:

> We were irreverent and unsatisfied,—
>   And so we are!" he said . . .
> He said: "We are the Great Adventurers,
> This is the Great Adventure: thus to be
>   Alive and, on the universal sea
>   Of being, lone yet dauntless mariners.[52]

"Lone, yet dauntless," was the way Henry Adams had described his heroine Esther, who was adrift without anchor in the sea of experience. When Clover committed suicide, the friend to whom she had written the irreverent letter about churchgoers expressed some anguish for her soul: "I can't help hoping that hers was 'invincible ignorance' and that somewhere and somehow she is learning better things."[53] Yet Clover's scepticism, yearning though it may have been for belief, was, like Stickney's, a matter of pride. The final stanza of Lodge's poem expressed an equally valid way to feel about her death:

> To fall with shattered pinions overwrought
>   With flight, like unrecorded Lucifers:—
> Thus to receive identity, and thus
>   Return at last to the dark element,—
> This is the Great Adventure.

Her eccentricity was neither invariably iconoclastic, nor was it always purely intellectual. Ideas could never be all of Clover Hooper's life any more than they had been all of Margaret Fuller's, whose powerful intellect provided little consolation for her lack of good looks: "I hate not to be beautiful," Fuller sadly wrote, "when all around is so."[54] Clover's features also seem to have caused her some anxiety. Before their marriage, Henry, with characteristic bluntness, wrote two letters to Gaskell remarking on Clover's appearance: in March he noted, "She is not handsome, nor would she be called quite plain"; in May he wrote, again, "She is certainly not beautiful, and her features are much too prominent."[55] Although Clover later became an excellent photographer—indeed professional by nineteenth-century standards—and would have easily been able to capture her own likeness, no close-up of her face exists. It is likely that Henry destroyed the one self-portrait she recorded making, but it is also possible that she did not admire the way she looked and wanted to leave no physical record of herself.

Two early portraits of Clover remain among the Hooper family papers: one is of a wide-eyed child of about eight—beautiful as all children are; the other is of a young woman in her twenties whose face is entirely covered by her sunbonnet as in a Winslow Homer print. Two other photographs have been reproduced with the volume of her letters: one on a horse, and the other taken in a group in England. The faces are too small to give any sense of the quality of her expression.

Included with Clover's childhood letters is an extraordinary story about her own death that she wrote when she was fifteen to entertain her cousin Annie; it is a simultaneously grotesque and amusing anecdote in the manner of Gogol or Mark Twain, that exposes her own vulnerability. Although the tale most deeply suggests a classical female castration resentment, it might also be interpreted as a story about the relation between appearance (or femininity) and death:

> It was a bitter cold night and the wind howled most fearfully. As the time drew near for her departure she felt a presentiment of death stealing upon her, and was loathe to depart, but at last summoning up all her courage she set forth attended only by one of the masculine tribe. She had passed in safety the three first crossings below Charles Street when arriving at the last crossing a sudden gust of wind caught her nose—that being the most prominent feature of her body, and whirling her through the air dashed her upon the frozen waters of Back Bay. The servant was seized by a

contrary wind and drowned in the waters of the
River Charles. A milkman riding in from the
country on Wednesday morning discovered her
body laying upon the ice. On looking at the face
he discovered that—it was minus a nose and
whilst returning to the land he perceived a nose
minus a head. A coroner's inquest will be held
upon this afternoon at 3 o'clock precisely, price
of tickets 25 cts, children half price. . . . en-
closed in this note is a pattern of blue for her
funeral riggings, that color being most becoming to her style of beauty. A customary speech
of hers was—"it's a weary world we live in,"
and just before reaching the 4th crossing was
changed to "it's a windy world we live in."[56]

The spoofing quality of the story, which finally included
the execution of her will to Annie—"a tea caddy will be
forked over subsequent to the inquest"—revealed Clover's
youthful wit. Whether the tale also suggests any perma-
nent anxieties about her sex and appearance is worth
pondering. At fifteen, Clover would have begun to realize that many roles available to the "masculine tribe"
were not open to her. That she should have imagined
herself somehow doomed by her nose (or finally her lack
of it) may make her fantasy appear less frivolous. Allowing for displacement in the dream image, we may conclude that Clover might well have seen her sexuality—
her loss of a prominent appendage—as a source of spiritual death. In any case, she did not see herself compen-
sated with feminine beauty for what she was losing in
the way of pre-adolescent freedom. Struggling to come to
terms with the role of appearance in defining female sexuality, she might even have momentarily considered
leaving the "weary world." Yet all teenagers worry about
appearance as part of their identity, and Clover's conscious good humor always seemed to save her from self-
pity, for she could usually jest about any situation and
laugh at her own flaws. In a later letter, Clover finally
seemed to be boasting to Ellen that one of the young men

going off to war with the 2nd Massachusetts Infantry had begged her for a photograph, so we might also assume that by then she had begun to discover that her "style of beauty" was not necessarily unattractive.

The contribution of appearance to any thinking person's self-esteem is hard to evaluate precisely. Henry Adams noted (as we would expect) that it was, after all, Clover's "intelligence and sympathy" that held him. Margaret Fuller's chagrin about her own appearance may still disappoint those admirers who think of her as a disembodied intellect, as Simone de Beauvoir's distress at aging disillusions more recent feminist philosophers. Even in Boston, Fuller's devoted followers would remark that her squinting eyes and long neck were disconcerting; and Fuller attempted to compensate for her looks by dressing with some flamboyance. In Washington, she was surrounded by many dazzling beauties whose values were far different from the charitable (and bearded) Elizabeth Palmer Peabody's. And Clover might have felt that good taste would be able to make up for nature's indifference. But the concern for good looks and style that emerged in her post-marriage letters may well have grown out of her anxiety to enhance her beauty so that she might be as attractive to her husband for her appearance as she was for her elegant wit.

That Henry Adams admired beautiful women can be readily documented by a glance at his correspondence with John Hay. It never would have occurred to him that the enthusiastic appreciation he showed for the other sex, which his wife sometimes shared esthetically, would have been in any way hurtful to the woman he described from the beginning of their life together as being as comfortable as old furniture. Yet self-esteem may be worn away by a variety of factors; we cannot help wondering how Henry, who was five feet three inches tall and had the legs of his furniture cut down, would have reacted had Clover—who was also small—constantly articulated a steady admiration for tall men.

Clover Hooper had first met Henry Adams in London after the Civil War when her father took her traveling.

But it was when Henry resumed his association with Harvard as a medieval historian that they saw each other frequently at Shady Hill, where Ellen and Whitman Gurney were guarding Charles Eliot Norton's home while the art historian was in Europe. This house, symbolically the center of Harvard's dawning concern for the arts, was one of the few places in Cambridge where Adams felt comfortable. Dean Gurney, who had been a serious candidate for the presidency of Harvard, was involved in as many reform efforts within the university as his wife was involved in reform from without. In their mutual interest in the founding of Radcliffe, both Gurneys' reform spirits merged. Because educating women was important to all of them, Whitman Gurney, moreover, gladly gave his spare time to tutoring Clover in Greek. In the presence of the Gurneys, with whom they happily shared their intellectual and moral concerns, it was easy for Clover Hooper and Henry Adams to fall in love.

Only two years before, Henry had written Gaskell, "My heart is now as immovable as a stone, and I sometimes doubt whether marriage is possible except as a matter of convenience."[57] Perhaps the eccentricity he found irresistible in Clover reminded him of the shadow of death that he had found so appealing in a twenty-year-old he described in the same letter: "Her only attraction is that I can flirt with the poor girl in safety, as I firmly believe she is in a deep consumption and will die of it. I like peculiar amusements of all sorts, and there is certainly a delicious thrill of horror, much in the manner of Alfred de Musset, in this pushing one's amusements into the future world." Fate seemed ironically willing to extend this "morbid" amusement into Henry Adams' future after his own wife's death, but, just before his wedding, he proclaimed himself "absurdly in love" and "gay as a lark."[58]

Prior to their marriage, Henry's usually sharp critical sense left him. He wrote an absurdly enthusiastic review of the book they chose together to mark their engagement, William Dean Howells' *Their Wedding Journey*, a novel that Henry James saw as an example of Howells' growing thinner and thinner. Never again, in fact, did Adams show any interest in the writing of Howells; but just before his own wedding this book seemed to him to serve as an example of the best in "American civilization" with all its "refinement and taste."[59] His failure to be intellectually critical must be sure evidence of Adams' being deeply in love, for it was hardly ever his manner to be effusive, even in writing reviews. Whatever Henry's feelings, his steady and remarkable control exemplified the education his father had once described with some regret as too deliberately restrained: "My nature is close and undemonstrative, perhaps even shrinking—hence I did not put any feelings in my instruction as I might and should have done."[60]

Henry Adams wrote three letters to his British friends before his marriage to assure them that he would never let love interfere with friendship and that he would never be persuaded to give up his British connections. Those friendships, more an outlet for epistolary social criticism than for emotion in Henry's case, played a strong and lasting role throughout his life. His many letters remain remarkable for their depth and brilliance, and, like Clover's, for their honesty. Unlike Clover's, they are beautifully organized—and unlike Henry, Clover did not realize that marriage might become a threat to the close relationships of her past.

Ironically, it was her childhood connections with friends and relatives that seemed to disappear after their marriage. Henry wrote point-blank that he never liked her Uncle Sam Hooper (Alice's father), and Clover later remarked that, after her marriage, she had not seen Carrie Tappan for seven-and-a-half years. The only people linked with Clover's past who remained close to the Adamses as a couple were Mrs. George Bancroft and Mrs. Sam Parkman, both strong intellectuals who had useful connections for a budding historian. Although Clover characteristically wrote one friend, Eleanor Shattuck, in March 1872, "I love you more because I love Henry Adams very much & it seems to be returned & you neednt try to think how happy I am,"[61] there is no evidence that Eleanor played any part at all in Clover's life after her marriage that June. Perhaps false modesty made Clover write "seems" instead of "is." Yet the circumspect nature of Henry Adams' character would necessarily make him an inconsistent lover. Although he had written to Brooks Adams that Clover was so far away superior to any woman he had ever met that he couldn't resist her, to Gaskell he noted that she had poor taste and that he would "improve" her. No less in love than she, but decidedly more critical, he wrote again:

> I hope you will soon find out that she is worthy of our society. I suppose I may now consider myself as comparatively settled and tolerably well able to decide whether I am likely to be contented with her or not. As yet I see no reason to doubt it. Life glides along very smoothly. If it weren't that I am such a sceptical bird, I would say that we two were a perfectly matched pair . . . but perhaps when one is in the lover's stage, it is safest not to look at the future.[62]

Clover was not so cautious by nature, nor was she so sceptical of her feelings; she was old enough at twenty-eight to know her own mind. Although she sometimes tried to keep herself under control to please the establishment side of the family, iconoclastic emotions more often seemed to dominate her. On a piece of stationery marked with a large "S," suggesting her identity with her mother, Clover wrote Ellen, before her marriage, a remarkably passionate letter describing a dream she had had about her family and Henry Adams. Perhaps because this letter is so intense, it was never included in the published volume of her correspondence; yet is it worth publishing in its entirety as a final picture of the young Clover Hooper:

> My dearest Ellen,
>     I shall tell you about a horrid dream I have had. I dreamt that for ever so many years you & I sat side by side with a high wall of ice be-

tween us & very often when I tried to look thro' it I saw something in you that was so like myself that it made me cold all over & I think it was the same with you—about four years ago the sun began shining so on your side of the wall that it began to thaw & then I looked over & saw you and Whitman & began to have a nice time with you but there I was out of the sun & my ice couldnt thaw. This winter when the very cold weather came the sun began to warm me but I snapped my fingers at it & I tried to ignore it. By & bye [sic] it got so warm that I tried to move & couldnt & then last Tuesday at about sunset the sun blinded me so that in real terror I put my hands up to my face to keep it away & when I took them away there sat Henry Adams holding them & the ice has all melted away & I am going to sit in the Sun as long as it shines thro' as Whitman says. I am a "Hooper" & if a feeling is very pleasant I feel as if it were wrong—& somehow you & I have done nothing at all but Whitman & Henry have waked us up—You tell me it grows better & peacefully *all* the time. Why! I've learnt that in less than a week—I always was quick at languages, when I put my whole heart into it—

You may show this to Henry because I want him to know what bad dreams I have had. Father has always said it is very vulgar to talk about one's dreams so we never will mention this again—[63]

Clover felt no reluctance about sharing her feelings in detail with Ellen, and indirectly with Henry. Risky as it is to attempt to analyze the dreams of the dead, it seems possible nevertheless to speculate that the wall of ice surrounding the two sisters may have been their sense of overwhelming loss at their mother's death—a loss so severe that even the welcoming hands of Henry Adams could not erase her impression of the dream as "horrid."

Her "real terror" might also include a fear of sexuality suggested in the image of the melting sun ("if a feeling is very pleasant I feel as if it were wrong"). Certain that she was leaving the security of her warm father and her loving, supportive family, Clover finally seemed to envision the establishment of her new emotion as part of a "bad" dream in spite of her satisfaction with the idea of sitting in the sun.

Although the awareness of her own quickness in languages enabled her wittily to interpret the language of love, the happy communication of intimacy, we notice that Clover saw her sister and herself as entirely passive in this experience: "Somehow you & I have done nothing at all but Whitman & Henry have waked us up." All the Hoopers' lifelong, conscious experience with the New England tradition of independent women finally appeared to be less important than their own unconscious needs to be dependent. And even as Clover approached marriage, it is clear that her father's opinions kept intruding on her own; she was still looking for his approval in rejecting her own vulgarity, as she would continue to look for her husband's by letting him know how "bad" she could be.

In contrasting Henry's letter to Gaskell about his love and approaching marriage, with Clover's letter to her sister Ellen, what seems most worth emphasizing is their disparity in tone. We easily perceive the difference between one human being carefully trained to be circumspectly intellectual, and the other cultivated to be intensely feeling. In the future, their intimacy would inevitably bring each one's approach to life closer to the other's.

# 6

# Europe and Harvard,
# 1872–1877

*Action is with the scholar subordinate, but it is essential.
Without it he is not yet man. Without it thought can never
ripen into truth. . . . The true scholar grudges
every opportunity of action past by, as a loss of power.*
Ralph Waldo Emerson, "The American Scholar"

**W**hen Clover Hooper's Aunt
Carrie went to Europe in 1857, Ralph Waldo Emerson
urged his spiritual sister to return:

We are the worse that you & those who are like
you, if any such there be, as there are not,—but
persons of positive quality & capacious of beauty—desert us, & abdicate their power at home.
Why not a mind as wise & deep & subtle as
your Browning, with his trained talent? Why
can we not breed a lyric man as exquisite as
Tennyson; or such a Burke-like longanimity as
E. Browning? . . . Our wild Whitman with real
inspiration but choked by Titanic abdomen, &
Delia Bacon with genius, but mad, & clinging
like a tortoise to English soil, are the sole pro-
ducers that America has yielded in ten years. Is

all the granite & forest & prairie & superfoeta-
tion of millions to no richer result. . . .

It seems particularly poignant that Emerson was describing the ten years that also produced *Walden* and
*Moby Dick* and *The Scarlet Letter*, for what strikes us now
is not the absence of talent but the failure of audience to
perceive it. Even the most receptive among us have had a
hard time feeling the shock of recognition that native
genius demands. The irony that pervaded this letter to
Carrie Sturgis Tappan surfaced in Emerson's own
ambivalence about the ultimate value of literature and
scholarly pursuits: "We still find colleges & books as
cramp & sterile as ever," he added, perhaps with a taste
of sour-grapes. And he concluded his letter with a
romantic glorification of what Carrie would never find in
Europe—"Nature": "As soon as we walk out-of-doors
Nature transcends all poets so far that a little more or less
skill in whistling is of no account."[1]

In 1870, when Henry Adams returned to Harvard to
teach medieval history and to take over the editorship of
the *North American Review*, he saw himself among those
"persons of positive quality" that Emerson had called
upon to take over the intellectual leadership of the country. He had not yet come to believe, as the American
Scholar asserted, that colleges and books were *cramp* and
*sterile*. In his earlier career as a Washington journalist,
Adams had already accepted Emerson's idea that "men
of aim must lead the aimless."[2] At this stage of his life, he
would not have been ready to accept the idea that a little
more or less skill in whistling was of no account. His
father, perhaps anxious to steer Henry back into a more
conservative career than journalism, urged the return to
Harvard teaching by appealing to his son's belief in power: "This is now the field of most influence in America,"
Charles Francis wrote, "It is . . . the teacher who can
make the greatest mark, who will make himself all
powerful."[3] So Henry took the Harvard job believing he
might be able to influence the thinking and taste of the

many potential leaders he would encounter there. He shared Emerson's sense of urgency and responsibility and believed that the "best and brightest" had to make this country self-sufficient intellectually as well as economically. Several years earlier, Henry had written his brother Charles:

> We want a national set of young men like ourselves or better to start new influences not only in politics, but in literature, in law, in society, and throughout the whole social organism of the country,—a national school of our own generation.[4]

Henry had never been deluded about the ease of achieving such influence; yet, when he took the Harvard teaching job, he saw himself joining an institution alive with possibilities for change under a new presidency. Able to define his own approach to history, he felt free to teach whatever he wanted in any manner he chose. To Gaskell he wrote again, "I don't believe in the system . . . and thoroughly dislike and despise the ruling theories of education in the university. . . . I shall quietly substitute my own notions for those of the College, and teach in my own way."[5]

Most appalling to Adams was the lecture system, which emphasized only one man's opinion and the great amassing of facts; small seminars held (after his marriage) in his own home were his preference. In order to help students draw their own conclusions rather than to give back his own, he innovated the idea of putting original material on reserve. Eventually, he would even urge President Eliot to allow one of his graduate scholars, Henry Cabot Lodge, to teach the same material as Adams, so that the students might benefit from two quite different analyses: "His views being Federalist and conservative have as good a right to expression in the college as mine, which tend to democracy and radicalism."[6] Getting his students to think was Adams' main concern; the creative results of his early graduate program remain astonishing. Many students never forgot Henry Adams' brillance as a teacher. But when he wrote Gaskell, "I am smashing things here, and have declared war against the old system of teaching," most of his fellow faculty—"twaddlers," he called them—would have laughed.[7] The power Adams yearned for within the university remained mythical.

Only Whitman Gurney, who had already lost the contest to become president of Harvard, seemed to show much sympathy for Adams' ideas. Made the first Harvard Dean, perhaps to compensate for missing out on the presidency, Gurney was considered remarkable for actually liking undergraduates. Dozens of anecdotes related his compassion and wisdom, but no statements of his beliefs remain (except anonymously) in writing. He belonged to that group of nineteenth-century individuals who defined their existence by the quality of their human relationships. Self-made, considerate, enormously learned, Gurney was a popular figure on the Cambridge scene. Family letters reported Clover Hooper's enthusiastic reaction to her sister's choice of a husband:

> Ellen Hooper is engaged to Mr. Gurney of Cambridge . . . a very delightful & intellectual person—Clover says it is so nice to have such a bright person come into the family: now she shall learn something.[8]

Gurney, as noted, was indeed one of the few Harvard professors who believed strongly in women's education, a belief, as Paul Buck has shown in a valuable essay on Harvard attitudes toward Radcliffe, generally detrimental to personal success at Harvard.[9] How different the history of education for women at Harvard might have been if Gurney, rather than Eliot, had been chosen president. Gurney had met Ellen Hooper, in fact, while teaching in the Agassiz School for Girls. It was natural for him to agree to tutor his sister-in-law Clover in Greek, and equally natural for Henry Adams, who valued both Gurneys' originality, to pursue his acquaintance with his future wife at Shady Hill. "To go to that home was a liberal culture," one of Gurney's students later wrote, "not only in 'the humanities,' but in human relations at their best."[10]

Like most of the great talkers among the Transcendentalists, Gurney left no monuments; the memorial festschrift for him that Henry Adams tried to organize among Harvard colleagues seems never to have been completed. Adams had described its possibilities to President Eliot as a testimonial to educational reform.[11]

When Henry Adams wrote his sympathetic review of William Dean Howells' *Their Wedding Journey* for the *North American Review,* he was publicizing, in an unusual manner, the book that he and Clover had chosen to consecrate their engagement. Their copy remains in the family with the inscription, "Clover Hooper-Henry Adams—February 27, 1872." That they should have chosen a realistic novel defining the social customs of Americans rather than any sort of conventional sacred text to mark their love for each other is characteristic of the freedom of thought they wanted their lives to represent. In choosing such a book they identified themselves, moreover, as being part of the scene—as standing for the representative Americans Howells tried to capture in his text. *Their Wedding Journey* has been labeled the most significant attempt to catalogue American life since *Leaves of Grass.* Henry Adams' own review called it a faithful picture of our American existence. He may have been pleasantly surprised by the "intrinsic interest and importance of commonplace American materials" in the book, underscored by Howells' satire of Basil and Isabel March's enthusiasm for European travel and their "recurrent efforts to make America more interesting by romanticizing it."[12] Both Henry and Clover would have been able to laugh at Howells' descriptions of Boston strengths and prejudices, which were suggested through the character of Isabel.

One of the passages marked with a tiny dot in the Adamses' copy must be seen as an indirect comment on the "eccentric" Bostonian, Clover herself:

> She was a woman who loved any cheap defiance of custom, and she had an agreeable sense of adventure in what she proposed. Besides she felt that nothing could be more in the unconventional spirit in which they meant to make their whole journey than a stroll about New York at 6:30 in the morning. "Delightful!" answered Basil, who was always charmed with these small originalities. . . . "You won't meet one of your own critical class on Broadway at this hour."[13]

If the typical Bostonian emerged in the story as unable to love the bigness and dullness of New York, Howells made the narrator at least able to appreciate the city's wonderful vitality as the "giant Mother of commerce." Not only did the novel introduce a rich variety of Americans, young and old, immigrant and Yankee, which the couple encountered on their honeymoon to Niagara Falls, but it also attempted to describe the marriage of a somewhat older pair of newlyweds like Clover and Henry.

When they married, the hero and heroine were already strong individuals; Howells did not play down their differences. Theodore Dreiser remembered *Their Wedding Journey* somewhat inaccurately, because there was "not a sentimental passage in it, quarrels from beginning to end, just the way it would be, don't you know, really beautiful and true."[14] Dreiser's memory exaggerated, but he nevertheless pointed up how unusual Howells' approach to married life was. The choice of this unsentimental novel to mark an engagement would emphasize once again the pride Clover and Henry always took in looking honestly at everyday experiences. Never narrow or romantically domestic, they too might have enjoyed the fictional quarrels as part of the richness of marriage so often ignored by more conventional writers. Although Howells' level of idealism, like their own, often ended up limiting his realistic vision of American life, the Adamses began their marriage with the belief that *Their Wedding Journey* was an accurate reflection of the richness of American possibilities.

Henry wrote his brother Brooks that he and Clover were not only independent of mind, they were also independent of means. To take a year off from his teaching job for an extended wedding journey that would include research abroad did not pose any financial difficulties. After living with Clover's father for a month before the wedding, unorthodoxly, as Henry noted, the pair were married in an entirely private ceremony and soon set sail for Europe. Boston seemed to follow them; on board the same ship were old acquaintances Francis Parkman and James Russell Lowell.

The wedding journey of the Adamses, as described in Clover's first series of letters to her father, was more harmonious than the one William Dean Howells depicted, if not less varied. Before she left, Clover wrote, "It seems to me more than I deserve to go from the care of such a kind father to a good husband and I am very grateful."[15] But it was less easy for Clover to accept the shift than for most honeymooners because any long separation from her home might have caused her to feel a repetition of the grief she experienced when her mother died. She wrote passionately to her father, "I miss you very, very much, and think so often of your love and tenderness to me all my life"; "I think of you always"; "I miss you all the time." Clover did not see her new role as wife excluding her old role as daughter: "Henry will be very busy and hard-worked and I shall come to you for advice and get very dependent on you."[16] Often she sent messages to Betsy, her old nurse, telling how much she missed her, begging for letters, and thanking her for remembering to write. Her sister-in-law Fanny described Dr. Hooper's ritual satisfaction in sharing Clover's letters with other members of the family: "We hear from Clover every week through her father's letters, & though she is happy and sees many interesting people, there is enough homesickness through them all to make Dr. Hooper quite cheerful."[17]

Perhaps many readers might feel some astonishment at the provinciality of Clover's letter home asserting that it was more worthwhile to plant peas in Beverly than to sightsee in Paris. Few New Englanders, on the other hand, would fail to sympathize with her request that her father send a bright red maple leaf so that the autumn in Europe might seem real. And many traveling Americans might still agree with the justice of her protest that it was impossible to grow fond of any place where you had neither home, friends, nor work. The Boston–Beverly world had provided Clover with a sense of her roots in a community where Henry Adams had seen only his own inner conflicts. She could not easily forget or hide her love for Boston, in spite of Henry's steady contempt for "Bostonian stupidity."[18]

Although Clover would later help Henry with his research, at this early stage of their life together her most useful gesture was introducing him to George Bancroft, her cousin by marriage, then American minister to Berlin, who provided the young historian with introductions to the greatest historical minds in Germany. Henry had earlier criticized Bancroft for his too consistent democratic fervor, but he nevertheless was glad to depend on the generous older man and his gifted wife for constructive criticism throughout his own creative life. In a comparative study of Bancroft, Parkman, and Adams as American historians, Richard Vitzthum has noted that, in spite of differences in emphasis, Adams, like Bancroft, remained committed to writing moral history, and that like the older man he also chose to believe that "American democracy" was "man's best hope." Democratic nationalism, Adams also admitted, "might move more men closer than any other kind, reaching the lowest and most ignorant class, dragging and whirling them upward."[19] At this stage of his life, however, Adams would be quick to label the religious or Transcendental elements behind Bancroft's thinking as "naive faith."

For Clover, the Bancrofts represented much more than useful intellectual connections. She truly regretted not finding Mrs. Bancroft, who was then too ill for the climate of Berlin. Elizabeth Bancroft, a distant cousin, had not only attended Margaret Fuller's Conversation groups with Clover's mother and Aunt Carrie, but she had also gone to elementary school with Clover's mother at Miss Cushing's Hingham Academy; she remained close enough to her dead cousin's children to help buy their clothes and to continue to shape the girls' intellectual interests. As late as 1883, Clover remarked that she was waiting for Mrs. Bancroft to send back her four volumes of George Sand's *Memoirs* for binding, suggesting the liberated interests the two women shared. It is not surprising that when Henry walked over to the Bancrofts to report on Clover's dispatches about her father during the old man's final illness, he found that the old couple had already heard from her.[20]

Clover not only shared Elizabeth Bancroft's interest in women writers but she also may have been imitating her cousin's personal letter-writing tradition as well as Abigail Adams' when she took care to record a variety of social customs in her letters home. Like Mrs. Bancroft's letters, published much later as commentary on the twenty-five years her husband was minister to England, Clover's correspondence retained a lively curiosity about how Americans stacked up against the British. "I think more highly of our own country . . . than before I came abroad," Elizabeth Bancroft had written: "There is less superiority over us in manners and all the social arts than I could have believed possible in a country where a large and wealthy class have been set apart from time immemorial to create, as it were, a social standard of high refinement."[21] Clover would write home with comparative concern: "The women were certainly better looking and better dressed than any I had seen before, though a party in New York or Boston would beat them hollow in both respects,—except for inherited jewels." Later she tried to distinguish the more compatible Britons: "Henry and I have found that the very pleasantest Englishmen are those in the 'upper middle class,' . . . whose brains and opinions are not entailed."[22]

Elizabeth Bancroft (who had remarked that many Boston Brahmins had snubbed her for marrying beneath her class) also devoted some attention to the baffling hierarchy of British servants. Clover frequently showed a similar interest, remarking that she had, with typical careless American generosity, given one of her British helpers a raise and elevated her title to "housekeeper." Such scattered comments on the habits and skills of the serving class reflect much more than the patronizing irresponsibility of upper-class women. Clover's letters suggest an ongoing egalitarian interest in the lives of a variety of workers: cooks, gardeners, coachmen, gravediggers, and sailors. Perhaps this interest was a direct result of her brief community involvement during and after the Civil War as well as of her family's interest in varying levels of reform. The diary of Alice James, who knew the Hooper sisters at Newport and who later showed some concern at Clover's death, suggests that it may have been relatively easy for American women of their social circle to identify with servants because the roles the women played were equally limited. They were all part of what Alice called "hemmed in humanity." Alice James, though she admired those who were able to admit that the game was too hard, had rejected suicide as an answer to her own frustrations. She nonetheless retained a compassion for powerless human beings that was more focused than Clover's and more intense than either of her writing brothers'. Clover Adams, like Alice James, if not committed to any concrete philosophy of social change, or to any specific reform movements, retained an awareness of working class people that gave her still another democratic dimension lacking in Henry.[23]

When Clover left Washington to nurse her dying father in Cambridge, Henry Adams spent much more time with the Bancrofts—as if he were reaching out for the people who had always mattered the most to his wife. He wrote Clover then that the old lady "talked much about your mother and father," going on to note also that the elderly historian "sent a pathetic little message to your father, regretting that he should go first." With characteristic cool comfort, Henry Adams added, "Indeed it is getting close on to the moment when the old man, for his own sake, would do well to depart."[24]

Although Clover's sharp tongue, often a signal of frustrated intellect, has become legendary, she never made a statement as detached from the feelings of anyone she cared about as Henry's remark about her father and Bancroft sounded. Her wit was directed mostly toward entertainment, following the cultural tradition of her class that woman's role was to amuse and please men. Her narrower comments suggest the deliberate gaucheries of the innocent abroad, or an earnest concern for her own New England morality, a morality, as Henry Adams noted, that was traditionally intolerant and full of weaknesses, but nevertheless "always feared the truth."[25] When she was rude, it was usually to uphold some principle she wanted to dramatize.

Clover had no respect for what have been called the pieties of English life: "the country house, the aristocracy, and the monarchy."[26] "England is charming for a few families but hopeless for most," she wrote, "and a large family is spoken of as a private and national calamity. . . . I like the people and they stand American 'sass' very good-humoredly. There was a question of precedence at our dinner Friday, so I told them they might fight it out among themselves, that their 'effete monarchical customs were a matter of no concern to me!'—and they enjoy such chaff."[27] Another time she boastfully remarked, "I let out my sentiments and those of my countrymen generally on Colonel Hamly and his snobbish behavior to General Barlow, and his writing about our war 'a screaming farce,' when he was being fed and lodged by Mr. Sturgis, who had a son, and a son-in-law, and three nephews, in the army."[28] Consistent with her native pride, New England conscience reached out as well in Clover's quaint judgments of "indecent" art, "immoral" theater, and "writhing" dancing girls. Although she had loved the free and innocent freshness of *Daisy Miller*,

Clover would later join the group who condemned the decadent estheticism of Oscar Wilde and the naughty escapades of Lillie Langtry. Her efforts to be broad-minded did not usually extend to sex.

On her wedding journey, Clover was not yet enough of an Adams to forget her own upbringing among spirited "blues." She noted with sorrow that she had to leave the English countryside before she could pay homage to the Brontë homestead, and she recorded her pleasure at discovering a charming woman who was "up on Margaret Fuller, Brook Farm and Hawthorne" with whom she could take tea. If Clover made little of discussing her iconoclastic background with Henry Adams there is nevertheless evidence to show that it remained important to her. Although she admired the Brontës, her reaction to Robert Browning was complete indifference; "I don't hanker to see him again," she wrote in the same letter. She concluded that the Dean of Westminster, who had introduced her to the famous poet, was like a "hungry little gray rat" who "skipped about in small clothes and silk stockings with big paste shoe buckles and a broad crimson ribbon round his neck."[29] Status or rank never impressed Clover Adams in the least. She would have been amused and incredulous that in the twentieth century, Bostonians would still think it worth their time to meet any puppet queen.

Although she later told a friend that she liked "to conquer prejudices," at this point she seemed to enjoy testing their validity.[30] Certain nations were decidedly better than others. "It will be pleasant to put the Alps between this land of saurkraut [sic] and beer-drinking warriors," she wrote of Germany, which contrasted with Italy, where the flowers were "as big as cauliflowers" and the sea looked "like boiling sapphires and emeralds." An ever-present awareness of death, which often appeared in her images, seemed to intensify her pleasure in living: "We picked huge bunches of wild flowers and were glad we had not died when we were babies, which was not the case in gloomy Germany."[31]

No evidence exists that Clover began marriage with

any of the anti-semitism that would taint Henry's later thinking. Although her Boston family's social circle included few "exotics," her mother's letters from Savannah, Georgia, described the role of Jews in society there with as much interest and objectivity as she described her son Ned's many Negro playmates. Like Grandfather Sturgis (whose diaries James Russell Lowell had just been urging her to publish), Clover thoroughly enjoyed all sorts of people; but, as we remember from her comment about Whitman Gurney, she particularly liked people she could learn from. In London, the Goldsmids, "a very rich old Jew family who have a fine establishment in Regent Park," often helped to enrich the Adamses' musical and intellectual lives.[32] And the Palgraves (Cohens) also provided them with steady enlightenment—not only about poetry but particularly about art. As her taste grew more sophisticated, Clover gave part of the money made from selling an early Vedder painting to Frank Palgrave to buy drawings; she tried to urge her father to do the same for the newly established Boston art museum. Her decision to profit esthetically from Palgrave's better-educated taste and to enrich America's cultural treasures prefigured the relationship later established between her Boston friend Mrs. Jack Gardner and another learned, sensitive Jew, Bernard Berenson.[33]

James Russell Lowell's obsession with the Hebrews as common ancestors clearly touched the Henry Adamses also. Henry Adams had always been equally interested in archaic connections, and he also appeared deliberately to imitate Disraeli as a model political novelist.[34] To Charles Gaskell, he noted, "It is rather curious that you and I should each have a brother-in-law of the same lineage and name (Cohen-Kuhn)." Another time Henry wrote, "Of late I have been a bit more Jewish than anything else."[35] His Puritan religious heritage and his eighteenth-century political awareness drove him to seek identity with the Biblical lawgivers and interpreters who shaped an ancient ethical civilization just as his recent ancestors had shaped a more modern one. Clover, later feeling pleased with her cleverness, would identify her own economic shrewdness as the "latent Hebrew which slumbers in every Yankee."[36]

As a young man, Henry Adams had gone out of his way to visit an American Jewish family that was being treated barbarously in its native Germany. He meant to use the dignity of his presidential connections to help establish their newly rich respectability. At that time, the democracy he stood for appeared infinitely more civilized than the old world he had come to for education. Henry's turning against the Jews after Clover's death suggests a measure of self-hatred—as much a turning against the "Jewish" civilized traits that the atavistic Yankee used to define himself—as the more obvious objection to crude immigrant hordes or sudden money losses that historians often use to account for this final hostility. In rejecting everything "patriarchal," Adams was rejecting his former rational, institutional personality from still another angle. It was typical of his extremism to replace the founding fathers with the Virgin Mary in his personal iconography. When he turned against law and science as guides to the good life, when he stopped believing that the trained intellect was an adequate force for good, it was easy for him to turn against the Jews—in spite of the fact that Jewish friends had provided him and Clover with much pleasure and knowledge during the early years of their "education" together.

Clover's tastes, even when delegated, remained those of the idiosyncratic moralistic Yankee. Her opinions were as fresh as Mark Twain's "innocents," or Henry James' *American*, Christopher Newman; she was not usually anxious to follow fashions. She thought the inside of the Vatican "vulgar," and she hated the stylish bronzes her Adams brother-in-law had commissioned them to buy. In art galleries, she remarked, "We often turn sadly from pictures which we wanted to see, getting nothing for our search, and as often find one that will never cease to be pleasant or wonderful to remember."[37]

It was her eccentric sensibility, so different from that of the majority of her rich fellow Americans, that rejected the popular work of William Wetmore Story: "How he does spoil nice blocks of white marble. Nothing but Sibyls on all sides, sitting, standing, legs crossed, legs uncrossed, all with the same expression as if they smelt something wrong. Call him a genius! I don't see it."[38]

By then she had also completely outgrown the work of another successful countryman, Elihu Vedder. Her pride in American craftsmanship was not adequate to compensate for what she believed to be bad art. "Vedder," she wrote, "had got a mania for painting stuffs and accessories in his pictures and he forgets they ought to be secondary." Perhaps reflecting on her own sense of what every wife should do for a gifted husband, Clover went on in this same letter to criticize Vedder's wife as "an ordinary little girl . . . who won't push him up to anything great."[39] Her ideas about the limitations of stuffs and accessories as means to characterize people must extend to her own life. The paintings she selected alone were distinguished by the intensity with which they mirrored her feelings. Clover described a watercolor that she bought as "so sad that my sensitive half wouldn't have it though he was fascinated by it." Of course, it reminded Clover of Boston:

> It looks like Boston common on a dreary November afternoon with a row of leafless trees and Park St. church seen through a grey mist. The artist is between thirty and forty and has already now a reputation, but he has lost his mind and is now in a maison-de-santé at Bonn. He must have painted this when he was breaking down. I'm not sure that I can part with this unless you want it.[40]

The idea that beauty could emerge from or be connected with breakdown must have been important for Clover as she read the many family letters her mother left behind. She wrote home that she and Henry had also visited the charming house at Sorrento where Tasso took refuge when he was broken down and insane. If all her reactions to her cousin Adie's breakdown have been removed from Clover's published letters, her general awareness of human vulnerability nevertheless remains.

It is generally accepted that Clover herself experienced some sort of nervous collapse during the Egyptian part of the wedding journey. Harold Cater's interviews with friends of Henry Adams suggest that there can be little doubt of such an illness even though clinical documentation outside of complaints that she could not organize her thoughts, remains unavailable.[41] The two weeks in which she ceased writing letters home along with a later note proclaiming that she had found a new lease on life support a general impression of momentary despair. Signs of great insecurity also appeared in the letters Clover continued to write. The strong self that had relished overcoming obstacles to see the Civil War parade and that had enjoyed telling off pompous European aristocrats had vanished:

> I have found it impossible to get my ideas straightened out at all. . . .

> I hate the process of seeing things which I am hopelessly ignorant of, and am disgusted at my want of curiosity. . . .

> I never seem to get impressions that are worth anything, and feel as if I were blind and deaf and dumb too. . . .

> I seem to have softening of the brain whenever I touch a pen. . . .

> I get so little while the others about me are so intelligent and cultivated that everything appeals to them. . . .[42]

What had happened? Perhaps the damage to Clover's personality at her mother's death—an incontrovertible trauma—was revived not only by the long separation from her father, but also by the appearance on the Egyptian trip of Samuel Gray Ward, a friend of her mother's circle who had published poems in those same early issues of *The Dial* that included her mother's work. Several of Clover's letters during this depressed period asserted that Betsy was "dreadfully" missed, as if she were particularly feeling the loss of those people who had helped to fill her need for maternal love. The slow realization that the intimacy with her father which she had planned to maintain was necessarily waning, would also cause pain. Being the youngest child, Clover had always commanded a special role in Dr. Hooper's affections. A letter to Mary Dwight Parkman noted that he was so "sick" when he learned about Clover's engagement that he too was unable to function—"to go to a dinner party where he was expected."[43] Henry belonged to a more self-sufficient intellectual world. "The Nile," Henry Adams wrote his student Henry Cabot Lodge during Clover's depression, "is not a bad place for study, and I have run through a library of books here."[44]

If there were unconscious reasons for Clover's failure to enjoy Egypt, however, there may also have been a valid conscious one. It is curious to compare her reactions to the ancient civilization with those of the old man Emerson, whose boat—thanks to the generosity of Clover's Aunt Carrie Tappan, who subsidized the trip—was sailing before them down the Nile. To her father, Clover reported that "Emerson when he was here a few weeks ago was not interested in Egyptian antiquities. . . . How true it is that the mind sees what it has the means of seeing."[45] If Clover's momentary failure to appreciate Egypt made her feel inadequate on one level, it may have also been an honest reflection of the Emersonian elements in her own intellectual background. Ralph Rusk reported that Emerson felt his journey down the Nile "a perpetual humiliation, satirizing and whipping our ignorance." "The people," Emerson wrote, "despise us because we are helpless babies who cannot speak or understand a word they say; the sphinxes scorn dunces; the obelisks, the temple walls, defy us with their histories which we cannot spell."[46] To suggest that Clover shared Emerson's belief that this ancient civilization could not teach anything to the nature children from the new world does not seem far-fetched; yet, in her self-accusing mood, she could never have had his educated assurance that her intuition was right.

Emerson's daughter, Ellen, who accompanied him, expressed regret that the cholera quarantine prevented her father from meeting up with the Samuel Gray Wards, who were sailing in a separate boat along side of Henry Adams and Clover: "A reunion with such a friend would have been," as Ellen read her father's mind, "an event of prime importance in any part of the world."[47] Indeed, Adams' description of Samuel Ward in *The Education of Henry Adams* as "bankerial and artistic" did not begin to do justice to the complexity of Ralph Waldo Emerson's old friend (so easily confused with Julia Ward Howe's brother, the Sam Ward who was "King of the Lobby," because they both went to George Bancroft's Round Hill School). Emerson's friend (and Margaret Fuller's) had been a young man of prodigious intellectual gifts.

Samuel Gray Ward and his wife, Anna, by then a semi-invalid admired by Clover for her persistent spunk in pyramid climbing, had been part of the original Transcendental circle that included Clover's mother and her Aunt Carrie. One of the most moving letters remaining in her mother's collection was from Anna Barker Ward— whom Emerson once called Margaret Fuller's Récamier— urging the invalid Ellen Hooper to come to the Berkshires to "spend a week or two with people who love you." "Elizabeth Peabody," Anna Ward continued, "is coming up on Saturday & she will take the best care of you."[48] That Clover knew of such correspondence is certain in view of her mother's legacy of letters and poems. The Wards would have unquestionably made Clover recall her mother. It is no accident that the most passionate letter Henry wrote about Clover's death twelve years later was to the Wards, who were, he insisted, "closely associated with the heaviest trials and the keenest pleasures of our life."[49]

The farm that Anna Barker Ward shared with Samuel Gray Ward during the early period of the intellectual flowering of the Berkshires was one of the first in America to yield both agricultural and intellectual dividends.

On his own, Ward tried to establish the validity of combining farming with intense intellectual activity; his success was impressive. While living in the Berkshires, he translated Goethe, wrote a series of critical essays, became an intimate of the Sedgwick circle, and achieved a rare degree of profit as a working farmer. Ward recorded his activities: "I got up a farmers' club to meet at each other's houses at stated times in the evenings, and to measure and compare crops."[50] When his sense of responsibility forced him to give up the farming that he loved in order to take over his father's brokerage business, the local farmers "resolved that the farmers' club deplore his loss as a member of the club, as a citizen and resident of Berkshire as a public misfortune."[51]

Ward's earlier cultural life had linked him closely with Margaret Fuller and Clover's Aunt Carrie as well as with Emerson. Ralph Rusk pointed out that there were paragraphs in Emerson's essay on "Friendship" that "echo the long debate by way of the Concord mail, with Margaret Fuller, Caroline Sturgis and Samuel Gray Ward."[52] A series of letters Emerson wrote to his young friend Ward were eventually organized by Charles Eliot Norton in 1899 as *Letters to a Friend*. Like Henry Adams, Ward preferred to remain anonymous in this volume, perhaps reflecting both men's final sense of failure to achieve any social identity they wholeheartedly admired.

Like many of his distinguished circle of friends, Ward possessed the desire to share his intellectual life with a greater variety of his countrymen. "Impelled by a determination to educate Americans in an appreciation of the masterworks of western culture, Ward had made a significant contribution of which both Berkshire and America might be proud."[53] Perhaps Sam Ward saw himself addressing Clover's generation when, like other Transcendental friends, he charged that the critical influence of England caused

> . . . all our own criticism to take the opposite ground, to overpraise that which we felt to be undervalued or invidiously regarded. . . . Although all original literature comes from and

> refers to the heart of the people, it cannot, ex-
> cept in a rude age, address itself to that people,
> except through a class capable of receiving it. If
> great works do not find such a class in their
> own age, they wait till time and their own influ-
> ence create it.[54]

It was no coincidence that Emerson felt free to write
Ward of his enthusiasm for Walt Whitman, or that Ward
came to perceive that the most important contribution
Americans would make to world literature would be the
creation of new forms.

By the time Clover and Henry shared their journey on
the Nile with the Wards, the older man suggested to
Henry simply the ease and polish of the cultured banker.
Yet, like Sturgis Bigelow with his Buddhism and Clarence
King with his secret Negro family, Samuel Gray Ward
emerges from the nineteenth century as still another individual close to Clover Adams whose life seemed to have
been split by opposing forces, as Henry Adams' own life
would be after her death. Ward's success at harmonizing
his conflicting lives may have been greater than the
others of their group when he finally decided to leave the
world of money and settle in Washington to live a life of
influence, rather than a life of action.

The letter that Henry Adams wrote the Wards after
Clover's death mentioned that Clover had delighted in
the peace the older couple had attained. At the same
time, he felt free to stress the peculiar democratic
awakening caused by his own suffering:

> During the last two weeks I have learned some-
> thing more about life than I knew before, but
> the saddest discovery of all was that I did not
> stand alone in my extremity of suffering.[55]

Adams concluded with the affirmation that Clover had
always been "warmly attached" to the Wards and regretted having seen so little of them—the kind of regret
that death so often accentuates. Samuel Gray Ward's

"peace"—the compromises of the man who felt "doomed" to leave his Berkshire plough for the business world—may well have been his own contented adjustment to the powerless good life that the Adamses tried to emulate in Washington. They all seemed to be seeking to fulfill Emerson's directive to Ward: "In this country we need whatever is generous and beautiful in character more than ever because of the general mediocrity of thought produced by the arts of gain."[56] Ward's peace of mind, like Emerson's, may also have resulted from a philosophical ability, to accept democracy theoretically and to adjust to its realistic flaws.

The letters of Charles Eliot Norton, Harvard's arbiter of good taste, written to Ward during Norton's retirement, give the impression that Ward had attacked Norton's precious medievalism. Ward believed that Democracy insured "teachable people"; he insisted that the nineteenth century was "the best century to have lived in since time began," and that men were no worse than they had ever been. He enjoyed challenging Norton's fondness for England, and pointing out "the prevalence and evil of caste."[57] Like his great mentor Emerson, Ward remained committed to the democratic present as a source of vitality for a new culture. The Adamses shared many of his attitudes.

Although no published biography of Samuel Gray Ward exists, his energies—when Clover and Henry encountered him on the Nile and in Europe—(like those of Henry James' fictional Adam Verver) seem to have been directed toward the acquisition of good art for America. He was one of the founders of New York's Metropolitan Museum. Just as in his student years he wanted to introduce European literature to America to provide touchstones for American writers, so in his commercial years Ward attempted to bring back European art—to enhance our native critical awareness with good examples, and to encourage American creativity. Whether or not the genius Emerson saw in Samuel Gray Ward—critic, translator, farmer, free-thinker, banker, and art collector—was fulfilled remains a haunting question. We cannot help believing that he should have left us more of the fruits of his remarkable mind.

Ellen Gurney, too, would write to the Wards after her sister Clover's suicide, thanking them for all their "tenderness for my dear Clover and my dear people."[58] We might conclude that Clover's failure to mention the Wards in her entertaining letters from Washington stems precisely from the fact that they had been so involved with the heaviest trials of her life that she could not bear to see them often. She was trying to forge a new life in Washington with Henry Adams, as Ward himself had done so many years before.

The thought of sinking into a "horrid vortex of shopping" (which seemed to be Clover's assigned role in Paris) did not please her as they started out from Egypt toward home. In Alexandria, she and Henry stopped, however, to buy another book they inscribed with both their names: a Holy Bible. Her spirits picked up as they turned west again. On board ship, she described her pleasure at discovering *Middlemarch*, and she renewed her attacks on British pretensions: "We have two lovely monkeys on board," she wrote mischievously, "who are much more amusing than the English swells." When they reached the Mount Cenis tunnel, the Adamses fired snowballs at each other to make up for their "winter of golden sand"; and when they finally set sail for Boston in July 1873—a year after their wedding journey had begun—Clover wrote with enthusiasm: "We are ready to come home and buckle down to hard work."[59]

The "hard work"—Henry's teaching, editing, lecturing, and history writing—Clover fully intended to share. Writing back to his friend Gaskell that fall, Henry noted a constant truth: "My wife seems to thrive under a tremendous amount of work and care." The following spring he would write again, "I have been hard worked and have deputed to my wife all that I could get her to do. . . . My wife is flourishing."[60] For a time Clover was able to make good use of her mind.

As important as the actual hard work Clover contributed toward Henry's many achievements may have been, however, he never credited her research officially;

nor would she have consciously resented his omission. Her greatest contribution to his intellect remains the reinforcement of his instinctive sympathies with the strengths and problems of being a woman. Although Henry Adams would probably never have acknowledged the idea that woman's training and experience should be exactly identical with man's, he had seen enough anguish in the lives of his grandmother, his mother, and his brilliant sister to realize that some changes in women's opportunities might be in order.

In 1869, just before Henry took over the editorship of the *North American Review*, his brother-in-law Whitman Gurney, who was editor for a short while, urged their friend William James to write a double review of John Stuart Mill's liberal essay on *The Subjection of Women*, along with Horace Bushnell's conservative *Women's Suffrage: The Reform Against Nature*. With characteristic grace and irony, James pointed out that Bushnell's clerical windiness added up to little. He noted that the reactionary Bushnell's defense of the nobility of suffering had "saved many a slave from envy and despair . . . but there has probably not been an unjust usage in Christendom which has not at sometime sought shelter under its wings. No well man or free man ever adapted it for his own use." James went on to proclaim, "Modern civilization, rightly or wrongly, is bent on developing itself along the line of justice." To show, as Bushnell had attempted, that women's interference in politics was pernicious, was to make "the strongest of women's rights arguments . . . that women are frivolous because they are irresponsible."[61] Mill, on the other hand, who was admired by James for his incisive thinking and "the wonderful fairness which has always been the secret of Mr. Mill's power to convince," nevertheless left him frightened. The "morality of justice," he predicted, would leave the competitive American male without any comfort:

> However he might shrink from expressing it in naked words, the wife his heart more or less subtly craves is at bottom a dependent being. In

the outer world he can only hold good his position by dint of reconquering it afresh every day:
life is a struggle where success is only relative,
and all sanctity is torn off of him; where failure
and humiliation, the exposure of weaknesses,
and the unmasking of pretence, are assured in-
cidents: and he accordingly longs for one tran-
quil spot where he shall be valid absolutely and
once for all; where, having been accepted he is
secure from further criticism, and where his
good aspirations may be respected no less than
if they were accomplished realities.[62]

Although James honored the "dependent being," the
kind of woman the historical Adamses had always found
so supportive in their political lives, he realistically
accepted the "ultimate tendencies of the democratic
flood." He envisioned Mill's "epoch-making" passion for
"absolute equality" with honest ambivalence: "The wip-
ing out of everything special in any man's relation to
other men—of every moral tie that can possibly be conceived of as varying in varied circumstances, and therefore as artificial—is but the inexorable outcome of the
path of progress on which we have entered." "Hereaf-
ter," William James concluded, John Stuart Mill's essay
*The Subjection of Women* would be regarded "as a landmark signalizing one distinct step in the progress of total
evolution."[63] He was, of course, right.

Although Adams' attitudes toward women mirrored
William James' ambivalence as well as his family's historical indifference to legal equality, it is hard to believe that
he could ignore the rational power of Mill's essay any
more than James could. Mill had always been one of his
intellectual heroes; he had once written his brother
Charles that John Stuart Mill was "the ablest man in
England."[64] At long last a political thinker emerged who
was actually answering Abigail Adams's cry to "Remember the Ladies." There can be little doubt, moreover, that
Henry's new associations with Clover's free-thinking
family influenced his own ideas about women's possibilities. The Gurneys' particular concern for women's educa-

tion had grown out of their more general interest in how women could make more use of their abilities.

Even before the Civil War, Clover's Grandfather Sturgis, defender of the rights of Indians and of mistreated merchant sailors, found it easy to speak up for "the weaker sex." To her sister Carrie, Clover's mother wrote with pride and humor:

> Father has struck for the "rights of women" one blow. He was a member of the committee for the Barnstable celebration and carried with some difficulty the point of admitting ladies to the dinner to be given. I suppose they will be served with toast and water.[65]

Carrie Sturgis, a lifelong reformer, allied herself firmly with John Stuart Mill's political point of view. To her "brother" Ralph Waldo Emerson she wrote in 1868:

> I think all women should feel and say that they are suffering from being governed without their own consent, not directly perhaps, but indirectly—losing the respect of every boy who grows up to manhood & his right to vote.[66]

How could women familiar with democratic ideals ever accept second-class citizenship? Knowing that Emerson (whom she lectured for not being positive enough about women's rights) was going to England in 1872, Aunt Carrie urged him to visit Mill to convey her appreciation for his advocacy of women's rights: "I should like to thank John Stuart Mill for being just & understanding that women are slaves still politically—& therefore socially—& for so nobly protesting against the injustice shown them."[67]

Still it was Horace Bushnell's book that remained in Henry Adams' library. If Clover adapted to Henry's ambivalence about the role of women and learned to live with the Adamses' hostility to woman's suffrage, it must have cost her a good deal of self-esteem, even if she herself questioned the value of women's rights as a panacea for women's problems. The attitudes we live with in daily intercourse more often shape our self-image than the ideas of the celebrated minds we admire. And Henry frequently made insulting remarks about feminists, as when he blamed "a vile gang of women's rights advocates"[68] for aggravating the Beecher–Tilton affair. Clover, with the natural scepticism of her mother and their apostle Emerson, may have also clearly understood the limitations of any one reform to develop human potential. Her mother had once written that reading books on women's rights made her feel like the downtrodden worm: "I try to equalize things by curtailing William's [her husband's rights], or substituting wrongs proper for men's use in their place."[69] Even Ednah Dow Cheney, a persistently active, committed, reformer, claimed that women's real emancipation in the nineteenth century was not merely the "extension of suffrage which is a partial and outward mark of emancipation, but the far deeper principle of freedom which reaches to the heart and mind."[70]

This New England circle of educated, wealthy, American aristocrats felt themselves free enough to consider suffrage a superficial issue, even irrelevant, to their own definition of the good life. Though Emerson had once chided the young Transcendentalists for not voting, John Jay Chapman preferred to see Emerson's ideas in a context deeper than politics:

> While the radicals of Europe were revolting in 1848 against the abuses of a tyranny whose roots were in feudalism, Emerson, the great radical of America, the arch radical of the world, was revolting against the evils whose roots were in universal suffrage. By showing the identity in essence of all tyranny, and by bringing back the attention of political thinkers to its starting point, the value of human character, he has advanced the political thought of the world by one step.[71]

Ideally the political system could free men to be apolitical. Henry Adams, although always involved in politics in one way or another, would boast to his student, Henry Cabot Lodge in October, 1874, that he wasn't registered to vote because he would not take the trouble to pay the poll tax. Many upper-class thinkers like Francis Parkman believed that universal suffrage had damaged the quality of life. To such minds, extending the vote to women would only increase the degree of government by the ignorant.

Although Clover generally kept quiet on this issue in her letters home, her opinions on the matter can be deduced from her ironic comment that Parkman's ideal woman was to be found in Morocco: "If I talked much with him," she wrote her father, "I should take the stump for female suffrage in a short time."[72] It was unlikely that Clover would have shared Brooks Adams' mirth at Edith Wharton's sister-in-law Nannie's expense, when, in an open discussion of a paper he delivered against suffrage, he suggested that any woman bored at home should find it her duty to run away with another man.[73]

If Henry Adams had early agreed with his elder brother Charles that a "division of activities and functions lay at the foundation of society," he was also driven all his life to explore the problem of establishing the "dignity of women as co-equals with men."[74] By the time he was an old man, in fact, he would write that, if he were beginning again, he would entirely drop the study of man "except as an accessory, and study the woman of the future."[75] Trying to clarify the significance of woman's role, the *North American Review*, under Henry Adams' editorship, continued to print relevant articles. A review of Dr. Clarke's *Sex in Education*, which remains on the list of Adams' unsigned contributions to the magazine, would surely have been as important to him for personal reasons as his criticism of Freeman's *Norman Conquest* (included in the same issue, but unlisted) was for historical ones.

The argument in Dr. Clarke's enormously popular book *Sex in Education*, that women were physically unable to endure the same education as men, had infuriated active feminists. Mary Livermore, another veteran of the

Sanitary Commission and an active woman's suffrage worker, called it a "monstrous assumption that woman is a natural invalid."[76] She attacked the "impertinent book" for trying to make certain that women would be helpless. Henry Adams' review made an effort at impartiality; the women he knew, after all, in spite of their capable intellects, also suffered physically—even Clover had frequent headaches. Whether such suffering could be the result of their constant frustrations was not an issue in the nineteenth century. Dr. Clarke had to be taken seriously; indeed, S. Weir Mitchell, America's foremost "women's doctor," was originally supposed to have written the criticism of Clarke's book that Henry himself turned in for the January 1874, issue of *North American Review*.

Adams' review acknowledged that what Dr. Clarke said about "the harm that may be caused by excessive brain work" was perfectly true—true of men as well as of women. "But," he went on, "it can only be said of the most excessive work, and to forbid well-regulated moderate study from fear of such extreme consequences is no wiser than it would be to denounce all care of the health for the sake of avoiding valetudinarianism."[77] Unfit fathers would result from immoderate study, Henry knew, as well as unfit mothers. Perhaps he was echoing many conversations with the Gurneys when he concluded: "That young girls should be denied the use of books, and left to their own frivolity and to greater idleness, would be, in our opinion, a lamentable result of Dr. Clarke's book."[78]

He may well have been recalling his brilliant sister Louisa when he commented also that the young woman frequently showed a facility for learning greater than that of her brother, "who very often does not begin fairly to work for some years later." Remembering his mother's anxieties in contrast with Clover's satisfaction from her many intellectual tasks, may have also caused him to conclude:

> Every physician knows the calming influence
> that intellectual work exercises over those who

feel themselves too sensitive to the temptations of the world, and we cannot help recommending some serious occupation of that sort to girls during the critical years of their early womanhood, as best worthy of their attention, and properly managed, most likely to save them from subsequent suffering.[79]

If Henry Adams saw woman's education as a good thing, he was just as reluctant as William James to support the idea that woman should be independent. He added finally that the education he believed in was "indispensable if women are at all anxious to adapt themselves for what is demanded of them by men who seek to make companions of their wives, and . . . to be able to understand what is going on about them." Understanding what is going on was never equivalent to shaping life, as Henry Adams ironically would come to realize about himself. Yet, in spite of the physical anguish he had witnessed among the women he knew, he could not share Clarke's view of woman as invalid. Perhaps the greatest testimony to her sex's strength was his final admission that "to resist the demand that women are making for education is a hopeless task."[80] Henry Adams may not have written the subsequent review in January 1875 of another of the redoubtable Clarke's books on women, *The Building of a Brain*, but, as editor of the *North American Review*, he would have approved of the final rebuttal: "There are plenty of tolerably healthy women among us, and these not merely Indians, working women, and servants, but such as can and do move with the foremost in their respected spheres."[81]

Many years later, when history appeared to him as "mere pedantry," he discussed women's vigor at length, knowing well that women were rarely content to be just ephemera. If he had read the letter to Clover's mother from her sister, Carrie, left in the papers for the Hooper daughters, Henry Adams would have never thought women inarticulate about their educational wants:

I galloped fast as any of them; I sang collegiate songs with them, rowed with them and really almost felt I was a boy. 'But they are gone they are all passed by' and I am again an inferior female—Ellen—do you think it is possible I shall be a female in the next world! I think they must have discovered the mistake before now & it only remains to be rectified—I longed absolutely to go off with the boys to college—and I sigh to look forward into the vista of female years.[82]

Although Carrie Sturgis concluded that she would resign herself to becoming a "mediocre female," her forced retreat into the dark wood "where there is no male or female" found expression in cultivated eccentricity, particularly in the exaggeration of her intuitive powers—a trait that would never have endeared her to the "scientific" mind of the young Henry Adams. Unable to train her intellect in any profound way, she concentrated on developing her psychic powers and learned to specialize in character analysis of handwriting. How could the friend of such overwhelming individualists as Hawthorne, Emerson, and Margaret Fuller resist trying her intuitive gifts on a younger individualist, Henry Adams. Of her new "nephew" by marriage, Carrie Sturgis wrote: "The man here portrayed holds himself aloof. . . . He wishes to be a force, a living force, and yet he takes no part in life's high destiny. He sits like a mountain, aside. . . . Advanced in thought, knowing and strong, he sees clearly, he acts mildly . . . he cannot act."[83] Small wonder that the trenchant Carrie began to play a much more modest role in Clover's life after her marriage. Educational disadvantages notwithstanding, Carrie's intuition would never have been honored as a substitute for accurate knowledge in the mind of the youthful Henry Adams—the character she perceived "setting himself before himself as the universe," nor would he have appreciated her prediction that, unable to act, he would take no part in "life's high destiny."

Conscious of having to clarify and define epistemological problems as he began to write biographies, Henry Adams tried to elucidate his own discipline when he included or wrote reviews of biographies for the *North American Review*. He criticized George P. Lathrop's *Hawthorne* especially for its use of "intuition" and its lack of proportion. George Ticknor's autobiography, on the other hand, he praised for its scientific accuracy: "The thoughts and impressions are as absolutely within certain limits as the habitat of a family of plants." History—he then believed—should be scientific too.[84]

When Henry wrote an essay on John Smith in 1866, it was meant to debunk the Pocohontas legend, and, to his own satisfaction, he proved that Smith had made up the story. But, circumspect as always, Adams began to ask himself about the power of myth as well as the actuality of fact. The primitive forces that represented salvation through Pocohontas—the female, the savage—had already begun to speak to another side of the scientific historian. Henry Adams was becoming one of the first historians to realize the importance of an anthropological dimension for interpreting complex reality. When Adams decided to leave Harvard and Boston for Washington, in 1877, he was searching for similar vigor in his own society. The identification of feminine vitality with democratic force already seemed connected in his mind. To Henry Cabot Lodge, he had written earlier: "I care a great deal to prevent myself from becoming what of all things I despise, a Boston prig (the intellectual *prig* is the most odious of all) and so I yearn . . . to get out of Massachusetts and come in contact with the wider life I have always found so much more to my taste."[85] The idea of "Culture" with a capital C was repulsive to him because he saw it as Emerson did—as a European derivative that denied the vital, primitive forces in American life. Although he himself had profited from European training, Adams feared becoming permanently part of the narrow continental traditions that dominated Harvard:

> Our men . . . talk "culture" till the word makes me foam at the mouth. They cram themselves with second-hand facts and theories till they

bust, and then they lecture at Harvard College and think they are the aristocracy of intellect and are doing true heroic work by exploding themselves all over a young generation, and forcing up a new set of simple-minded, honest prigs as like to themselves as two dried peas in a bladder. It is an atmosphere of "culture" with a really excellent instinct for all the very latest European fashions in "culture." . . . Our young people have all the most novel intellectual fashions crammed into them. . . . But I am aghast at the result. Such a swarm of prigs as we are turning out, all suffering under a surfeit of useless information is new to human experience. Are we never to produce one man who will do something himself?[86]

Save for the sharpness of tone and the vague sexual suggestiveness of the imagery, Emerson might have been preaching still. Like Clover's old family friend, Henry Adams had also tried to put the individual pupil first, to teach self-reliance. He had achieved a high degree of success as a teacher, but, by 1876, Adams felt his usefulness among a society of "icebergs" at an end. To Gaskell, he wrote, "I regard my university work as essentially done. All the influence I can exercise has been exercised. The end of it is mere railing at the idiocies of a university education."[87]

Whether Clover—who would have once been grateful to share such idiocies—agreed, we do not know. She was familiar with the endless tribulations of her brother-in-law, Whitman Gurney, in trying to institute such modest academic changes as broader entrance requirements and voluntary chapel attendance at Harvard, and she loved the idea of the more active life of behind-the-scene reform politics. Even after the Civil War, she had written the artist Elihu Vedder that she was happily busy with "work and politics."[88] If Clover regretted leaving her family and her beloved New England, the idea of playing a new role at the center of American political life along with helping Henry with his historical research would have been exciting to her. Besides, the two of them planned to return to Beverly every summer.

By the time Henry Adams delivered his Lowell Institute lecture in 1876 called "The Primitive Rights of Woman" he had been married for four years. The Lowell lecture was meant to discuss woman's universal power in primitive cultures and how the vigor of primitive types had long since been converted into the silent suffering of Christianity under the protective influence of the modern family and the development of property law. He meant to praise the contemporary institutions that protected women; yet his descriptions of women's strength in earlier societies remain the most memorable aspect of this talk. Strong women emerged in Adams' imagination, as they never could politically in his own family, to dominate the institutions that restrained their vitality. Such women as Hallgerda, who murdered three husbands, and Penelope, who shrewdly outwitted all her suitors, were a far cry—and a curiously attractive one—from the patient Griselda. Although Henry Adams meant to commend the family as it emerged through the protection of civilization, the ambiguity of his feelings can be sensed. The fierce vitality of archaic women striving to be individuals remained the fascinating truth of the lecture. Like Cooper, Melville, Thoreau, and Mark Twain, and, more particularly, his later friend Clarence King, Adams was beginning to share the strong ambivalence toward civilization that seemed so foreign to his ancestors. Trying to understand the sources of vitality and power remained a fascinating problem to Henry Adams throughout his life, perhaps the core of his efforts to define what education should be. He was reluctant to relinquish the primitive, sustaining vigor of women through the training of the civilized male establishment.

# 7

# Washington and Europe, 1877–1880

*The evolution of a highly-destined society must be moral;*
*it must run in the grooves of celestial wheels.*
Ralph Waldo Emerson, "Civilization"

**W**hat is man born for but to be a reformer, a remaker of what man has made; a renouncer of lies; a restorer of truth and good?"[1] charged Emerson, expressing an idea that must have been deeply lodged in Henry Adams' mind when he returned to Washington, the city where his ancestors had achieved so much. "Here," Adams wrote Gaskell when he finally settled in, "I can fancy that we are of use in the world, for we distinctly occupy niches which ought to be filled." With unusual enthusiasm, Henry Adams continued, "I belong to the class of people who have great faith in this country and who believe that in another century it will be saying in its turn the last word of civilisation."[2] With Ulysses S. Grant turned out of the White House and with a good number of reformer friends in powerful positions, Adams envisioned himself able to "bullyrag" his own generation for the good of this civilization. Once again, he could delight "in the barbaric simplicity of our native legislators," as he opposed their primitive vitality to the more "effete" decadence of the British parliament. To Gaskell he had earlier pretended to be afraid of our southwestern congressmen—as "when I meet a Sioux warrior on the plains."[3] But, in 1878, he was glad to be once again in the one place on this "miserable little planet" where Adamses were less insignificant than elsewhere. Enjoying the belief that, behind the scenes, his ideas and values would now be seriously considered, he wrote with pleasure, "We make informal evening calls on the President, the cabinet, and the Diplomates."[4] [sic]

The letters Clover sent back to Boston during her first year in Washington reflect her own persistent interests; such letters, she wrote her father, would be her way of keeping a "diary" of her own activities. Full of colorful details, they did indeed suggest the varied, useful life Henry predicted would be available to both of them there. To her father she once protested that he should not in his letters to her be a sundial, recording only happy hours. Had she seen the letter Emerson and Fuller wrote to subscribers explaining the title of *The Dial*, as a measure of sunshine, a cheerful, "rational voice among the din of mourners and polemics?" Her own life, as she described it to her father, reflected a similar dedication to the positive. Except for statements about headaches or minor ailments, or reported refusals to attend the many social functions that Henry relished, unlike a true diary there is nothing at all introspective about Clover's descriptions of daily life; there is hardly ever a complaint, or any psychological analysis that might be compared to Alice James' self-awareness. Clover seemed happy to approach life uncritically, to record just what happened, or what her wit caused to happen for her father's special pleasure. The emotions expressed in her letters seem entirely directed toward the outer world; if she had any moments of doubt or hesitation about the life she was leading, she did not articulate them. The emotionalism of Clover's teenage years had given way to an ideal of restraint that was not entirely the result of becoming an Adams. In her father's desk was his own hand-copied maxim for living, which she also attempted to follow:

C'est qu'on savait vivre et mourir en ce temps-
là; on n'avait pas d'infirmités importunes. Si on
avait la goutte, on marchait quand-même et en
faisant la grimace, on se cachait de souffrir par
la bonne éducation.[5] [sic]

There is no reason to believe that Clover experienced
any personal suffering that she might have wanted to
hide when she was working side by side with Henry on
research for his biography of Albert Gallatin. Nothing
made her happier. Clover wrote in December 1877: "This
week I have been working at the State Department with
Henry. If you want to know how we look see Cruik-
shank's illustration to *Old Curiosity Shop*—Solomon and
Sally Brass on opposite stools. The rooms in the new
building are superb."[6] Although Henry never gave Clover
any official recognition for her contribution to his historical work, her letters reveal that she collated every one of
Jefferson's letters with him, and she read over the letters
in French from Voltaire to Gallatin's grandmother (fifty-
three in all) for the preparation of Henry's definitive
biography of Jefferson's Secretary of the Treasury. Such
tasks provided her with a happy sense of usefulness;
nineteenth-century women were not eager for individual
recognition as the selfless work of Francis Parkman's sister and the monumental copying labors of Tolstoi's wife
continue to remind us. Women were often able to find
real satisfaction in identifying with the men they loved;
to feel worthwhile they had only to be able to contribute
skills or advice to some larger project. In one of her letters home Clover declared happily, "I wish the Sundays
wouldn't come so fast—not because I must write a letter
but because I hate to see the milk going out of the bowl."[7]

If having no children sometimes made Clover Adams
unhappy (her niece remembered her saying that all
women wanted children; and she once requested that
her father *not* record births in his letters to her; in the
Adamses' library also was a copy of *Clinical Notes on
Uterine Surgery with Special Reference to the Management
of Sterile Conditions*), Clover nonetheless managed to

divert some of her maternal needs into protecting Henry and watching over a number of dogs and horses. During the summers she would also help care for and amuse her brother's daughters. "One consequence of having no children is that husband and wife become very dependent on each other and live very much together," Henry wrote.[8] Although it is probable that anyone so interested in ancestors would have regretted not having descendants, Henry Adams managed consistently to think of his work metaphorically as his offspring.[9] He also openly protested, "I myself have never cared enough about children to be unhappy either at having or at not having them, and if it were not that half the world will never leave the other half at peace, I should never think about the subject."[10] The historical rumors about his impotence must, of course, remain just that, whereas the remaining text on uterine surgery suggests that Clover at some point blamed herself for this void in their lives. It is harder for a woman with no professional distractions to ignore the world's demands.

Although Clover Adams did not relish crowds of people, and certainly never justified entertaining for the frivolous sensations of the moment, she managed to use her many new associations either for increasing her own knowledge or for preaching New England principles. Perhaps she remembered the extraordinary letter left among her mother's papers defining social activity:

> I have never felt that social life was quite right—one looks at its meetings too much in the light of successes or failures, a natural abstract wish for perfection, but not the best spirit of sociability— . . . I think the true way is to invite visitors with their books, most everyone has a book he can never get time to read at home & put up a placard "No talking allowed here except urgent" and then we should have a feast of thought. But to know two days beforehand that

you are to be lively for three hours in the evening is enough to drive one to stimulus or
chloroform.[11]

The stimulus Clover found may have been partly in the
wines the Adamses served during the teetotaling administration of Rutherford B. Hayes; but more important in
her enjoyment of Washington social life was the reality
that, as independent people, the Adamses could choose
their new acquaintances with care: "The rules of etiquette
are a delightful hedge, for unofficial folks as we do not
hanker for a large circle of congressional friends."[12] If
they did not read books at their parties, they could nevertheless make sure that there were serious intellectual conversations, or planned discussions of controversial political issues involving the passions of their guests. They
had no social obligations to members of any one party or
to people of any one caste.

Clover's own reform interests remained alive even in
the southern city. She would not, as her mother warned,
"prate with idle men of idle things."[13] To her, the Civil
War period, a time of clear-cut purpose and community
action, still loomed large, for it was the period that had
shaped her sense of American possibility. Clover particularly liked reporting her impressions of Southern opinion
to her father; she quoted one fox-hunting, Virginia
schoolmistress as knowing only one person in Virginia
who regretted having the institution of slavery. She also
liked exposing the Mississippi prejudices of Senator
Lucius Quintus Cincinnatus Lamar, who, she noted, "in
common with almost all Southerners had supposed [slav-
ery] a delightful status for the negro."[14] Lamar, in the
process of arguing with her, became a good friend; she
enjoyed getting the better of him:

Now Mrs. Adams no negro could make such a
brilliant remark as that. I wouldn't believe it
unless a man as reliable as your husband told
me it was said to him. I merely answered the

remark was made to my brother who is quite as reliable as my husband: I've known him much longer.[15]

But although Clover grew fond of many southerners as individuals, she did not share Lincoln's compassion for the erring South. When one believer in "slavocracy" described "the destitution among the once rich people—now Miss Middleton bakes and sells bread," she reported self-righteously, "I wanted to say 'serves her right.'"[16] No respect resounded from her description of a White House reception where Mrs. Hayes beamed "alike on the just and unjust."[17] Judgment had to be part of the New England reformer's role.

Clover tried at one point to sustain her family's interest in the Freedmen's Schools, but somehow failed to find any part for herself in Washington; the area had no community to sustain or encourage her work. "Our enthusiasm for negro proficiency in the three r's," she finally reported, "was postponed indefinitely."[18] Henry Adams' circle of friends remained behind-the-scenes political reformers working within a more conventional framework. John Hay excepted himself, Adams, and Carl Schurz when he wrote that he generally loathed reformers "because they are loathely,"[19] a statement typical of the mixed messages Clover always had to live with. She later wrote home that she had avoided the "all pervading" Caroline Dall, a famous female reformer from her mother's Conversation group days. Dall, who, with Clover's good friend Mary Dwight Parkman, was instrumental in the founding of the American Social Science Association, would have alienated Clover more by her imperious manners than by her egalitarian principles when she sent a message by Henry James ordering Clover to call on her. Indeed, Dall's personality, which was the same morally assertive type as Clover's own, injured her cause more than once: the Boston Women's Club and the American Women's Suffrage Association both blackballed her out of leadership in 1868. Caroline Dall would have easily fit Hay's description of the "loathely" reformer.

Alms-giving continued to play a modest role in Clover's life. Although she shared her brother's interest in teaching art, her priorities reflected a broader culture when she wrote that she would no longer support one art school "now that it is well afloat with many paying scholars. . . . There are many pitiful calls for help here & when it's art versus starvation, art must wait."[20] Yet Clover never failed to send money to Ellen for the new Harvard Annex for women, a project that reflected her own kind of starvation. To suggest that Clover Adams made any personal sacrifices to support the causes that concerned her as her philanthropic cousin Effie Lowell did would not be accurate. Effie's sense of charity demanded that "a constant and continued intercourse must be kept up between those who have a high standard and those who have it not," and her way of life demanded that "the educated and happy and good . . . give some of their time regularly and as a duty, year in and year out, to the ignorant, the miserable and the vicious" in order "to raise the standard of decency, cleanliness, providence and morality among them."[21] Clover, who once shared her cousin's way of life, no longer saw social action so simply. Unlike the widowed Effie, who organized middle-class women in Consumers Leagues to boycott stores that mistreated and underpaid workers, Clover did not feel free to involve herself in politics. Even her involvement in charities was less time consuming than the charity work of Henry Adams' fictional Esther. If she remembered her mother's poem to the grasshopper,

> Wailing brings no doing!
>   Moaning brings no rest
> In acting & pursuing
>   Alone is perfect rest[22]

she nevertheless felt that her arena for action was primarily private. She would not sit "sad & lonely" on a

mossy stone, but try to create her own sphere of influence. Like many Transcendentalists, and like Emerson in
particular, she always had trouble championing specific
reforms; instead, she wanted to establish around herself
an atmosphere of general moral criticism of the culture. It
is no accident that the novel Henry Adams picked (reminding us also of his admiration for *The Blithedale Romance*) as a companion volume for *Esther*, was *Among the
Chosen*, an inspirational story of a spirited woman's struggle against the head of a reform community.

Her Grandfather Sturgis' intense concern for the
American Indian also remained alive in Clover's letters
from Washington. General Miles, she noted, spoke "very
kindly & tenderly" of the Indian; he wanted "the government to let one of its usual forts on the frontier be used
for a school for 6 or 7000 young men and women among
the prisoners—have them taught useful things & then
sent back to their tribes,—but he said he could get no
hearing—his only chance is to go back & be killed by
which possibly something might be done."[23]

For many years after the Civil War, her brother and
sister remained involved with the teaching programs of
the Freedmen's Bureau—a means to integrate the black
man into white culture. How appealing to Clover's New
England soul would have been the idea of liberating the
Indian through similar conventional education. That the
Native American's culture could not survive side-by-side
with the European American's was only just beginning to
be understood. In another letter, Clover reported that
General Sherman told her that the Great Plains Indians
would die out simply because they were not willing to
work. Of Carl Schurz, one of their most frequent visitors,
she wrote, reflecting her own concern, "The Indians lie
heavy on his soul."[24]

The connection with the West that their close friend
Clarence King's geological explorations represented may
also have reminded Clover of the pioneering bravery of
her beloved Grandfather Sturgis. There can be no doubt
that King, for all of his "insanity," was the character both
Adamses admired most. He seemed the perfect balance

between eastern education and western vigor; he was as comfortable discussing British art with John Ruskin as he was living secretly with his black wife and children. Henry Adams wondered why the creator had made so few men in this mold—so perfectly versatile. Whenever King came to Washington to ask Congress for expedition money, Henry and Clover put all other plans aside. One of Clover's treasured possessions was a basket King gave her made by the sister of the Pi-ute chief who was buried in King's dress coat—later described by another authority on Indian languages as a bonnet which women wore and also used for picking berries. A more remarkable present Clarence King sent her was the head of an antelope that he had shot himself. For all of Adams' railing against the crudity of men from west of the Alleghenies, the friends the Adamses grew closest to in Washington, the group they called the "five-of-hearts" (Clover, Henry, John and Clara Hay, and Clarence King), were all people who had strong connections with the democratic West. Henry himself would much later take pains to point out that none of these close friends had anything to do with his specific Harvard background. The "five-of-hearts" represented instead the natural democratic aristocracy of talent that both Jefferson and Emerson believed should be most influential in a successful democracy.

Frequently, the politics of the reform Republicans were debated in the Adamses' living room. Clover relayed concern for Civil Service, open-trade agreements, and the problems of free silver, along with descriptions of a cast of political heroes and villains, in entertaining weekly letters to Boston. Although the printed collection of *The Letters of Mrs. Henry Adams* does not include correspondence from the earliest years in Washington, the volume still provides the reader with a detailed political background of the times and gives thorough footnotes and appendices on all the issues that absorbed the Adamses. Their political positions remained consistently moral and disinterested—even on issues like silver. They enjoyed great freedom as behind-the-scenes reformers. When Carl Schurz, who regularly came to play the piano, was made Secretary of the Interior, Clover told him that "his conversation was not half as pleasant now that he is in the cabinet & muzzled."[25]

Even then, Clover did not forget those issues that involved women. "General Taylor," she noted, "disbelieves in democracy & universal suffrage as firmly as Mr. Frank Parkman—but is too much a man of the world to wail over the inevitable."[26] That Clover identified universal suffrage with democracy gives us a clear sense of where she stood, in spite of the fact that she played no active role for women's rights.

During this period of their life in Washington, Clover frequently mentioned her erratic cousin, Adie, and the presents they continued to exchange; she also continued to send her deep love to Betsy Wilder, her loving, supportive housekeeper. At one point, she managed to press the bouquet the President's wife had given her as a souvenir for the old nurse, as well as to make her a little cap that Clover insisted Betsy wear. Clover also often asked Betsy's advice on domestic issues, like how to make a stiff meringue. There was no sense of helplessness in any of these letters; Clover clearly felt happy and in control of her own life. Missing, however, were any references, except the most perfunctory, to the rest of the Adamses; perhaps, for her own salvation Clover managed to see to it that they played no emotional role in the life she and Henry shared.

Letters to Boston never ignored the special rewards of living in a milder climate; the abundance of flowers in Washington always delighted Clover. She was particularly pleased with the profusion of roses George Bancroft pressed upon her (like Parkman, he was an amateur horticulturalist who helped develop the American Beauty rose). Later she would hire his gardener; she enjoyed cultivating her own garden. At one point, she described the perfection of the weather—"beautiful sunny days neither warm nor cold—but like little silver hairs."[27] The loveliness of the Potomac countryside seemed to fulfill another of her important needs. Like Emerson, Clover found spiritual sustenance in nature that she never found in any institutional religious experience. On the daily horseback rides she and Henry took in the woods she described her tremendous delight with the profusion of azaleas, blood-root, and dogwood that characterized spring in Washington—the profusion that Henry would later identify with the forces of primitive sensual splendor and that T. S. Eliot would dismiss as spiritually unsustaining in his personal search for traditional faith.[28]

Clover's own "religious faith" remained as sceptical in Washington, "a pious city," as it had been in Boston. Wanting to avoid invitations to church, she declared, "I think I'd best announce that I'm a Buddhist or a Mormon." Glorying in her own kind of Emersonian naturalistic materialism, she made fun of the gaudy house of a more religious acquaintance, which was colossal and bewildering: "Folks must fall back on spiritual comforts who live daily in the presence of such upholstery & bric-a-brac."[29] No church away from home could provide her with a community; she would always be an iconoclast.

American women married to striving men are rarely allowed to luxuriate in their emotional attachment to any one place. No sooner did the Adamses begin to feel comfortable in Washington than Henry felt they must return to Europe. He had finished all the research he could accomplish in this country after having worked steadily for six hours a day; but neither of them was pleased to leave their new associates or their family of dogs and horses to cross the rough ocean again. Clover admonished a younger friend to never marry anyone who had to go abroad for samples: "Why that lie yclept history can't be agreed upon in America, I dont see"; and to her father, she complained, "Europe is a beast & I wish it was dead."[30] But Clover good naturedly resigned herself to yet another adventure. "Women," Henry Adams proclaimed, "commonly accept everything and die smiling and what they call resigned," which means, he deduced, "that they feel they are powerless." Later, he might have wondered at the astonishing glibness of his own conclusion: "Is life worth living? I should say not under such conditions."[31]

If a large part of Clover was reluctant to leave the beautiful Potomac countryside, the stimulating companions, and the Portuguese and Greek lessons (she had rejected French because she disapproved of the "unwashed Jesuit" Henry had chosen as teacher), another part was momentarily glad to give up the role of "genteel restaurant keeper." Perhaps she saw a new role emerging for herself as Henry's research assistant; a sense of an identity shift is apparent in the way that she signed her letters. Although all early notes to her father were signed "Clover," on this trip, she became "Marian Adams," or "M. A.," and there were fewer calls to Betsy in her affectionate remembrances. Perhaps she also saw herself taking on the split cultural position of European and Westerner that Clarence King seemed able to balance so well. She usually began these letters "Dear Pater" and ended them "Adios." But her fondness for Europe grew slowly and uncertainly.

The people the Adamses sought in England on this second trip were essentially the same old friends—not the "swells," but the intellectual elite who often, however, carried titles as well as intellects. Clover thought British parties were less interesting than their own affairs in Washington: "To my prejudiced mind good talk is more skerce here than in our brighter, lighter air." She also chided English provincialism: "The social savoir-faire and ease is what one would expect in Pawtucket Centre; the suppers, barring the absence of pie and pickles, resembling those of a remote village in New Hampshire. For all that, the men are poets and painters and the women are intelligent and have fine handles to their names."[32]

"Marian's" sense of elegance drew her again to Lady Goldsmid, now a widow, who was "interested in everything nice." Because her old friend's nephew was about to depart for America, Clover wrote him a letter of introduction to her father, urging the old man to share their own hospitality, to put him up at the Somerset Club, and to make sure he met Oliver Wendell Holmes. Clover and Lady Goldsmid also discussed their mutual interest in women's education with a "Girton scholar who was much pleased at hearing about the Harvard Annex experiment."[33] In May, 1880, the two of them went down to Cambridge to look at Girton, the new women's college of which Lady Goldsmid was a friend and benefactress. There they "lunched with a Greek tutoress, a pretty Miss Herschel, a Don, and took tea at the rooms of a young Jew, a nephew of my protector."[34] For Ellen Gurney's enlightenment, no doubt, Clover described the women's rooms: "Each has her parlor and bedroom & some are charmingly fitted." Another enjoyable part of her education centered about trips to the British Museum with the scholarly Dr. Ginsburg, whose wisdom she liked to quote.

When Clover described Lady Goldsmid, "unwearied in her kindness to us" as "a mother in Israel," and noted that there was "a theory that England is so much in the hands of the Jews that the English are the twelve lost tribes," she seemed essentially naive.[35] She may have felt herself expressing still another facet of Lowell's cultural atavism, which sought to identify all vitality with the same primitive roots. Yet in a later description of Disraeli as a "jew bagman with quack medicines," perhaps ironically meant to criticize Disraeli's own hostility to democratic ideas, she was also revealing some resentment that was not part of her earlier relationships; more likely, she had absorbed more of Henry's mixed feelings about the great Jewish Prime Minister. Gladstone, however, would fare no better by Clover's pen, and many of her Yankee neighbors fared worse. Although Clover's permissive upbringing and freewheeling interest in all sorts of people make it hard to label her "prejudiced," she continued to enjoy categorizing national types, a nineteenth-century pastime, as did also the most cosmopolitan and open-minded, William James. The French, for example, Clover labeled a "race of monkeys," the same term Henry Adams would later use for the Japanese. It was a self-enhancing game.

Just as many Brahmins failed to face the absolute necessity of identifying the best with the worst in their own democratic culture, so they also found it easy to separate individual Jews like the Goldsmids and Ginsburgs, and later, in Henry Adams' case, Bernard Berenson, from the mythical force they saw taking over the west. The threat of "the Irish and Jews, downtrodden races," avenging themselves (a fear that Adams would describe to Gaskell) became a dread reality to the Yankee imagination.[36] That such revenge might ever become a positive force in a democracy was inconceivable to many of the elite who, like the Adamses, felt the responsibility to impose their own aristocratic values on all society; to this elite, individuals were intended to be the only measure of quality. In their efforts to establish a world of intelligence, taste, and political morality, the reformers could not live without judgment; their most extreme generalizations would have been considered by them merely honesty—an essentially corrective force in an egalitarian society.

The British music world, which Lady Goldsmid introduced to the Adamses, was naturally accessible to Clover after her Agassiz School training, but the avant-garde London art world was harder for her to accept. After six years of marriage to Henry Adams, who had once admired John Rogers' statue of Chactas taking a thorn from Atala's foot as "a flash of real genius," Clover's taste had grown more conservative.[37] Now she relied on the critic Ruskin or the sculptor Woolner's judgments as much as on her own taste to pick paintings; and she was no longer interested in buying the work of unknown artists. The Bohemianism of even the conservative art establishment distressed her. At the Royal Academy Reception she noted, "Every art rag-bag seems to have been ransacked to adorn the women. They look like illustrations to Christina Rossetti's *Goblin Market*—fat figures in pea green; lean symphonies in chewing gum color; all in a rusty minor key."[38] But Clover nevertheless loved the "classical" paintings she found there; she returned twice to the Royal Academy to enjoy the Reynolds, Gainsboroughs, Hogarths, Turners, and Holbeins, "as I don't expect to come abroad again." Regretting not being able to share her pleasure with her brother, who was then raising his five daughters by himself, she wrote, "I hope

Ned will see them in another world if not in this," reflecting the curious sense of transcendental identity that was so often real for her. The more modern Grosvenor Gallery, on the other hand, she found "hung with many shocking daubs." "Whistler's largest piece, five by six feet, is all that Ruskin could ask to justify his charge that it was flinging a paint pot in the face of the public."[39] Recalling her many trips with her father to the lunatic asylum, Clover concluded intolerantly, "Any patient at Worcester who perpetrated such a joke would be kept in a cage for life." She nevertheless admired Whistler's more conservative etchings. Her brother Ned, a much more adventuresome art collector than Henry Adams was, would later commission Whistler to do a portrait of one of his five daughters, requiring only "brains"; "You can give as little paint, paper, or canvas as you please."[40] Even in England, the American Indians remained important to Clover; she took Henry by the hand to see the display of Native American artifacts at the Kensington Museum, which was "on the whole nothing new to an average Yankee who has been wallowing in bric-a-brac at home."[41] The art they took back with them to enrich their own American scene finally included much that was simply fashionable. A Turner painting, their most experimental purchase, may well have been a fake.[42] "If our ship goes down," Clover wrote her father, "you miss: Turner, Mulreadys, Copley, Fielding, Zuydeem, Moorish Cabinet, Salamanca embroidery & eight pretty Worth dresses."[43]

Clover prided herself on originality and often praised "Shaker simplicity" and the "New England freshness and tidiness" she grew up with in contrast to what she saw in Europe—"more fearful taste to the square foot than human imagination could conceive." "Only royal revenues could command such horrible curtains."[44] She nevertheless failed to assert her belief in simpler styles and accepted Henry's decisions on such matters as fashionable dresses by the great designer Worth. Henry and her cousin Adie Bigelow, who was then traveling in Europe, "bullied" Clover into getting Worth gowns, Clover feebly protested, "for the praiseworthy purpose of increasing my self-respect." Enchanted by Worth's lovely black poodle and his keen sense of craftsmanship, Clover enjoyed sharing the vision of her prospective elegance and often sent snips of material home to Betsy for her approval. As intense and serious as Clover Adams was, she was not immune to what has been called the real curse of Eve, "the perpetual hunger to be beautiful."[45] Such vulnerability made her all the more human. The time she spent on this trip with Mrs. Jack Gardner, admired by Clover as an even freer spirit than she could ever be, may have taught her that great style could also compensate for many other flaws.

Clover could no longer derive self-respect from her work with Henry. Her husband had to spend more and more time in the archives alone, and "mousing" about shops and museums grew wearisome to Clover. She also did not share her friend Henry James' imaginative appreciation of life in a country manor: "I would rather live in more squalor & have less paraphernalia. The more I see of English Country House existence the more it bores me," she wrote, and "the means drown the end." At one dinner, she found herself seated beside a man whose talk was exclusively of "fox-hunting, saddles, & patent stirrups." Though she was a horsewoman, Clover could not resist concluding, "Such a dinner is now and then very resting to the brain."

The general inequities of the British social system continued to bother her:

> It must ruin these poor lords to have to keep up such places, and only the sight-seeing public get any fun from it. We find a great change in six years. At this Belshazzar's feast, not only we see the handwriting on the wall, but the givers of the feast do too; and they are scared, and say it's giving way. On all sides are wails of unlet farms, discontented tenants, no money, good servants who wont wear livery. The 39,000,000 who get no cake and ale, think it's about time for the 1,000,000 who do to treat.[46]

Clover, unlike Henry, expressed compassion for the "kind and sympathetic" populace. She also shared his theoretical vision of himself as a Radical, which coincided with her mother's transcendental concerns about injustice. Talking of the downfall of prime ministers, she proudly boasted that her sympathies always went with the Radicals.

Similar social sympathies enabled her to communicate with writers she otherwise avoided. Robert Browning, whose voice was "like steel—loud & harsh & incessant," became suddenly interesting to her when he spoke of Margaret Fuller, whom he had known well in Italy, during the revolutionary phase of her life, and "liked much."[47]

Clover's own reports on George Eliot's unconventional marriage to a much younger man echo Margaret Fuller's earlier comments about the irregular life of George Sand: "She takes rank in society like a man, for the weight of her thoughts. . . . I suppose she has suffered much, but she has also enjoyed and done much, and her expression is one of calmness and happiness."[48] Writing to her father with a sympathy for her female contemporary that she was later unwilling to extend to Oscar Wilde, Clover proclaimed "We declare that 'a woman of genius' is above criticism. . . . The comments are likely to be many & hard; they're going to be stabbed by sharp criticisms."[49] That society forced unusual behavior upon gifted women who had fewer conventional outlets for self-expression was, in this instance, a point she wanted to underline. During this visit to England, Clover sought out still another gifted and liberated woman. Henry James arranged a final meeting with her teenage idol, the bohemian Fanny Kemble. What they talked about, however, was never recorded.

Matthew Arnold, first admired because he reminded her of the critic George William Curtis, another related member of the Brook Farm group that touched her background in so many ways, was "facile & gay & full of talk & curiosity about America & its people which he wished much to see." Clover urged her father to help Arnold visit America: "If the trustees of the Lowell Institute made him a tempting offer to deliver a course of lectures next autumn I should think it might please him and them. He is poor and has a family to support."[50] She assured Arnold that he had many readers on our side, but warned him that "abusing us it might not be the same." Whether Henry's more austere judgment influenced Clover's opinions is hard to say precisely, for she prided herself on independent thinking, yet she later charged that Arnold seemed "less of a heavy-weight and *slopped over* too much."[51] When Clover copied out a poem for her aging nurse Betsy Wilder about Angelica Kauffman's cupids, however, she was not much worried about slopping over; she remembered affectionately that Betsy had "an eye for sentiment."[52] Lecturing in America, Arnold made his criticisms of democratic values outweigh their shared concern for defining the best; Clover found him "snobbish." Her old friend George Bancroft, ignoring the justice of many of Arnold's complaints, continued to defend democracy's superiority; he called Matthew Arnold's American lectures "twaddle."

Although the Adamses entertained the distinguished American historian Francis Parkman, one of Henry's older friends and an active foe of women's rights, Clover's reaction remained less than enthusiastic. Her independence asserted itself indirectly in her comment that his conversation had not changed at all in three years, either in opinions or in topics. He had grown "no less conservative," she reported; in fact, she saw him as "immutable as Faneuil Hall."[53] Her later photographic portrait of Parkman, seated on a chair in the woods with his derby hat on, graphically reinforced this view.

A more favored visitor was Henry James. Always appreciative of Clover's spirited intelligence, James became a constant companion in England, often staying until midnight to argue the eternal debate about Europeans versus Americans; he reported home how much he had enjoyed "abusing the Britons" with the Adamses. Although he found Clover more "toned down" than in the Newport and Boston association of their youth, Henry James still relished her play of mind. Describing his intimacy with the Adamses to his father, James wrote, "Henry is very sensible, though a trifle dry, and Clover has a touch of genius."[54] Clover continued to lecture James on the need to return to America for a transfusion of vitality. She called him "frivolous" and wrote that it was "high time Harry James was ordered home by his family—he is too good a fellow to be spoiled by injudicious old ladies in London. . . . He had better go to Cheyenne & run a hog ranch." That James felt misunderstood by his countrymen he tried to show by bringing Clover the savage notices of his biography of Hawthorne in American newspapers. She refused to sympathize. Hadn't the Adamses always experienced similar hostility in their political struggles? "He had better not hang around Europe much longer if he wants to make a lasting reputation," Clover concluded.[55]

If her analysis of James was superficially wrong, Clover's perception of his peculiar need to see himself as an American was not. In their mutual efforts to define the *best* in a democratic society, they often felt complete empathy. Yet Henry James could no more define his artistic role in a simple, chauvinistic way than the Adamses could narrow their political focus along simple party lines. They always understood each other's conflicts and enjoyed arguing about them at length; they valued their own complexity. The basic moral qualities they shared enabled the three of them to remain close friends throughout their lives. They were all, James assured his mother, "very excellent people."[56]

Clover might have anticipated finding her ideal American writer in the westerner Bret Harte, whom she looked forward to having "a field day" with in London, but the acquaintance did not flower into friendship. Was Harte exploiting his "western" traits too much as a form of self-promotion, as the contemporary papers suggested? Such ostentatious behavior would have surely put off the Adamses, but Clover did not comment. She did mention another western writer to her father with consistent enthusiasm for his work. Mark Twain was the man to read in "moments of depression" when life seemed "like a blank." No evidence exists, however, that the Adamses ever tried to meet Mark Twain or even William Dean Howells, whose steady production Clover continued to follow closely. Never impressed by the trappings of success, however, she came to believe that it might be better *not* to meet the writers one admired most if one intended to go on reading their work. When the Adamses set out for the continent again, though, she wrote home with her usual sense of pride in their American identity: "The second act of the *Innocents Abroad* is now beginning."[57]

Although both Adamses approved of the more "democratised" France that had emerged since the breakdown of "the vulgar Bonaparte Dynasty" ("vulgar" meant pretentious as opposed to authentic simplicity), Clover felt less comfortable in France than before. The presence of her cousin Adie, however, who shared her sympathies and her judgmental approach to life, made the hours pass more quickly when Henry retreated to the archives. Other American friends enlivened Paris as well. Henry James followed them across the Channel, and Mrs. Jack Gardner joined the group for pleasant evenings of good restaurants and risqué theaters. Clover even relaxed enough to enjoy a "very indecent and charmingly acted play" they thought might be justly interrupted by the police. As might be expected, she found the more institutionalized official drama at the Comédie Française "as dull as King's Chapel."[58]

She sometimes tried to emphasize her own ever-present desire to startle by omission—"I won't trust myself to enlarge upon the weather as my language might shock you"—but she herself could not bear the more socially shocking drama of Zola's *L'Assommoir*. The world of the "gruesome and terrible," which she had once confronted in the insane asylum, was too excruciating for her to watch on stage. "For ten minutes at least in a delirium tremens scene worked up in a London hospital, I could not look on, and was even driven to putting my fingers in my ears." The destruction of the rational mind—lack of control—was intolerable to Clover; death would be preferable to a life of instability and anguish.

Later that same year, she commented sympathetically on the suicide of another early Newport friend, the artist William Morris Hunt, as "putting an end to his wild restless unhappy life." "Perhaps," she argued, "it has saved him years of insanity which his temperament pointed to."[59]

Although there can be no doubt that the nineteenth century was on more intimate terms with death than the twentieth century is, Clover's frequent comments sometimes reached the morbid extremes of Emmeline Grangerford's poems in *Huckleberry Finn*. At one point, she wrote home, "I'd rather winter in a first-class American coffin than in any house on this side." Another time she commented, "Still the rain came down and we thought that death to us would be a welcome alternative to Madrid." She also reported all the macabre details of the tribulations of James Russell Lowell's wife with the conclusion that he "yearned for six feet of clean gravel over him."[60] Because Clover as a child had not only experienced the terminal illness of her mother but had also been with her Aunt Susan Bigelow when she took a fatal dose of arsenic, she must have felt peculiarly intimate with death. She grew up—as Alice James had—accepting the idea of choice in life or death as part of her own definition of freedom of the will.

When she had significant work to do, however, Clover was always happy to be alive. In Spain, her superior linguistic skills managed to get Henry into archives that were otherwise closed. She liked to talk to strangers on trains and sometimes even found them helpful to Henry in his work. Back in England, she would resort to bribery to get her historian into a house that was sealed for the holidays: "Silver and brass—feminine brass—open all doors in all lands," she wrote home boastfully.[61] If Henry saw such behavior as compromising the higher moral principles of the Adamses, he did not write as much; he was grateful for her help.

Although their stay in Spain was saddened by the terrible health of Mrs. Lowell, who apparently had typhus, which involved frequent mental breakdowns,

Clover nevertheless managed to be a support to the Lowells as well as to Henry. And again she was enjoying adventuresome learning: "I plunge in wildly, regardless of verbs, nouns, and genders, and am picking up something everyday." Before returning to England, she acknowledged that she had gained a better understanding of the Spanish philosophy of "tomorrow," but her Yankee desire for accomplishment "today" struggled hard. Clover also perceived that the government in Spain looked even more hopeless than the governments of England or France:

> The Spaniards are the most kindly, sympathetic, child-like, unpractical, incapable, despondent people I ever saw, with a magnificant country which they are utterly unable to develop, a rotten old church in which they don't believe, a king whom they don't know and declare to be a puppet, a longing for a republic which can't manage, and a lurking conviction that the Anglo-Saxon race is going to crush them out.[62]

England, in spite of its familiarity, would not make Clover feel much more at home, even though she again worked side-by-side with Henry in the British Museum. Although she enjoyed mocking them, the endless rituals and traditions in Britain made Clover uncomfortable. She had been trained to be a free spirit, not a diplomat— "these old pageants & ceremonies seem like a joke & I rejoice that I am alien & belong to a race who kicked out of this old harness so long ago." She "wriggled out" of going to the Ascot Races because she'd heard that the only excitement there was "the women's dresses"; "I feared such a mass of it would cause hopeless idiocy," she ridiculed.[63] During a visit to Parliament, Clover took obvious pleasure in noting that "one of the more advanced liberals chewed a sheet of paper and scratched his bald young head" while the royal family were prayed for. The great Queen herself would not escape Clover's critical eye. Victoria appeared "fat & red-faced and ducked her old head incessantly from side to side."[64] Such ongoing irreverence would feel at home only in one country. Clover and Henry always took care to separate themselves from the horde of Anglophiles that Boston constantly sent their way, no matter how much they too enjoyed what was civilized about England.

By the time the Adamses were ready to return to America, when "the object which brought Henry over" was accomplished, Clover wrote that she had begun to feel "like a machine which says a few incoherent words when the lever is pulled." The thought of returning to Beverly "for a little visit & to vote," cheered her immensely.[65] Women in Massachusetts had won the right to vote for school committee in 1879, a privilege that the politically aware Clover did not mean to neglect. If suffrage was not a prime commitment for her, neither was it an issue of indifference.

The "genuine New England soul" of Clover Adams did not find the time she had spent with Henry in Europe ultimately profitable. Leaving England, she wrote, would cause no more regrets than finishing a pleasant story that one does not care to read over again. But she had once again, perhaps much more consciously than in her younger days, left an indelible impression on the mind of her countryman, Henry James. James wrote to their mutual friend Grace Norton from England in September, 1880:

> I go in an hour to bid farewell to my friends the Henry Adamses, who after a year of London life are returning to their beloved Washington. One sees so many "cultivated Americans" who prefer living abroad that it is a great refreshment to encounter two specimens of this class who find the charms of their native land so much greater than those of Europe. In England they appear to have suffered more than enjoyed, and their experience is not unedifying, for they have seen and known a good deal of English life. But they are rather too critical and

invidious. I shall miss them much though—we have had such inveterate discussions and comparing of notes. They have been much liked here. Mrs. Adams in comparison with the usual British female is a perfect Voltaire in petticoats.[66]

Henry James would imagine many heroines in terms of the free-spirited, irreverent qualities of the "Voltaire in petticoats" he so steadily admired in Clover Adams.

# 8

## The Final Years

*I have tried here and there rather to suggest
than to assert . . . the inevitable isolation and disillusionment
of a really strong mind.*
Henry Adams to Henry Cabot Lodge, October 5, 1879

Home suits our tastes and tempers better than your effete old monarchies," Clover had written.[1] Whether she got to Beverly to exercise her new right to vote for school committee before settling back in Washington in October 1880, seems unlikely; the town's voting records are not that complete. That she was aware of the opportunity, however, tells us much about her alertness to the issues of civil rights for women. In 1881, only 149 people of both sexes voted for school committee in Essex County. If Clover felt any ambiguity about the ultimate effects of universal suffrage, moreover, it would not have extended to education. Women were expected to be an influence for good in public policy. As early as 1875, there were women on the Boston School Committee. The privilege of voting for others became a cultural mandate as well as a right.[2]

When Clover began to shape a political salon in Washington, it became, in a sense, her own kind of school, a source of moral enlightenment that was free of institutional or party connections, where men could learn from educated political thinkers. Worthington Ford, who edited the first volumes of Henry Adams' letters, described Clover's salon: "There was the best school of politics in that house, for the leaders of higher politics frequented it and one had only to listen to learn." Visitors to the Adamses often described a place where "host and hostess offered the best, a house almost unique in its composition."[3] Yet what appeared unique in post–Civil War Washington had clear-cut moral antecedents in pre–Civil War New England. Both Clover and Henry were projecting Emerson's ideal of the "unconscious radiation of virtue" upon their new associates.

Clover's letters to her father during the final five years of her life in Washington expressed a kind of newspaper columnist's excitement in reporting all the details and gossip behind the political scene. During these years, Henry Adams was not only talking about history and shaping the ideas of men making history, he was also writing it—without Clover's help. Enormously productive during this period of his life, he was not only deep into his nine-volume *History of the United States During the Administrations of Jefferson and Madison*, but he was also writing biographies and novels. He and Clover no longer worked side by side. Clover contributed some superficial details to his books, particularly the novels, but she was less able to feel herself his intellectual equal because Henry isolated himself for five or six hours, sometimes for as many as ten hours a day, when he was writing.[4]

Their late afternoon horseback rides in the Potomac woods became their greatest source of intimacy during the day. Yet Henry continued to try out his writing on Clover's "typical" democratic mind. To John Hay he wrote, "I make it a rule to strike out ruthlessly in my writings whatever my wife criticizes on the theory that she is the average reader, and that her decisions, are in fact if not in reason absolute."[5] The idea that Clover's capacity to reason had not been adequately educated, that her intuitive faculties enabled her to identify with the masses in a way that Henry's "snobbish" education did not, remained important to him. The image that he used to describe the free-spirited Clover-Esther—a ship without a rudder—was also an image he extended to the great democracy itself: "How could a ship hope to reach port when the crew threw overboard sails, spars, and compass . . . [and] unshipped their rudder. . . ."[6] Adams made the European mind speculate about "American Ideals" in his first volume of the *History of the United States*.

When many people, among them Clover's Aunt Carrie Tappan, whose close association with such women as Margaret Fuller and Catharine Sedgwick would have given her good cause to believe in women's intellectual potential, asserted that it was Mrs. Henry Adams who had written the anonymously published novel *Democracy*, Henry was outraged: "My wife never wrote for publication in her life and could not write if she tried," he protested to John Hay.[7] Clover, all too willing to accept his judgment, joined Henry in declaring Aunt Carrie a ninny.

Clover must have frequently heard Henry rail against women with intellectual pretensions. Sympathetic as he often was with the cause of education for women, he also saw it as a reason for the loss of their emotional strength. Before his marriage, he had written of Charles Gaskell's distinguished intellectual aunt that it was "worse than useless for women to study philosophy; the result was to waste the best feminine material, and to make very poor philosophers." Going on to express his own capacity for identification with the female sex, he concluded: "Her mind only fed on itself and was neither happy nor altogether free from morbid self-reflections which always come from isolation in society, as I know to my cost."[8]

In the same letter that had condemned university priggishness, Henry complained: "Our young women are haunted by the idea that they ought to read, to draw, or to labor in some way, not for any such frivolous object as making themselves agreeable to society, nor for simple amusement, but to 'improve' their minds. They are utterly unconscious of the pathetic impossibility of improving those poor little hard, thin, wiry, one-stringed instruments which they call their minds, and which haven't range enough to master one big emotion much less to express it in words or figures."[9] Finding a woman historian listed on the American Historical Association program in 1885, Adams was outraged enough to protest violently against the irrational forces taking over the AHA—"cometary theory & female story telling."[10]

Whether Clover's ego was strong enough to separate her own mind from the simpler or more pretentious minds of her sex, in order to maintain her self-respect, seems questionable. She continued to study Portuguese and Greek (at a time when her brother-in-law Charles was fighting compulsory Greek at Harvard as superfluous) perhaps as much for Henry's amusement as her own satisfaction. He enjoyed all her esoteric accomplishments, and he liked to show her off. But Clover acknowledged freely that her education added up to little. At one dinner party, she and another younger woman "deplored to each other the vast sums our respective and respected parents had vainly 'fooled away' on our education. The deem'd total being useless. 'Have you the apricot of my aunt?' 'Has the baker the coat of the tailor?' though excellent exercise in themselves, are as useless in the sea of real life as a dory without oars," Clover complained.[11] Clover nonetheless continued to support her sister's work for the Harvard Annex to help educate other women. After a visit to New York, she agreed to aid Clarence King's mother in founding an art school in Charleston "to help educate and cultivate a vanquished foe. . . . Allston and Richardson show that there is seed worth forcing in that barren land." An American art and architecture had to be encouraged and supported.[12]

It would be hard to separate a commitment to education from a commitment to democracy. In spite of protesting the uselessness of her own training, Clover would not, however, advocate the entirely "useful" education that Charles Francis Adams, Jr., was trying to sell President Eliot at that time. Her own definition of the "best" would follow her mother's Transcendental vision that al-

ways included the good and the beautiful. She shared
her parents' and Emerson's and Whitman Gurney's
sense of responsibility to the cultivation of broader values
in American life. Art schools were undeniably important;
she knew that Carrie Tappan, whose family later gave
Tanglewood to the Boston Symphony Orchestra, might
also be interested in supporting this project and urged
her father to enlist his sister-in-law's help.

Only the educated are finally able to scoff at the frivolity of education. Henry Adams' contempt for his
own intellectual training reflected what George Santayana
called "the longing to be primitive" that remains "the disease of culture."[13] Clover did not share such a longing;
hungry for more education, she celebrated and sought
knowledge whenever she got the chance. If Henry's
ambivalence about educating women influenced her, her
enthusiasm for women's education also caused him to
modify his prejudices. After he made fun of Grover
Cleveland's sister Rose for carrying "an atmosphere of female college about her thicker than the snowstorm outside my window," he ended up admitting that he greatly
enjoyed her seriousness: "We talked chiefly of George
Eliot's biography which she takes in an earnest spirit,"
Henry wrote Clover when she had gone home to nurse
her father in 1885. That his wife's values may have been
accentuated even at this time by her absence appeared in
his firm decision to return to the White House with Clover to visit Miss Cleveland again: "I liked her and became
quite intimate with her."[14]

Although Clover Adams' letters describing settling
back into Washington in the 1880s revealed her to be a
pioneer consumer of some magnitude, she was never
entirely contented buying furnishings and organizing
her household. She often grumbled about details and
complained, "I don't have time to breathe and yet do
nothing." She was troubled by the idea that "we are
working very hard, but it is all for ourselves."[15] When she
finally established their home as a place "to alleviate the
lot of strangers in this city by feeding and protecting
them," she felt more useful.[16] Both Adamses put a good

deal of thought and energy into the newly rented house at 1601 H Street to make it hospitable; finally, Clover wrote that they were so fond of this old house that they would "never leave it."[17] Indeed, she never did.

The house they established was meant to be as artistically stimulating as it was politically interesting. Clover Adams accepted Charles Eliot Norton's idea that art was necessary to provoke the imagination and to enrich the dimensions of history. Like Emerson, Norton had also warned that in America "the practical concerns of life" were too engrossing: "nowhere were the conditions of life more prosaic; nowhere the poetic spirit less evident, and the love of beauty less diffused."[18] Henry Adams' family was still waiting to produce its generation of artists. Indeed, Charles Francis Adams had confessed himself a Goth for not having made his first trip to the Boston Fine Arts Museum until after it had been open for seven years. Even then he went only to hear William Wetmore Story, who was once greatly admired by Henry but who remained Clover's idea of the epitome of artistic phonies. The elder Adams enjoyed Story for his simple manners and was impressed by the crowd; he reported that the museum "looked very well at night, and the assemblage was of the best."[19] Yet, although Clover, unlike Henry, had grown up with art and had once felt sure of her taste, she now continued to give in to his need for the advice of European experts. Thomas Woolner, sculptor, poet, and art dealer, became their British scout and artistic mentor after they settled back in Washington. In exchange for his advice, they attempted to sell Woolner's offerings to American friends to enrich the American scene in general, as well as to embellish their own walls.

Woolner possessed an attribute not usually essential for an artist, but essential for the approval of an Adams—he was a "gentleman." He shared the Adamses' sense of decency and their awareness of "moral chaos." "The works which the chiefs of fashion support are so outrageous I can scarcely think they are believers in what they do," Woolner wrote to "Mrs. Adams"; the pre-Raphaelites he turned away from as distressingly sensual. Appealing to Clover again as one of those "who think for themselves," Woolner persuaded her that Bonington was as distinguished as Turner.[20] The Adamses ended up with four Boningtons in their art collection, but they were not frequently misled. By 1885, their collection of drawings included examples of Flaxman, Rembrandt, Blake, Mantegna, Murillo, Rubens, Michelangelo, Watteau, and Claude Lorrain, as well as a number of less impressive craftsmen.[21] If they were conservative about paintings, their choices of graphic art were unusually sound. Clover reported her satisfaction at gathering a collection that was pleasing both to Elizabeth Bancroft, who professed a general indifference to elegant possessions, and to Marianna Van Rensselaer, the sophisticated and distinguished art critic of the *New York World*. In her letters to Woolner, Clover countered his pride in the richness of the European environment by emphasizing the pleasures of the "wild Indian life" they were leading in America.[22] She attempted to send him Aztec vases and Tiffany glass, as well as flower seeds and books on Mexico and American mountaineering as responses to his somewhat patronizing statements that he was offering the kind of treasures that could only be found in Europe. Her presents made him wonder if he too might not someday become "weary of civilization."[23]

Although Clover and Henry agreed on the importance of art as an educational moral experience, they did not always agree on what was beautiful. Clover bought two modest Joshua Reynolds figures in spite of the fact that Henry hated portraits. A verse she wrote for a Boston accent reflected their differing tastes:

> *Jack Sprat dislikes portraits*
> *His wife dislikes paysages*
> *And so betwixt them both*
> *The choice is very large.*

"Henry can look the other way," she concluded defiantly, without inferring that such differences in taste told a good deal about the differences in their personalities.[24]

Clover deeply enjoyed all kinds of people; Henry's social preferences were more limited.

As the "first Heart" of the group of close friends that included Clarence King and John and Clara Hay, Clover extended herself generously to these closer intimates. Although it seems unlikely that she would originally have had much in common with the silent, shy Mrs. Hay, perhaps the suicide of Clara Hay's millionaire father in 1883 brought them closer together. Clover would always be able to understand the deep suffering brought about by separation or loss. John Hay, Abraham Lincoln's personal secretary and biographer, was during these years a particularly close friend of Henry Adams, although Henry grew more and more intolerant of Hay's undiscriminating taste in people. To his English correspondent Robert Cunliffe, he wrote an honest description of John Hay, the Westerner: "I never knew more than two or three men from west of the Alleghenies who knew the difference between a gentleman and a swindler. This curious obliquity makes [John Hay] a particularly charming companion to me as he knows intimately scores of men whom I would not touch with a pole, but who are more amusing than my own crowd."[25] Henry came to feel that Hay compromised his moral principles too easily. As early as 1884, Adams wrote that he no longer talked politics with him as they were on "opposite sides."[26] When Hay finally became Secretary of State, he became, in Henry's imagination, still another example of the corruption implicit in power.

Clarence King, who was as comfortable with John Ruskin as he was with any Pi-ute chief, remained the archetypal American hero to the Adamses. William Dean Howells pointed out King's remarkable and consistent democratic "feelings for the people who do the hard work of the world so that others may enjoy their ease"; King was always a failure, Howells noted, at driving his own workmen.[27] John Hay, too, was moved to write about King's overwhelming compassion for "the most wretched derelicts of civilization."[28] If Henry Adams did not share such compassion, he nevertheless was able to admire it. Adams never made any critical comments about King's steady admiration for black women; there is some sense, moreover, that his own interest in primitive women, "old gold," particularly in his travels after Clover's death, was stimulated by King's belief in the remarkable intuitive powers of women with dark skin.

The "Five of Hearts" played a minor role in Washington at the time the Adamses were settling in again for the second time. In 1882, Henry Adams noted ruefully that all of their best friends were broken down:

> Hay had heart palpitations; King suffered from an old rupture; Richardson had 'Bright's disease'; Wendell Holmes was 'very weary'; Alex Agassiz, 'another invalid'; not to mention the state of my brother, Brooks. . . . These are the jewels of my generation, all the friends I have that count in life.[29]

Clover Adams found comfort in the warmth of her family. Unlike Henry, she still remained emotionally close to her New England clan. During her travels, she had expressed frequent concern for Ned's wife, Fanny, whose health deteriorated rapidly after she had given birth to five daughters in seven years. Was it a son the Hoopers wanted most? If Clover envied Fanny's motherhood, she also recognized the high price Fanny was paying for her children. Once a spirited reformer, Fanny, who was also a fellow Sanitary worker, had spent a good deal of time with the family of James Freeman Clarke, the distinguished liberal minister active in the fight for women's rights. She had worked, too, with the Women's Educational and Industrial Union to improve the lot of working women in Boston. If Fanny had any time at all for such sympathies after her children arrived, no record of her later activity remains. Clover had wanted to help take care of her invalid sister-in-law: "I will be nurse or read story books all day long or play games or anything to fill any gaps."[30] But understanding her intense sensitivity, the Hoopers shielded Clover from the seriousness of Fanny's illness; in fact, when Fanny died in 1881, they even managed to keep her from attending the funeral by sending news of the death by slow mail instead of by telegram. "Fate has strange ways of dealing," wrote Clover later, contrasting the death of such a full life as Fanny's with the continuing vigor of an empty one: "Poor Aunt Anne who has and gives no pleasure to anyone and may live to bury all her contemporaries—and others called off from a full feast. The moral is to make all one can out of life and live up to one's fingers' ends." Aunt Anne's final suffering had been derived not only from the Civil War death of her son, but also from the mysterious illness of her lively daughter Alice, remembered by her antics on the school bus and her fine description of the Civil War commemoration ceremonies. What caused Alice's death at the age of thirty-eight remains unclear. "As much as I wanted to write to her I could not help feeling that she would never see a letter, and that it would be added pain to Aunt Anne," Clover wrote.[31]

When her cousin, Adeline Bigelow, who had always been her good friend and her close companion on two trips to Europe, experienced the dreaded breakdown they had once jested about, Clover was deeply concerned: "Can she be sent to some more soothing climate? Where the sound of church bells & her mother's voice can never reach her poor tired brain. I know from her own lips her horror of insane persons & of those who have been sent to asylums—if they can by any possible means ward off that crisis it will save her years of misery."[32] Yet Adie's mental state, seemingly related to the fierce religious ministrations of her mother, finally landed her, to Clover's great distress, in the Somerville Asylum. "I cannot bear to think that what she most feared has come to pass—for such sweet cheery creatures it seems a cruel fate. . . . a life one cannot grieve with any sense of loss. I wish it might have been Worcester instead of Somerville which is such a smelly hideous place." She knew the difference between such institutions. "Best love to Adie," Clover continued to write, trusting her father to reach the cousin with whom she could no longer communicate. "Can't her mother go to Somerville when she comes out?" she demanded, adding that "S. Weir Mitchell is going to write a new book, 'The Divorce of Mother and Daughter.'"[33] Herself motherless for so long, Clover may have found it easier than most of her contemporaries to perceive the destructive force in such close mother–daughter ties, or she may have rationalized that they were unnecessary. Whether she could have joked about the divorce of father and daughter in the same way is another question. Yet respect for the authority of the family would never be, in any case, any more automatic in Clover's mind than respect for any of the other institutions society cherished.

Although the remark about S. Weir Mitchell was semiserious, Clover had been pleased to count Mitchell, the greatest contemporary authority on women's mental illness, among her friends. He often took tea with the Adamses in Washington, and he sent Clover a volume of his poetry. Although it seems unlikely that she would have ever felt free to discuss family problems with him, she was sensitive enough to Adie's anxieties to suggest that her cousin not return to Boston upon her release from the asylum, but spend some time instead with the Adamses in Washington where "among entire strangers she would feel less conscious."[34]

Another close old friend, Tom Kinnicutt, also ended up in an asylum. Clover urged her father to make sure to visit him at Worcester on one of his lifelong medical missions, as Tom was "broken down and paralysed in bed; all his profession gone, and money too"; he needed "cheering."[35] That she worried about her own fate in a world so full of instability is certain. At the trial of the maniacal Guiteau for the assassination of President Garfield, which Clover and Henry regularly attended, there was, as Charles Rosenberg reported, "a strained attempt to minimize the importance of heredity in the etiology of insanity at a time when neither physicians nor laymen doubted its significance for a moment."[36] Clover appeared to be taken in by the attempt. Like the judge, she wanted to believe in the power of free will; to her father, she wrote with satisfaction, "The witnesses that day smashed the hereditary insanity theory pretty thoroughly."[37]

Clover's greater range of sympathies enabled her to cope better than Henry with the individuality of their servants; she had few pretensions. Although she thought decorations ostentatious, she kept mum about the velvet band her coachman enjoyed wearing in his hat. She even made an attempt to pacify the furious German workman who, protesting that nothing could please Henry Adams, ran home in a rage from his construction job and subsequently murdered his hapless wife. Yet commitment to social reform that was similar to her early work for the Sanitary Commission was as absent from her new life in Washington as were truly close friends. One such loyal friend, however, returned to America to visit the woman he had long ago described as the genius of my beloved country.[38]

Henry James had written Clover a safely flirtatious note reminding her that in London she had promised that it "would be over there that we shall really meet *familiarly.*" "I am prepared to be intensely familiar," he concluded, signing himself, "impatiently and irrepressibly yours."[39] Once in Washington, he again spent a good deal of time with the Adamses. He enjoyed the absence of commerce in the capital city although he found the place still "too much of a village." James also enjoyed the "perennial afternoon teas—two or three times a day" at the Adamses' house—and the "frequent dinners at a little round table"; he described their Washington life to a mutual English friend:

> I find here our good little friends the Adamses, whose extremely agreeable house may be said to be one of the features of Washington. They receive a great deal and in their native air they bloom, expand, emit a general fragrance. They dont pretend to conceal (as why should they?) their preference of America to Europe, and they rather rub it into me, as they think it a wholesome discipline for my demoralized

spirit. One excellent reason for their liking Washington better than London is that they are, vulgarly speaking, "someone" here.[40]

To be "someone," Henry James went on to observe, did not mean, by the Adams definition, sharing the life of the many corrupt or compromising politicians that swarmed over the Washington scene; yet the Adamses could not help being interested in the lives of the corrupt. James was amused that they thought the company he kept "very bad," but were nonetheless anxious to hear what he had "done and heard at places which they decline to frequent."[41] He, after all, being an outsider, as well as an artist and not a reformer, felt no need to set an example. Meeting Oscar Wilde or James G. Blaine, anathema to Clover and Henry who were trying to exemplify the best American life, was merely enriching experience for Henry James. What Clover saw as James' own exotic limitations also continued to bother her:

That young emigrant has much to learn here. He is surprised to find that he can go to the capitol and listen to debates without taking out a license, as in London. He may in time get into the "swim" here, but I doubt it. I think the real, live, quick-paced world in America will fret him and that he prefers a quiet corner with a pen where he can create men and women who say neat things and have refined tastes and are not nasal or eccentric. "Let everyman be persuaded in his own mind," we say.[42]

Clover was not acting inconsistently. Because, unlike James, she wanted to accept and to live in the culture where people were nasal and eccentric, she felt she had to be more discriminating on a moral level; she declined, she once wrote her father, to eat lunch with forgers. When Henry James modelled two characters on the Adamses who said "let us be vulgar and have some fun—let us invite the President," he captured part of their dilemma. "For Washington their society was a little too good"; they too must have often been bewildered by the responsibility and the ambiguity involved in seeking out the best.[43] When Charles Francis Adams, Jr., referred publicly to the anonymous author of *Democracy* (to Henry's delight) as "coarse and half-educated," he revealed just how hard it had become for even the most self-assured to evaluate authenticity. Life in England, Henry James noted, was less of a strain: "There we needn't be always making the best of things. One may make the worst of them and they are still pretty good."[44] The picture Henry James had drawn of alienated Americans in *Portrait of a Lady* (a novel he wrote almost directly after spending time with the Adamses), Clover recognized as "a cry from the heart," but she had little patience with the growing intricacies of his style. Her famous statement that "he chaws more than he bites off" seemed a dismissal of his craft, but it was also in keeping with a sense of the democratic responsibility to make art accessible.

What seems worth dwelling on in connection with *Portrait of a Lady* is how much the novel might suggest a cry from the heart in connection with Clover's own life. No more poignant fable exists about the irony of freedom; nor has any writer ever shown more sympathy with the adventuresome female spirit trying within a limited sphere to choose a creative rather than a conventional life. James describes Isabel Archer's imagined ideal in terms that might easily be applied to Clover: "Her notion of the aristocratic life was simply the union of great knowledge with great liberty; the knowledge would give one a sense of duty and the liberty a sense of enjoyment."[45] The confinement she found herself in was the opposite of what she sought. That Henry James' genius, as Ezra Pound pointed out, was aligned always with "human liberty, personal liberty, the rights of the individual against all sorts of intangible bondage," suggests an easy alliance with the ideas of his friend from adolescence.[46] When Gilbert Osmond, the corrupt expatriate in *Portrait of a Lady*, wants to mock Isabel Archer's intensity of belief, he finds it easy to say "her sentiments were worthy of a radical newspaper or a Unitarian preacher."⁴⁷ The Transcendental heritage that Clover Adams and Henry James shared from the connections their parents passed down to them from Emerson and Swedenborg made them both more idealistic than they may have been willing to admit. That the freedom their heritage led them to appreciate might ultimately be illusory remains one of the terrors implicit both in the *Portrait of a Lady* and in the life of Clover Adams.

Clover was also pleased to find herself identified in another Henry James story, *Point of View*, with the masculine character of Marcellus Cockerel, whose enthusiasm echoes many of the letters Clover had written her father:

> The vastness and freshness of this American world, the great scale and great pace of our development, the good sense and good nature of the people console me for there being no cathedrals and no Titians.⁴⁸

If such patriotic fervor suggested Clover to James, it also recalled the inspiration of Emerson. When Henry James eventually returned to England, he wrote a final note to Clover Adams that she sharply reported to her father:

> He wished, he said, his last farewell to be said to me as I seemed to him "the incarnation of my native land"—a most equivocal compliment coming from him. Am I then vulgar, dreary, and impossible to live with? That's the only obvious interpretation, however self-love might look for a gentler one. Poor America! She must drag on somehow without the sympathy & love of her denationalised children. I fancy she'll weather it.⁴⁹

Clover's insistence on the possibility of identifying the best in democratic culture with political life encouraged a wider variety of acquaintances than James imagined possible for the Adamses. She boasted that she liked to "get off our own beat" and meet "any man or woman going"[50]; she preferred the stories of Nevada senators to the conventional status-seeking quests of Bostonians for titled Europeans. Her loyalty to Massachusetts did not extend to its representatives: "Dawes and Hoar show themselves greater asses everyday—it's a shame to represent the old Bay State through such poor white trash."[51] Although she had visited the Lawrence mills and might have been expected to understand the mill workers' support of Ben Butler, she hated what she regarded as his corrupt and vulgar ways and urged her brother to vote against giving him an honorary Harvard degree. She had wanted to extend her own knowledge by increasing her social circle, but her honesty and her judgmental nature often made it impossible for her to take much satisfaction from the democratic scene. It had been easier for the Adamses to believe in the success of American democracy when they were living in Europe. At the heart of the governmental process, the present appeared grim in spite of all its possibilities. Both Clover and Henry began to look more toward the future for the fulfillment of their democratic ideals:

> This city is getting to be a great centre for travellers—scientific men as well as hungry politicians on the make or unmake—I hear many doctors are here now though none have turned up here . . . "the music of the future" as they are pleased to call it is that which gives H. & me the greatest pleasure. When one is forty & on the home stretch it's consoling to find it suits one better to look ahead than behind.[52]

Similarly, the heroine of Adams' novel *Democracy*, Madeleine Lee, argued that it was unfair to judge American democracy by its contemporary fruits: " 'You want peaches in spring,' said she. 'Give us our thousand years of summer and then complain if you please, that our peach is not as mellow as yours.' "[53]

Clover enjoyed the excitement of entertaining people
as varied and bright as Matthew Arnold and Perry Belmont, Carl Schurz and Aristarchi Bey; she had assured
her father that Washington was "a good town for health
of minds" because "one never had time" to think of oneself—"the variety of people and interests" was so
incessant.[54] Yet there remained a question about the quality of all these relationships. She was, after all, a woman
raised in an environment of deep emotional commitment.
When Henry finally wrote Gaskell in 1885 that he "had
no close intimates" in Washington "except George Bancroft who is 85, and various lovely women," he may have
been speaking for his wife as well.[55] It is curious that he
had by then taken over the loyal old democratic historian
as his special intimate although the original connection
was Clover's. When Clover spoke of her special satisfaction with middle-aged friends, she might well have been
deliberately limiting the role lovely women played in
their daily lives as well.

We know from Clover's letters that she had a falling
out with Emily Beale, whose wit and beauty Henry particularly enjoyed. And her intimacy with Elizabeth Cameron assuredly never matched Henry's growing devotion to
the Senator's beautiful wife: "I shall dedicate my next
poem to you," he wrote to Mrs. Cameron in 1884; "I shall
have you carved over the arch of my stone doorway. I
shall publish your volume of extracts with your portrait
on the title page. None of these methods can fully express the extent to which I am yours."[56] The few letters
Henry Adams wrote Clover never reflected such intense,
idealized passion; yet, although Henry loudly protested
his love for Elizabeth Cameron, he made a point of re-
specting "Mrs. Don" for her loyalty to the "lump of clay"
she married. Whether Clover felt any more jealousy than
Henry might have felt toward a number of men who
stayed to chat by the fire with her when he went off to
parties is questionable; but the physical intimacy this
group shared even in social affairs must have created a
good bit of sexual tension. Henry seemed to find the idea
of sexual competition exciting; he described to John Hay

a scandal involving the President as "slander which I think if addressed to your wife or mine, would make you and me skip and jump with youthful ardor."[57] A letter of the young Bernard Berenson, which is quoted by Ernest Samuels in *The Making of a Connoisseur*, seems to capture the way this generation of Americans tried to make the most of their sexual fantasies:

> After all, it is a delightful thing to keep one's self in hand. I have enjoyed the effort not to possess, no less than the delight in possession. Think of the hundreds of women one has desired without love, and refrained from, even when one could have had them. Such suppressed desire immensely enriches life.[58]

Sexual morality was no more an issue, for this circle of nineteenth-century Americans than was political morality. Their repressions were so deep that they allowed platonic friendship to develop to an unreal, often extremely uncomfortable degree, as in the case of Emerson and Margaret Fuller or, later, with more tragic consequence, Henry James and Constance Fenimore Woolson. The vision James reproduced in *Daisy Miller* and *Portrait of a Lady* of the free-spirited American woman intimate with men without any sexual involvement, if baffling to Europeans, seems nonetheless accurate among the innocents of his own social group; it may have been one realistic source of their anxieties as well.

Whether Clover's new friendships with the many young women who surrounded them both, provided any of the intimacy she had cherished either with her cousin Adie, or with Henry James himself, seems debatable. She played a somewhat motherly role, giving advice and presents to Anne Palmer and Rebecca Rae, who valued her warmth and generosity, but Clover's letters do not indicate that these young women matched or rewarded any of her own intensities. During the final period of depression, Henry thanked Rebecca Rae for making Clover smile; yet momentary amusement could not ease her deep pain.

Writing his nine-volume history during these years gave Henry Adams a more purposeful role to play than the mere "twinkling" he had earlier described to Gaskell. ("In the middle of confused politicians and idiotic society I go on grinding out history with more or less steadiness.")[59] The limitations of an entirely social life, even when seen as a part of democratic political education, emerged sharply. In 1882, Henry wrote, "I write & ride & dine & chatter all I can with all who care to waste their eternal souls in that frivolity."[60] He warned his student Henry Cabot Lodge to stay away from politicians: "Politics deteriorates the moral tone of everyone who mixes in them. . . . Politicians as a class must be as mean as card-sharpers, turf men, or Wall Street curbstone operators. . . . I have never known a young man go into politics who was not the worse for it."[61] Immersed as they were, even as reformers, in all the ugliness of the American political scene, it seemed realistic for Henry Adams to conclude that the life the Adamses had been leading accomplished little and contributed much to Clover's final depression. A month before her death, Henry wrote, "The worst effect I have noticed from the pursuit of politics, apart from the fact that it spoils men's morals, is that it depresses their spirits & hurts their tempers."[62] Clover herself must have arrived at a similar conclusion even earlier, for, in 1883, she began to put her considerable energy into a more satisfying creative occupation than entertaining: photography.

Failing (like Madeleine Lee in *Democracy*) to develop any deep emotional attachment in Washington, Clover reassessed her life. Her insistent high morality had ironically narrowed the range of acquaintances she had wanted to expand; Henry James' complaint that a salon like the Adamses' seemed designed to leave out more people than it took in was often true. Clover's letters home sometimes degenerated into petty personal complaints about drunkenness or pretentiousness that she herself must have felt out of keeping with an essentially generous nature. Perhaps, like Isabel Archer, "she who of old had been so free of step, so desultory, so devious, so much the reverse of processional" saw herself now confined by the patterns of a life where there was "a certain posture they must take" and "certain people they must know and not know."[63] Clover Adams must have realized, as William James was just then asserting, that "real culture lives by sympathies and admirations, not by dislikes and disdains; under all misleading wrappings it bounces unerringly upon the human core."[64] When she started taking pictures in earnest in 1883, she bravely attempted to switch the direction of her life away from increasingly meaningless social activity toward a positive realm of professional fulfillment.

"I grudge every day which does not show progress in my work," Henry had written.[65] That Clover, who had no patience with women's activities in Washington and often identified herself with "masculine" women, would have felt the same restlessness seems inevitable. In Henry's novel *Esther*, he described his heroine's sense of letdown when she finished decorating the church modeled on Richardson's Trinity in Boston:

> She could no longer work in her own studio without missing the space, the echoes, the company, and above all, *the sense of purpose*, which she felt on her scaffolding. She complained to Wharton of her feminine want of motive in life. "I wish I earned my living," she said. "You don't know what it is like to work without an object" [italics mine].[66]

For all his querulousness, as long as he was writing his enormous history, working "without an object" in life never became a dilemma for Henry Adams; it did for Clover. When she took up photography, she went about her work with incredible zeal, perhaps reflecting another of the fictional Esther's protests about her art: "If I were able to be a professional, do you think I would be an amateur?"[67]

Yet in the novel, Esther does not succeed in becoming professional; it is essential to her charm and helplessness as a character that she does not. Her tragedy must relate to her ultimate dependence on other people. Talent and training could not spare her emotional pain—"Whichever way she moved she had to look down into an abyss and leap."[68] Clover imagined herself to be freer.

In the two and a half years before her death, Clover Adams managed to establish herself as a remarkably gifted photographer. Considering that she was in a state of extreme depression during the last seven months of this period, her photographic legacy is all the more astonishing. If Clover was not a "professional" in the narrowest sense (she did not need money), newspapers nevertheless cited her for her talent and acquaintances requested her to make portraits for them. Because the art of photography at this time was so technically demanding, the line between professional and amateur was fine. Robert Taft, in his survey of photography in American life, noted that early photographic societies included both amateurs and professionals: "The amateurs in these societies took their labors quite seriously. . . . In fact, it can be said that for many years these organizations were largely responsible for any growth in the art."[69] Clover belonged to such a society; she proudly included a review of their show in a letter to her father in November, 1883, which pointed out that Mrs. Henry Adams' work was "very skillful."

Although in May 1883, Clover had attributed the success of a picture of Henry to the advice and help of Clifford Richardson, the Chemical Expert for the District of Columbia, she worked hard over the summer to perfect her own skills. Henry Adams protested that his wife was doing nothing but taking photographs; by fall, she was more sure of herself. Notebooks reveal the analytical way she approached her successes and failures, measuring exposure time, sun and clouds and movements, and noting her own mistakes as any scientist would. It was clearly not her intention to be a dilettante. By December, 1883, Clover was so involved in her work that she often put off her Sunday letter to her father in order to develop prints or to enhance her knowledge in other ways. One letter gives a sense of her delighted commitment:

It was science plain & simple which took up all
my morning on Sunday & left me sleepy in the
p.m. A wonderful process of printing from
negatives has been perfected lately & the man
who owns the patent gave an exhibition of the
process at the photographic rooms in the
National Museum on Sunday. Mr. C. Richardson very kindly smuggled me in as the only
woman—we were three hours there though the
process is really very rapid. I shall buy of
Siebert the right to use his patent for a trifle and
will send you a proof.[70]

Once again, in an environment where women were not
encouraged, Clover appreciated being treated as an intellectual equal. Perhaps Clifford Richardson's helpfulness
overcame other doubts about her abilities; so often gifted
women need to feel that some man believes in them in
order to believe in themselves. There is no question,
however, that Clover loved photography and that she
flourished doing work that was both science and art. In
her own way, she had found a purpose for her life that
exactly paralleled Henry's: she would record American
history with her camera.

One souvenir remained from her 1865 trip to Washington to watch the final parade of the Union army: a little
booklet of Matthew Brady's *War Views*. Brady had
attempted to describe the war honestly in visual images
just as an historian would use words. His was not a
romantic vision; even Clover's souvenir book included
pictures of the dead. Photography seemed a perfect
medium for conveying the possibilities of the American
scene with integrity as well as with hope; it would
emerge as the most democratic art form, the most accessible both to the artist and the audience. If Clover's personal world, moreover, was limited, it could nevertheless be
recorded by the camera as one valuable segment of the
American scene.

Perhaps she had also taken note of some of the pictures in Matthew Brady's ambitious attempt to publish a

*Gallery of Illustrious Americans*, the first half of which was printed in 1850, and later supported in Congress, ironically, by the vulgar Ben Butler. Her own attempts to photograph their distinguished friends reflected a similar concern for illustrious people—the democratic aristocracy singled out by her mother as "the Nobl'y Born" in a favorite poem of Emerson's. Her own brother-in-law Whitman Gurney eloquently argued at Harvard that history "should be recognized to have other sides than the political and legal."[71] Clover's pictures all added up to an attempt to capture the beauty and intensity of the life she knew best; the human beings she recorded would suggest the fulfillment of democratic possibility. Her subjects would speak for themselves about the quality of American life.

In one group of photographs she tried to capture the New England simplicity she had so often missed in Europe: the wicker furniture, the hammocks and pony-carts, the elegant white clapboards and spacious porches, the open lawns, the cornfields, and the cat-boats that spoke for an environment she loved, much as Winslow Homer's woodcuts did. Several of her pictures of people looking out to sea trying to expand their vision of life seem almost derivative of Homer. It was probably no coincidence that her brother, Ned, collected a number of Winslow Homer prints and watercolors that paid homage to the same retreating civilization. Homer had once thought of himself patriotically as the Walt Whitman of painting.

Another group of her pictures followed Brady's attempt to catalog the illustrious. Clover knew many people of achievement: H. H. Richardson, the distinguished architect; John La Farge, the artist; Oliver Wendell Holmes, Jr., the young jurist; John Hay, the writer and statesman (whose picture she took as a spoof with *Democracy* under his arm); and her own illustrious Adams in-laws who shared so little of Clover's life. Her work also included the historians, Francis Parkman and George Bancroft who were themselves equally concerned with the idea of representative men.[72] Like Julia Cameron in

England, if considerably more inhibited, Clover attempted to record the heroic figures of her own intellectual world.

All her efforts, as might have been expected, were directed at honesty. If the camera had not yet learned to flatter, neither had she. Clover described one day of intense involvement with her work including a chaperoned trip with Henry to photograph the southern Senator, Lucius Q. C. Lamar:

> Printed photos for nearly two hours—seizing a bright sun which is rare of late—then H & I drove to Senator Lamar's rooms. . . . to take his photo. L. brushed his long hair to the regulation smoothness & then I refused to take his likeness until he had rumpled it all up. I took two shots of him & one of Gordon (General Gordon of Georgia) who has a deep hole from Antietam in his left cheek as you'll see next summer.[73]

The Civil War remained in her imagination as one of the overwhelming experiences of Clover's life. Her last tribute to the Union dead was a photograph of Arlington Cemetery showing row after row of white tablets. "Death, death, death, death, death"; her own vision reflected Walt Whitman's. Next to the picture, she quoted German and Latin—her only comments in the entire album—on the sleeping dead who would remain alive in memory.

Clover also took a number of pictures, like that of little Jerome Bonaparte blowing his horn, as favors for Washington friends, and she made prints of the people, as well as the dogs and horses she loved. Particularly fine were her pictures of George and Elizabeth Bancroft: "Hers is good technically but not a pleasant likeness—it is exactly like Judge Davis' bust in the Athenaeum [It was through the Davises (Clover's grandmother Sturgis) that Clover was related to Elizabeth Bancroft.] Mr. B. is very good—sitting at his library writing table writing history—

a profile view—his hair & beard came out silvery and soft in the print—I must send you one if I print any more."[74] This picture of George Bancroft impressed John Hay so much that he urged Richard Watson Gilder to publish it in the *Century:*

> Mrs. H. A. has made a remarkable photograph of George Bancroft in his study. He is now eighty-three, and one of these days will be gone I suggest that you get a copy of it and put it in the hand of your engraver—in time.[75]

But Henry Adams objected strenuously to this proposal. His irrational tone suggested the hostility to "fathers," he would later acknowledge, as well as his mixed feelings about Bancroft's history. The idea of according national publicity to Clover's talent may also have offended the man who at least pretended to relish anonymity. Including his wife in the editorial "we," he wrote to John Hay: "We have declined Mr. Gilder's pleasing offer. You know our modesty. . . . As for flaunting our photographs in *The Century*, we should expect to experience the curses of all our unphotographed friends."[76] How realistic was such an objection when everyone understood that Bancroft, an honorary member of Congress forty years older than Adams, well deserved the tributes years of government service and historical accomplishment could bring. Clover, however, did not protest. In the manner of the good nineteenth-century wife, she wrote her father of the offer as a matter of fact:

> Yesterday I was amused to get a letter from R. W. Gilder, the editor of *The Century* magazine asking if I would let him have a photo of Mr. Bancroft. Someone had spoken to him of it with a view to its reproduction in the magazine & writing Henry to write an article on Papa Bancroft of 7 or 8 pages to go with it. I've just written to decline & telling him Mr. Adams does not fancy the prevailing literary vivisec-

tion. The way in which Howells butters Henry
James, & Henry James, Daudet, & Daudet
someone else is not pleasant. The mutual
admiration game is about played out or ought
to be.[77]

That such admiration could ever be sincere seemed out of
the question to Henry Adams. One of his most poignant
letters to John Hay described his own reaction to personal praise from Hay;

I am not used to such language. Mrs. Hay must
be permanently suffused with crimson if you
are so complimentary in your conversation with
her; and the children, I foresee, will be
hopelessly spoiled. My amiable one, I am used
to cuffs, not compliments. . . . Never do so
again.[78]

There was little danger that Clover would ever be "permanently suffused with crimson." If Henry praised any
of her work as a photographer there is no record of it. We
know, however, that although Henry himself took many
pictures, he had little respect for photography as an art.
He had ridiculed Emerson for either "extreme sublimation or tenuity of intelligence" for asserting that photographs gave more pleasure than paintings. After Clover's
death, Henry declared, "I hate photographs abstractly
because they have given me more ideas perversely and
immovably wrong, than I ever should get by imagination."[79] Yet Clover often knew when her own
work was good, and Henry supported her in his own
reticent, ambivalent way. He even let her go to New York
alone for a few days in 1883 where she announced with
pleasure that she would visit "various artists and out-of-
the-usual-line people. . . . We shall see pictures and
studios and not shops for two days."[80]
    While in New York, Clover wanted to visit Saint-
Gaudens' studio (then expressing relief that it was he and
not William Wetmore Story who was designing the great

monument to her cousin Bob Shaw), and she went to the "American Artists" exhibition. She also tried to see her philanthropic cousin, Effie Lowell, who was currently involved with work on prison reform and improving the administration of poor relief. Josephine Shaw Lowell intensely felt the "indifference and ignorance and harshness" expressed by her own class against working people. She would eventually resign her position on the State Board of Charities to help organize retail workers in the Consumer's League. At the time of Clover's visit, however, Effie was in Albany working with the State Legislature on the problems of the indigent. Clover managed during this brief holiday to renew her acquaintance with another artist, also, Frank Millet, later to be coordinator of the mural work at the Chicago Exposition of 1893. She frivolously stayed over an extra day to see Barnum's circus, making Henry protest finally that he was "glad I enjoyed *my* week, but that it's his last alone." "It would not happen again," he said; "he doesn't propose to stay behind in a big lonely house."[81]

If Henry Adams could not bring himself to pay public tribute to George Bancroft in writing, he never discouraged Clover's deep affection for the ancient couple. To her father in 1884, she penned her own private tribute describing "the old man" as wonderfully bright and full of talk, and she wrote of the old lady with the sustained admiration she had always shown her distant cousin and spiritual companion:

> Mrs. Bancroft looks very frail and has been in her room for six months, but reads & discusses everything from Henry's history to the Supreme Court decisions—her will bids fair to keep her alive as long as she chooses unless death catches her in a nap.[82]

Clover could see intellectual vitality and purpose in Elizabeth Bancroft's life where she failed to see it in her own. "It's read, read, read till I loathe the very sight of a book," she wrote, reflecting the chaotic nature of women's education that Elizabeth Bancroft's friend Margaret Fuller had criticized so many years before.[83] A glance at Clover's reading at any period of her life would substantiate this lack of focus; not only was she studying Portuguese, Spanish, and Greek, but she was also reading books as different as *Tent Life in Siberia*, Bacon's *Life of Henry VII*, Gibbon's *History*, Carlyle's "latest trash," George Sand's *Memoirs*, and, of course, the native writers she admired, William Dean Howells, Bret Harte, and Mark Twain, and the work of a neighbor she did not know, Frances Hodgson Burnett. "She picks up all she knows without an effort and knows nothing well," Henry had written of his fictional heroine, Esther; he did not ask if she had any alternatives.[84] When he described the final illness of Esther's father, a man doomed by inactivity to a world of books, Henry Adams caused the old man to protest, "Indiscriminate reading is a fiendish torture. No convict could stand it."[85]

Clover's escape from such torture lay not only in photography, but also in her continued closeness to nature. Emerson had defined his meritocracy to include people "who know the beauty of animals and the laws of their nature, whom the mystery of botany allures, and the mineral laws, who see general effects and are not too learned to love the Imagination and power and the spirits of Solitude."[86] In spite of the time she spent in society, Clover wanted this definition to describe herself as surely as Thoreau did. Like Thoreau, in fact, Clover sometimes compared the progress of the same season in different years: "We met a cherry tree in flower last Friday while riding but no peach trees yet; in 1878 they were fully in bloom by April 1st." There can be little doubt about the ecstasy she felt riding in the woods when her horse seemed "flying in a dream . . . ready to jump over the moon." Together, she and Henry imitated pioneers looking for wild bits of country off the beaten track: "No one knows a tenth of the beauty of this neighborhood unless they explore it on horseback." Another time she exclaimed, "Our rides this week have been rapturous."[87] A better sport than Henry, Clover drew an amusing illustration of herself in a puddle after her horse, Powhatan, had thrown her; she did not hesitate to ride him again, but when he threw Henry, she put Powhatan up for sale. Two weeks later she wrote, "I have sold Powhatan. . . . he became unmanageable with Henry & fighting a balking horse on these slippery asphalt pavements is very dangerous to both horse & rider." She was relieved to report to her father that "so handsome a beast had found a good mistress."[88]

Some of the feelings Clover experienced riding reflect so much of her mother's poetic sensibilities they seem worth recording as a diary of ecstasy:

> Yesterday a lovely ride through the white country roads, the atmosphere like essence of opal, brooks still running.

> We rode for two hours before breakfast over soft roads into which frost has not yet gone and through an atmosphere of liquid sapphire.

> We have beaten the country far and near in the saddle, finding new paths in the forest, fording streams and coming home decked out with cherry, peach and unknown flowers.[89]

More and more the Adamses preferred "the frogs singing gaily and the maples hanging out spring tassles," to the political crowds that descended upon them. In fact, they shifted the time of their rides to fit in with Henry's work schedule, thereby cutting out a good deal of social life or, as Clover wrote home, they "lied" themselves "out of almost all invitations."[90]

The silent beauty of death, which Clover had tried to articulate in her photograph of Arlington cemetery, she also tried to describe in words: "We rode to Arlington Friday P.M. and it was lovely with its fifteen thousand quiet sleepers; no unsightly iron flummery and granite lies there, there's no lovelier place in the world as I know it than Arlington with a sunset behind it and a view in front." As much as she enjoyed living, dying provoked no fear. "Praise! praise! praise!"—she might have echoed Whitman—"for the sure-enwinding arms of cool-enfolding death."[91]

The simplicity that Clover found in the marble tablets in Arlington Cemetery and admired in New England clapboards and Shaker traditions, she did not see in the work of Henry Hobson Richardson. She could appreciate his amusing, forthright personality, and she admired his institutional buildings, Sever Hall, for instance, which her brother Ned had managed to get Richardson to build at Harvard. But there is evidence in her letters that she had misgivings about the great architect's ability to create the kind of home she would have liked to live in. She recorded her doubts about the "stern and severe" house Richardson had built for Henry's friend, Nicholas Anderson because it had "fireplaces for show," not use. But she rationalized that perhaps the western tastes of the Andersons were responsible: "I doubt if they ever really use the open fire places. . . . I do not think people learn west of the Alleghanies to understand cosiness in the New England sense." Clover added, "John Hay in his expensive house in Cleveland has *no* fireplace in the large elaborately fitted up dining room & unsightly steam heaters in every room."[92] If Clover had been against the building of the Adams–Hay combination mansion in Washington, she was also willing to modify her opinion to please Henry, because building such a house would become another source of purpose in life. "I like to change my mind of a sudden—we are *not* as happy as once," she confessed to her father.[93]

The idea of the Hay house and the Adams house being connected on one lot was interesting to Clover and promised, as the newspapers reported, to add to the distinguished architecture in Washington. She kept writing home that such an arrangement could provide them with "a plain cheerful sunny house . . . totally different" from Richardson's "usual somewhat heavy monumental style."[94] Whether she saw the simple house she dreamed of being built remains doubtful, although Richardson wrote scornfully to Henry Adams, promising to "put a double check on my vulgarity and sacrifice all my 'whims' to save your reputation."[95] Clover had particularly admired Richardson's "neo-agnostic" capabilities, which were perhaps embodied in the seashore house he had built for the Gurneys at Beverly, but it was harder to express simple radical ideas in the elegant official atmosphere of Washington. The dogs Henry and Clover had asked for as carvings on their arches, for example, Richardson turned into lions. And he allowed a cross to be chiseled across the facade, which filled Henry's "heart with sadness" and steeped "his lips in cocaine." "The whole thing seems to me bad art and bad taste," he wrote his secretary; he planted ivy to hide the carving.[96]

Planning the details of the house seemed to become Henry's particular pleasure (one cannot help thinking of Gilbert Osmond's palazzo); he took charge of everything—except the building of the stables for Clover's beloved horses, which she discussed at length with the architect. When Henry jested that *he* would teach Richardson architecture, he was, as usual, hiding true feeling in irony. But even Richardson, who was used to Henry's quirkiness, remarked to him about worrying "when I am with you or writing to you about the house that there's something around that might 'go-off.' The tendency is to muddle me."[97] Not only was the building far from Clover's cosy ideal, but the construction was slow and expensive. The newspapers took as much interest in reporting all the expenses as in appreciating the architectural addition to Washington. Adams and Richardson bantered constantly about details, making the building of the house every bit as full of tension as it was of promise.

Early in the project, Henry wrote with proud eccentricity to John Hay that Richardson went in with "enthusiasm for all my peculiar idiocies. In my opinion I shall have a house which will be the laughing stock of the American people for generations to come. Quite unutterably unutterable."[98] But Richardson grew tired of Henry's constant interference; two years later, he rebelled against being taught academic building style by an ignorant

historian: "Viollet-le-Duc has been warping your naturally well-balanced perceptions; the poor man never understood and was never able to create an architecture. . . . It
is a common saying in Paris that even well bred horses
shy at his buildings."[99] When, as might have been expected, Henry Adams asserted that he preferred John
Hay's half of the building, Richardson countered vigor-
ously that Hay had made no effort to interfere with the
architect's original vision.

Although Clover took several pictures of the architectural details of the houses during their construction and developed a number of the plates Henry took,
she felt little emotional involvement with the building of
their new house. It would be easier to argue that she was
more reluctant to leave the rented home she herself had
made cosy and notable for hospitality. Although she
liked the idea of letting a great American architect show
off his talent, her rose garden may have meant more to
her than the mere architectural chic of living in a new
building that was "unutterably unutterable." That the
commercial society Adams' social group was so wary of
would tear down Richardson's "ultimate" building—the
creation Henry Adams had wanted to leave for the
amusement of the American people for generations to
come—remains a final irony.

# A Gallery of Representative People and Scenes

### 1883 – 1885

*Henry Adams and dog*

*George Bancroft*

*Mrs. Bancroft (Elizabeth Davis)*

*George Caspar Adams and Mary Ogden Adams, nephew and niece, at Beverly Farms*

*Mrs. Bancroft (Elizabeth Davis)*

*Charles Francis Adams, Jr.*

*Charles Francis Adams and Abigail Brooks Adams*

*Henry Adams*

*Jerome Bonaparte*

*Miss Minot*

*L.S., an unknown black woman*

*Mrs. Pratt, Mrs. Howe, and Adeline Pratt, neighbors at Beverly Farms*
*Miss Graff in hammock*

*Nelson Miles*

John Hay

Francis Parkman

*Betsy Wilder and Dandy*

*Virginia Farmhouse*

*Oliver Wendell Holmes, Jr.*

*Dr. Robert William Hooper and Kitty*

*John La Farge*

*Pitch Pine Hill*

*William Evarts*

*H. H. Richardson*

# 9

---

# Suicide

*The life of Truth is cold and so far mournful;
but it is not the slave of tears, contritions, and perturbations.*
Ralph Waldo Emerson, "Experience"

Looking out at Niagara Falls
—that dominant symbol of nature's sublime power in
nineteenth-century America—Esther Dudley, the heroine
of Henry Adams' novel, smiled, remembering that it was
Sunday morning: "A ludicrous contrast flashed on her
mind between the decorations of St. John's with its par-
terre of nineteenth-century bonnets, and the huge church
which was thundering its gospel under her eyes."[1] Here,
confronting nature, she felt the sources of her spiritual
identity. If Henry Adams took the name of his heroine
from the politically conservative Esther Dudley of Hawthorne's Province House legends, he clearly identified her
religious ideas with the more liberal Transcendentalists
and Emerson.[2]

Decidedly not an atheist, Esther emerges as a romantic
pantheist, a free-thinker who could never find any honest community for herself within the confinement of institutional religion. "I should be a scandal in the church,"
she cried, "Some people are made with faith, I am made

without it." When she refuses marriage to Hazard, the minister she truly loves, because she cannot share his beliefs, he challenges her much as friends and family must have challenged Emerson when, as a young man, he refused to honor the same sacrament that she rejects—"Do you mean to separate yourself from all communion?" Hazard demands. Defining communion in a deeper way, Esther replies, "If you create a new one that shall be really spiritual, and not cry: flesh—flesh—flesh at every corner, I will gladly join it and give my whole to you."[3] Emerson had attacked communion as a meaningless product of the "hollow, dry, creaking formality" that had sapped vitality from the church.[4] Esther's words and intensity, which are derived from the Transcendental tradition, might have been Clover Adams' as well.

Organized religion had never provided the Henry Adamses with either a sense of community or with spiritual comfort. If Clover was not brazen enough to sit, as her Aunt Carrie Sturgis had done, sewing at her window on Sunday mornings, flaunting her indifference when others went to church, she nevertheless continued to comment on the churchgoers with irreverence from behind a screen as she wrote her weekly letters home.[5] In one dispatch to her father, Clover jested about the piety of her genteel relatives: "I tried for an agnostic cook—in humble imitation of my evangelical cousin Russell Sturgis Jr. who advertised in a Boston paper—'wanted a Christian cook—none other need apply'—lo, I went him one better & tried for a free thinker but had to compromise on a hard shell baptist."[6] Once again, Clover's defiant spirit emerges in contrast to the conventionality of her peers.

Institutional religion did not strike Clover as spiritually liberating; rather, she considered it intellectually stultifying, and often destructive. She noted that it was a sense of "eternal damnation" that had driven one of Henry's mother's friends to the Somerville Asylum, and she could never forget the fate of her cousin Adie, whose apparent failure to respond to her own mother's religious demands was somehow linked to her breakdown.[7] Clover thought that the mother of her young friend Anne Palmer was similarly limited by religion: "Mrs. Palmer, I do not like. She is a bigoted Episcopalian with no more mind than a waterbug."[8] Clover's father, who sometimes argued with Clover about her harsh political judgments, never seemed to respond to her hostility toward religion; he may have enjoyed her irreverence. In one letter, she described Agamemnon, who was about to sacrifice Iphigenia, as a "dyspeptic Congregational"; another time—clearly to amuse—she reported a concert where "a young female sang a few feeble ditties about angels & heaven to propitiate the orthodox. . . . Certainly the devil had all the best tunes."[9] Throughout the novel *Esther*, in which, Clarence King declared, Henry Adams had "exposed his wife's religious experiences," the church appears representative not of civilized freedom, but of barbaric coercion.[10]

Although Clover continued to explore the role the church played in society by adding such tomes as Bishop Wilberforce's *Life* in three volumes to her eclectic reading, such books, she insisted, did not increase "one's reverence for the established church." Yet she would have been as reluctant as Esther Dudley looking at Niagara to proclaim that there was no force in the universe greater than the individual. At one time, Henry reported that Clover had been converted by the nineteenth century's most powerful rational defender of religion, William James. After Clover read James' essay *Rationality, Activity and Faith*, she talked of "giving five dollars to Russell Sturgis' church for napkins," Henry wrote facetiously; but, he concluded, "as the impression fades, she talks less of the napkins."[11] It was during Lent, when others stayed at home, that Clover proclaimed the Adamses' social life most lively.

Clover, did not, however, dismiss religious reality; the metaphors of the church remained real for her even if the rituals did not. In a letter to her father that began, "I shall be surprised, if I ever get to Heaven, to find a better day than this," she concluded with a description of her delight as she put her pen aside to listen to the birds "sing Sunday hymns in their new furnished choirs."[12] In time of crisis, however, the spiritual forces she believed in might well have drawn her into the beauty of infinity, instead of providing her with reasons for staying alive. Henry Adams would characterize Emerson in terms of his "immortal longings and oneness with nature."[13] Thinking of her mother's transcendental verse, Clover might have readily accepted the idea that what was harsh in life would dissolve into the heavenly ideal that rolls through all things. The Transcendental contempt for worldly values that sustained her mother may have suggested to Clover that the unity in death—the ultimate democratic identity—would restore her soul to worthiness; the disappointed freethinker would at last find the best of earth's possibilities in becoming one with the oversoul. Clarence King's suggestion that the unhappy heroine Esther logically should have thrown herself into Niagara Falls was entirely consistent with a Transcendental point of view, for becoming a part of all earthly beauty would translate suffering into joy. Ellen Hooper, in a poem about her own death, articulated the idea of extending the richness of life into "unknown spheres":

> Father from out this world of self-distrust
>     And doubt of all things, lead me forth today
> High thoughts and proud are not for things of dust
>     Heaven's secrets for the child of yesterday
>
> And memories so blessed bore she hence
>     Of all she knew in these few earthly years
> They served as lovely models, whence
>     To shape the hopes she formed for unknown spheres.[14]

Becoming part of nature would be a way to identify with the best for eternity; the "lovely models," the hopes and dreams of earthly years, would become the paradise never achieved in reality.

The idea of reconciliation with lost loved ones after death could have been as real for Clover as it was for her mother, and it would have provided her with a logical reason to end her life. Much later, after the death of

Clover's reliable brother Ned, William James wrote to comfort Henry Adams: "His departure enriches the other side and makes me more willing than ever to go"—suggesting that the belief in spiritual reunion was irresistible to the scientifically trained mind as well.[15]

Members of the James family, however, were more receptive to mystical ideas than the men in the Adams clan; yet Henry Adams felt comfortable writing that "most women," on the other hand, "were more or less mystical by nature."[16] One of the truly curious books in Clover's library is a sentimental religious text, *Old Lady Mary: A Story of the Seen and Unseen*, inscribed "MA from HA, 3 March 1884." Before her marriage, Clover had acquired such polemical tracts as *La Donna e la Scienza o la Soluzione del Problema Sociale* from her sister; the books Henry Adams gave her were not designed to sharpen her interest in woman's social role, however, but to reinforce her sensibilities and to strengthen her position as a sensitive guardian of culture. He added a number of volumes to her collection of poetry, and he encouraged her efforts to learn Greek with presentations of the *Iliad*, the *Odyssey*, and the *New Testament*. *Old Lady Mary* is about the reality of spiritual contact after death. A rich old lady who dies without making a will for the destitute orphan who took care of her returns to earth as a ghost and leaves the missing legal document in the closet. What may be most impressive about the tale is not simply the idea of spiritual survival, but the idea that the old woman is given a second chance to communicate her love. Ignorant people judge Old Lady Mary harshly, but her poor, charitable servant remains loyal, and is ultimately rewarded. The ideal triumphs; the story ends in "pardon and in love."

Although Henry was the most passionate of the Adams men, he was trained *not* to communicate his feelings. It is possible that he often identified with the indifference of Old Lady Mary and tried to compensate with his later interest in the charitable Queen of Heaven. If his novelistic record of father–daughter love in *Esther* suggests his jealousy of the honest intensity of Clover's relationship

with her father, strengthened weekly by her devoted letters home, it was with good reason. Intense devotion
between fathers and daughters was accepted (as heterosexual love could not be) as emotional reality in the
nineteenth-century world of duty. In *The Golden Bowl*,
Henry James would show that such profound attachment could easily interfere with successful marriage.
Henry Adams knew that he could never compete emotionally with the double role that his own father-in-law
had played in his wife's life. It is not surprising that,
immediately after Clover's death, Henry burned all the
old man's letters, for they were likely to be as intense
as the other Hooper–Sturgis correspondence. Henry's
own letters to Clover had to express feeling by understatement and irony.

In *Esther*, Adams tried to work out his personal uneasi-
ness about extreme father–daughter relationships. Published a year before Clover's father actually died, the
novel manages to look at marriage from a potential
father-in-law's point of view. The older man, Henry
fantasized, would wish the young husband dead, knowing that he would interfere with his comfort. When the
heroine's father eventually dies, Henry intuitively understood that Esther Dudley, in her excruciating suffering,
would want to join him: "She wanted to escape, to turn
away, to get out of life itself rather than suffer such pain,
such terror, such misery of helplessness."[17] When Dr.
Hooper died of heart disease, life turned description into
prophecy, and Henry Adams was helpless as well.

The early years of the Adamses' marriage were not
solely years of intellectual satisfaction. If they read Schil-
ler's *Thirty Years War* in German for nightly amusement
during their honeymoon, they also had more relaxed moments. In Paris, the dangerously amoral city that Clover
never appreciated, Charles Francis Adams, Jr., dropped
in unexpectedly on Clover and Henry, "the most married
couple I have yet seen," to report to his wife:

> At 7 I knocked the mature Henry out of the
> arms of his Clover, for he's always in Clover

now (Joke! ha! Ha!) and the wretched long-
faced little ass sat on the sofa yawning with a
shawl wraped [sic] round his wretched legs.[18]

The tone is typical. Even Charles Francis Adams, Sr., had
noted that the Adams family were "more or less given to
a degree of severity upon others which they do not desire
& which is not really meant."[19] The quote also suggested
that Henry's marriage had become more important to
him than his venerable family; if the sexual innuendo
was accidental, it was nonetheless real.

Henry often amused Clover with presents of flowers,
books, and dogs (they frequently had more than two), as
well as visits from fascinating people. We know for a fact
that she found his historical work interesting and enjoyed helping him. "How did I ever hit on the only
woman in the world who fits my cravings and never
sounds hollow anywhere,"[20] he wrote, significantly to
John Hay, as a protest of devotion. But his lifetime of
critical habits, illustrated by many insensitive comments—from the earliest ones about her appearance to
the later ones refusing to let her publish her Bancroft
picture—was not easily altered. Feeling perpetually frustrated by his nature as a thinking man and as a man who
relished power, Henry Adams could never have been an
easy man to live with; he clearly lacked, as Lindsay Swift
pointed out in Henry's obituary, "the joy of small
achievement."

It is apparent from all her letters home that Clover
could never consciously acknowledge any hostility toward Henry's deliberately analytical ways, or any resentment for being isolated from his deepest intellectual
world. Although she was a defiant spirit, Clover nevertheless accepted all his judgments about her self. Conventional Freudians might argue that her final lengthy
depression signaled her revolt:

The occasions giving rise to melancholia for the
most part extend beyond the clear case of a loss
by death, and include all those situations of

being wounded, hurt, neglected, out of favor, or disappointed, which can import opposite feelings of love and hate into the relationship or reinforce an already existing ambivalence.[21]

When she turned against herself, it could be argued, she was also turning against him for not providing enough support, for self-reproaches are also "reproaches against a loved object which have been shifted onto the patient's own ego."[22]

The novels Henry Adams wrote about women's dilemmas were failures not so much because they were inadequately conceived, but because the emotional conflicts they attempted to depict seemed unreal. At the time the novels were written, Henry found it difficult to articulate deep feeling; therefore, the conflicts he described remain purely intellectual. Moreover, Adams' early writing often reveals a vital flaw—his inability to communicate compassion for human suffering. The artist Wharton's wife in *Esther*, for example, who had attempted suicide in sheer disgust of life, emerges as "coarse and melodramatic," not pathetic. When Adams tried to account for her hysteria by writing that "doubtless this excellent woman [had] faults, owing to a defective education," he almost seemed to be mocking the educational concerns of all his Hooper in-laws, rather than providing insight into, or understanding of, his character's tension.[23] Adams concluded his biography of John Randolph with the self-righteous dictum that "neither sickness, nor suffering, was an excuse for habitual want of self-restraint."[24] A person as sensitive as Clover would have had good reason to feel Henry's ambivalence about any human weakness, no matter how solicitous his behavior in time of stress.

In one of Clover's last letters home before she returned to Boston to nurse her fatally ill father, she reaffirmed her belief in the success of the Civil War. Although the intervening twenty years might have given her many occasions to lose faith in the Union, the inauguration of Grover Cleveland suggested once again the harmony of rich and poor, man and woman, North and South that was so essential to the American dream of unity out of diversity. Clover wrote with special pride that the bands were playing "Dixie" and "The Union Forever" in the same parade, and that "everyone looked gay and happy & as if they thought it was a big country."[25] The newspapers reported that the Adams house had celebration candles in every window; Clover also encouraged the servants to attend the festivities so that they might share the sense of idealism that had shaped her youth.

It seems certain that Clover carried her good humor North in March 1885. The political wheel had turned again, and many of their good friends, people of "sense and character" were once more coming into power. If, as Henry later suggested, the general political scene contributed to Clover's final depression, it need not necessarily have done so. Grover Cleveland's administration might have reinforced Clover's faith in democracy which was always stronger than Henry's.

Dr. Hooper faced his final illness with the good cheer and stoicism demanded by the French maxim that Clover would later save from his desk. She had commented earlier that a mutual friend comparing father and daughter had noted that it was "ridiculous that any man and woman should be so like one another as you and I are," but she conceded that her father possessed the better temperament: "I wish I were sure of being so congenial to my fellow critters as you are when I've turned seventy." To another friend, she wrote the final tribute to her father: "He was unselfish & brave & full of fun until he lost consciousness"; the desolate Clover sadly concluded: "No one fills any part of his place to me but Henry so that my connection with New England is fairly severed as far as interest goes."[26]

Losing her connection with New England meant losing the supportive family community that had given her so much love from the moment of her mother's death until her marriage to Henry Adams. This community had been responsible not only for her passionate belief in American possibilities, but also for all of her iconoclastic ideas, and her eccentric behavior. Henry left no records of these people with his own papers; not only are there no letters to Clover from her father, there are also no letters from her sister Ellen, Betsy Wilder, Cousin Adie, or from any other relative who might have written to Clover as an adult. Henry burned them all.

The letters Henry wrote to his wife while she was away nursing her father were not, I think, "devoid of tenderness," as Ernest Samuels has asserted; indeed, it might be possible to argue that they were more authentic in their loving understatement than the much more conventionally effusive letters he later wrote Elizabeth Cameron. The letters do remain singularly egocentric, however; there is no sense at all that Henry, in spite of his prophetic novel, was able to empathize either with his wife or her father. Adams wrote to Gaskell that Dr. Hooper's death (on April 13, 1885) altered their situation "only so far as it severs one more tie."[27] When a sad and exhausted Clover returned to Washington, he gave up much time trying to cheer her, planning different expeditions through the summer to distract a wife who was "off her feed," and who could "do nothing."[28] Whether anything Henry Adams could have done during the seven months of her sinking depression—short of never leaving her for an instant—would have saved Clover's life, remains conjectural.

The most detailed description of Clover's final breakdown and the circumstances of her suicide (December 6, 1885), caused by swallowing the potassium cyanide she had used in developing photographs, was written by Ellen Gurney to their close friend and neighbor at Beverly Farms, Mrs. James Elliot Cabot. This letter emphasizes for the last time the enduring ties between the Hoopers, and Emerson and the Transcendental circle. James Cabot was not only Emerson's literary executor but also a collaborator on his late essays, and one of Emerson's first biographers. Just as Henry Adams had turned to George Bancroft and Samuel Gray Ward at this time of crisis, the others close to Clover Adams instinctively looked for intimacy and comfort to those loving spirits whose connections remained with the idealistic philosophy hardly ever

associated with the Adamses. Because this important letter has been neglected in the past, I shall include most of
it here:

> What comes so close to us I cannot have you
> wholly in the dark about—and I will try to pain
> you as little as possible. . . . Whitman, my
> brother and I started for Washington getting
> there 24 hours after Clover's death. After the
> anguish of that week I never had so deep and
> abiding sense of peace—it seemed as if the
> heavens opened there and have not closed yet.
> The shock was largely for you outside—we had
> been consumed with anxiety—and probably
> others think if we had only done this or that &
> have shown feeling! We did the best we knew
> how—and we know no better now. I think any
> other course would have been cruelty. The
> courage & manliness & wisdom & tenderness—
> and power of feeling so intense a misery for
> days and nights—months & months—at first
> looking for the cloud to lift within a few
> months—finally satisfied it might be years be-
> fore it did—what Henry Adams went through
> we only knew—his family were wholly ignorant
> of it—and we felt it might kill him or worse.
> The week before Clover's death she struck out-
> siders Alex Agassiz & Richardson—who had
> seen her before—as much better—she slept
> well—In truth we knew Henry thought her not
> better—in [sic] the contrary. He went to the Den-
> tist's for a short time Sunday morning and
> when he returned—she was at peace. God only
> knows how he kept his reason those hours. But
> when we got to him he was as steady and
> sweet and thoughtful as possible—almost like a
> child in his touching dependence. His brothers
> came on. We sent for Edward Hall [a Unitarian
> minister]. She is laid on a sunny slope in a most
> peaceful church yard—very old part of it—with
> room for us all if we wish it, near the soldiers

home and soldiers cemetery—a place which they often went to together and where the spring comes early. In her last note to me—never posted—which no one has read—'Twould break their heart—she says, "If I had one single point of character or goodness I would stand on that and grow back to life. Henry is more patient & loving than words can express—God might envy him—he bears & hopes & despairs hour after hour—Henry is beyond all words tenderer and better than all of you even"—and more too—

No, not break your heart—perhaps heal it—you can't imagine what she was this summer—She told Whitman and me [her] heart as never before—She was so tender and humble—and appealing—

When no human help could do anything—sorry for every reckless word or act—wholly forgotten by all save her—the constant cry was "Ellen I'm not real—Oh make me real—you are all of you real!" I see now what she meant. I never felt so real before or now.

Henry Adams is getting on far better than we dared to hope even. He, I trust, gets into his new house—next the old one—today.

After we left him Sunday after he went back to their room—where after the Wednesday she was taken from it—Whitman & I slept at Henry's wish. He couldn't have gone back there at once. He has living with him—a namesake of Mrs. Dwight . . . full of tact, soothing companionable.

Reads Shakespeare aloud evenings, sleeps better,—and is like a wise child—and really peaceful.

We are very happy & cheerful & peaceful all of
us. I live in the past & present, dont look
beyond the present hour.[29]

Ellen Gurney, who two years later after a period of similar torment would die under the wheels of a train,
emphasized the peace Clover had attained. Perhaps she
remembered how often her sister had remarked that falling apart at once like the one-hoss shay was preferable to
any lingering illness. One of Clover's challenges to organized religion criticized the Episcopalians for praying to
be delivered from sudden death. To become a sorrowful
burden to others, or to end up in the asylums that she
and her cousin Adie had both rightly feared, would have
seemed infinitely worse to Clover than death.

That such self-destructive acts were not only an effort
to spare others the burden of care, but also an angry
reminder that society failed to value adequately the gifts
of brilliant women must be considered as well. Ned
Hooper managed to conquer his depressions for most of
his life through his hard work for Harvard and for various Boston cultural institutions that wanted his advice,
but no Boston institution was able to reinforce the Hooper sisters' belief in their own intellectual potential. No
letters of encouragement for her scholarship or gratitude
for her role in the establishment of Radcliffe College remain in Ellen Gurney's scattered papers. Like the other
Adams women, ironically, Clover's talents became entirely subsidiary to or complementary to her husband's.
There was nothing more for her to do when he sat down
to write. The discrepancy between this dependent role
and the sense of possibility for greater individual fulfillment, which their varied education and the Emersonian
tradition of self-reliance engendered, must have caused
both Clover and Ellen inevitable pain. What society ultimately reinforced was their lack of self-esteem. Both sisters may also have felt guilt and anger too for failing to
fulfill their mother's hope that her children would sur-
pass her own accomplishments; they could not articulate
their ambivalence.

A part of the intellectual community Clover Adams belonged to, moreover, did not look down on suicides; she had always seen herself as much a Greek as a Christian, and the Greeks honored suicides.[30] A considerable number of her fellow Brahmins—not only the James family, but also James Russell Lowell, and even her own Adams in-laws—entertained the idea of suicide, the exercise of choice, as the ultimate freedom, a legitimate answer to life's anguish. In one letter to Gaskell, Henry Adams described a "very worthy neighbor" who "being out of spirits because he had too much of all he wanted in the world except content . . . blew his brains out." Henry summed up the death succinctly: "There was no flourish, no pathos, no tragedy about it. We are a practical people."[31]

Henry may have perceived that Clover's death at the age of forty-two was a greater tragedy because she was clearly such a capable person, but he never made one comment to that effect. His own sense of guilt, anger, and sorrow, which mirrored Clover's own, may have been too great. He would later write in the story of his *Education* that tragedy "was no new thing in feminine history," yet he could not bring himself to write even one conscious word about his wife as an individual.[32] Of all their close friends, only John Hay managed to articulate an eloquent tribute to the woman who had provided so much for so many. Hay wrote to Adams: "Is it any consolation to remember her as she was? . . . that bright intrepid spirit, that keen, fine intellect, that lofty scorn of all that was mean, that social charm which made your house such a one as Washington never knew before and made hundreds of people love her as much as they admired her."[33] One old admirer, Henry James, would simply record that, by succumbing to hereditary melancholia, Clover had found "the solution of the knottiness of existence," pointedly suggesting that even in such a death the possibility of intellectual choice remained.[34]

After Clover's death, James stopped writing humorous tales about the international scene. In the years immediately following her suicide, he wrote two stories ending with the suicides of women, *The Modern Warning* and *The Patagonia*, and still another about an American heroine whose "inflexible conception of what is good and right" leads her to an isolated end, *A London Life.* Although the heroine of *The Modern Warning* may be much less assertive than Clover Adams actually was, it is hard to escape the idea that James was remembering all the "international" conversations he had had with the Adamses when he described the patriotic character of Agatha Grice:

> The sentiment of her nationality had been culti-
> vated in her; it was not a mere brute instinct or
> customary prejudice—it was a responsibility, a
> faith, a religion. She was not a poor specimen
> but a remarkably fine one; she was intelligent,
> she was clever, she was sensitive, she could
> understand difficult things and feel great ones.

Recalling his earlier letter home about the excellence of his real American friends, he delineated his fictional characters, too, as "all superior people."[35]

Yet Agatha Grice poisons herself when she is unable to reconcile her British husband's critical book on America with her feelings for him and for her intensely chauvinistic brother. To suggest that Henry James identified the more European aspects of Henry Adams with the English husband who sees the modern warning implicit in "the horrors of democracy," may be partly true, but does injustice to the complexity of both men; in fact, Henry Adams could still behave like Agatha's brother, Macarthy, who wanted to identify himself as "a passionate democrat and unshrinking radical."

What seems worth extracting from *The Modern Warning* is that the invidiousness James once objected to in the Adamses becomes a destructive force. Dogmatic opinion cannot be reconciled with emotional allegiance. The egalitarianism of Agatha Grice, who had never before realized that she was "a democrat or even that she had a representative function," takes precedence over her allegiance to her husband.[36] As she remembers her Irish immigrant ancestors and the feelings she still shares with them she cannot tolerate his aristocratic notions; their love disintegrates. Indeed, her suicide is related to the idea that the ideological struggle has killed her love (an admission that she is not free to make to her brother, whose arrival precipitates her violent act). Like the heroines of Henry Adams' novels, Agatha Grice allows her ideals to deprive her of the emotional life she also desperately needs. In *The Patagonia*, the suicide of Grace Mavis (named by an author well aware of Puritan rigidities) also stems from her realization of emotional impoverishment. Engaged to a man she does not love, Grace bestows her affections on an unworthy young man who cannot take her seriously and finally she leaps from a ship to her death rather than face her fiancé. Although Henry James is overwhelmingly sympathetic to the women who choose death over living with men who are emotionally incompatible, he suggests no easy answers to the intensity of their suffering. The life of renunciation and self-sacrifice is available neither to every good character in fiction, nor to every sensitive human being in life. James accepted suicide as one solution to the "knottiness of existence."

Ellen Gurney's letter to the Cabots was meant to comfort the living by emphasizing the peace Clover had found in death. It must also have left its readers uneasy by pointing out the deep sense of unworthiness that flooded over Marian Adams during her period of depression. Why, indeed, should such a gifted, privileged person end up seeing herself without "one single point of character or goodness?" Why should she have found the only solution to the knottiness of her existence in suicide? There are no easy explanations for certain kinds of human agony. I have tried to show the ways in which the grudging, dilettantish nature of Clover's education and the critical temperament of her husband might have contributed to her self-diminishment. But to assign blame in any manner would be simple-minded, especially when Clover had also learned a good deal and had profited in many ways from everything that was stimulating in her environment. There can be little doubt that she enjoyed her life with Henry, and, in many dimensions, her life was always admirable, and satisfying, and surprisingly fulfilled.

Those classical Freudians who would link the suffering brought on by Clover's mourning for her father with a recurrence of the pain she had felt when her mother died, and felt again briefly at the separation from her father on her honeymoon, can present much satisfying evidence to back their claims.[37] The loss of a parent during childhood leaves any ego vulnerable to self-doubt in a way few other traumas can (in the twentieth century, Sylvia Plath might be an example of this shock); yet Clover had a loving network of substitute parents while she was growing up: Betsy Wilder, Grandfather Sturgis, Aunt Anne, Aunt Eunice, who lived long enough to find herself in Clover's picture gallery, and her ever-indulgent, adoring father. If such deep wounds can ever be healed by a loving environment, Clover's would have been, for her family made every effort to supply the love that her mother's death denied her. But the anger at being abandoned by someone she loved so intensely (perhaps the source of her sharpness and deep sensitivity) might have finally turned against her self. The other side of her intense capacity to love may have also been an equally intense capacity to hate. There must also be a terrible sense of irony in the truth that the training and development of the sensibilities sometimes leaves human beings less equipped for survival. Their very capacity for feeling seems to prevent them from acting deliberately enough to save themselves—they lose hold of physical reality and become vulnerable to their own ideal values.

A number of other factors contributed also to Clover's low self-esteem. She had doubts about her appearance, about being a woman, about her writing skills, about her photographic work, and about her physical stamina; she worried steadily about the superficial nature of her education. The education that exposed her to so much—but did not want her to take any of it seriously—left her unable to cope with, or to channel her own active aggressive nature; and the society she lived in reinforced all her doubts about the kind of life an intelligent woman could lead. Watching Henry accomplish so much every day could only have emphasized her own lack of achievement. Committed to literary-historical means for avenging the death of his fathers' values, Henry Adams wrote obsessively during the years of his marriage. When he later fostered a view of his introspective self as Hamlet, he may have sensed that Clover, like Ophelia, had been cut out of the most intense struggle of his intellectual life.

Nineteenth-century middle class women, encouraged to be subservient, flocked to enjoy Hiram Powers' marble statue of a naked woman described in one of Clover's mother's letters: "My consolation now is the Greek Slave! Take the earliest time to see her when in Boston for you will never have seen enough." (It should be noted, however, that her independent friend Margaret Fuller thought the Greek Slave's reputation the result of "drawing room rapture and newspaper echo."[38]) Another popular marble statue, the manacled Queen Zenobia also provided an identity for many gifted women; if they were, on one hand, treated as queens, they were, on the other, captives of a society that made them the victims of conflicting demands. Fanny Hooper, Clover's sister-in-law, who had been active both in the Sanitary Commission and the Women's Industrial Union before giving birth to five daughters, paid homage to the statue. The sculptress of the great Queen Zenobia was Harriet Hosmer, who had been educated at Miss Sedgwick's School in the Berkshires in the same liberating atmosphere Clover enjoyed during the summers of her youth. Harvard's ambivalence about women had not caused Hosmer to question her professional aims (though cynics might still suggest that she should have); she persisted as one of the pioneering professional women artists of her time. She was most proud of becoming self-sufficient, of establishing a tradition for future professional women artists. Although her sense of self was uncomplicated compared to Clover's, both women had experienced common influences. The statue of Zenobia was important not just as a tribute to the many queenly women who felt themselves enslaved, but because it inspired Hawthorne to use the name for his unsubmissive, intellectual heroine in *The Blithedale Romance*.

The force of Hawthorne's Zenobia, thought to have been partly inspired by Margaret Fuller as well, is unquestionable. Zenobia saw the world (she might have included her creator, Hawthorne) taking common cause against the woman "who swerves one hair's breadth off the beaten track."[39] And she, too, chose suicide as her solution to the knotty problems of existence. Both Julia Ward Howe and Perry Miller have convincingly suggested that Margaret Fuller may have exercised a similar choice in her own "accidental" death. Although the fictional Zenobia was clearly endowed with a powerful intellect like Fuller's, a loveless life was no more acceptable to her than to Henry Adams' less passionately conceived heroines. Indeed, the successfully defiant female spirit of Harriet Hosmer was more difficult to find in fiction even than in life. American writing often celebrates independent, rebellious men (perhaps a tribute to our revolutionary origin) but has been more hesitant to honor defiant women. We recall that Henry Adams commended Hawthorne's description of Zenobia's death to Gaskell as an example of one of the finest *representative* passages in American literature.

Although Adams later complained that his own life was a failure, and recognized Clarence King's suicidal existence in the same terms, he might have noted that the *men* he admired were at least permitted to fail in an active sense. They had received the kind of education that, if not professional enough to make them the fittest for survival and too moral to insure great financial success, nevertheless encouraged them to develop their talents and supplied them with adequate tools for self-expression. If glory did not crown the endeavors of the Adamses' circle of male friends, they all led lives, as Henry would perceive, "more or less worthwhile." The women, on the other hand, presented a more complex problem, for, as Charles Francis Adams, Sr., wrote to

Henry, "to be happy in life is possible, so far as it depends on oneself, only by being busily occupied upon objects that seem worth doing."[40]

Most women found their sense of purpose in motherhood, but there were always women like Clover's mother, for whom child rearing was never enough to absorb all their intellect and capacity for achievement. There were also women like Clover, who had to look for a wider realm for self-expression because they had no children or remained single. "All the contented women are fools," one of Henry's female characters protested, "and all the discontented ones want to be men."[41] The statement is distorted: what they wanted was not to be men, as Margaret Fuller kept insisting, but to experience more of the encouragement and the opportunities so readily available to their brothers. Over and over in Clover's family papers, we find bright women succumbing— as they had in the Adams family—to depression and eccentricity because there were so few ways to make good use of their minds.

In a family that put heavy store in the value of education for everyone, it was natural that the women would think more adequate schooling might solve many of their problems. Both Carrie and Ellen Sturgis urged their reclusive mother, often "out of spirits" or "stricken in mind," to try to do more with her intellect, to go on learning German, or to study astronomy. "Every time I begin a new study," wrote Carrie to encourage her mother, "I feel as if a new world opened before me. . . . You would find it so if you began. . . . If you should begin astronomy which you love so much, you would find that most magnificent discoveries are being made in which you could not fail to be interested. Studying with another person you will find much easier and pleasanter than doing so alone." Another time Carrie wrote that studying something would "make you young again."[42]

When Carrie Sturgis had felt depressed about her own life, Hawthorne's philanthropic sister-in-law Elizabeth Peabody tried to urge her to action: "You feel very strongly the deficiencies of the present system of educa-

tion," the philanthropist wrote. "Why do you think Providence has brought you to feel them? Is it not that *you*
may be stimulated to alter this state of things? Do not get
into the cage of Despair—then—and leave all this evil in
the world as you found it."[43] The Hoopers, however,
were less single-mindedly optimistic than Elizabeth Palmer Peabody; the "cage of Despair" regularly opened its
doors for all of them. Clover's mother summed up her
personal fatalism in a letter to her sister Carrie: "I am
filled with a deep compassion for mother and could I
but see how she might have escaped her fate, how
there was more than a bare chance for her, I should be
glad. . . . You believe in influences. I believe life is a
struggle with powers of darkness, and he who stands
at last forth to the light, stands there pale and worn and
scarred."[44]

The experience of too much pain—her mother's un-
predictable irrationality, her brilliant sixteen-year-old
brother's accidental death at sea, the consumption that
would soon take her own life—made Ellen Sturgis Hooper less affirmative than most Transcendentalists. If Clover
Adams and Ellen Gurney absorbed many positive values
from their family letters they also absorbed the uncertain-
ties. If, for example, Ellen Gurney carried the torch from
Carrie Sturgis for women's education at Radcliffe with
Clover cheering her on, both sisters ultimately found
themselves too "pale and worn and scarred" to cope with
the many obstacles they encountered on the way, to carry on a cause indefinitely.

Clover had used the image of the "dory without oars"
to describe the way she felt about her own education—
helpless. And Henry Adams sought to emphasize the
bravery of such a voyage in that fictional description of
Esther Dudley, who was, he said, "a lightly-sparred
yacht in mid-ocean. . . . She sails gayly along, though
there is no land in sight and plenty of rough weather
coming."[45] Would he have wanted her to be better prepared for life? Henry Adams believed that Esther, who
knew much without effort but who knew nothing well,
nevertheless seemed to understand everything. Her in-

tuitive insights might have been sacrificed in the kind of education that provided men with access to worthwhile work, for being practical seemed to stifle the discovery of what was best in life—"The reach and quality and capacity of human nature." Henry James claimed he had learned these values from "restless," "helpless," "impractical" Minny Temple.[46]

Although Clover Adams, free like Minny Temple and the fictional Esther, appreciated the intellectual security of professional work and might often have regretted playing the role of "second-rate amateur," she could never have committed herself to a life of deliberate narrowness. One of her letters recorded her interest in a woman doctor who gave up her medical career—after discovering "what nonsense" it [medicine] was—to take care of seven children, two of whom were adopted.[47]

Modern minds might see Clover's ambivalence as complete confusion, which led, quite naturally, to a final sense of unreality. There can be little doubt that she must often have felt herself pulled apart by extremes. Her idealistic upbringing trained her to define the best in life in terms of the richest possibilities rather than the easiest choices. Her lifetime had been the chaos of mixed attitudes that most intellectual women experience. Instead of being able to train the mind that had flowered at the Agassiz School, she had to devise her own outlets for her intellect in the traditional woman's role as guardian of culture. Although she enjoyed this role, and made more of it than any of her contemporaries, Clover was sensitive enough to see its limitations and to wish herself better trained. But she took as many chances as seemed legitimately possible, and never gave up learning new things.

Her plight was not, however, entirely a feminine one; the men who admired her, Henry Adams, Henry James, and Clarence King, who were also trying to enrich society's cultural possibilities, often possessed the same sense of impossible ambiguity. A more remote member of the Hoopers' circle, James Elliot Cabot (the biographer of Emerson) recorded his own values as a reflection of the positive beliefs shared by their class:

My discursive habit of mind, though it has been
fatal to success, has not much, if at all, dis-
turbed my enjoyment of what the day has sent.
My life has thus far, been a very happy one,
and very much because of the varieties of my
interests and sympathies. In my younger days,
"culture," which is the cultivation of this tendency, seemed to many persons the end of education. Nowadays the stream runs the other way,
"liberal culture" is called "dilettantism"; I have
come to think the modern way, upon the
whole, nearer the truth; but it ought not to prevent us from seeing that deliverance from narrowness and prejudice is one of the constituent
elements of education.[48]

"I like to conquer prejudice," Clover had written. In so
doing, she may have been undermining most of the traditional props that could have prevented her suicide. The
role of the unaffiliated free-thinker remains the most
dangerous.

If Freud is able to persuade us of one kind of explanation for Clover's suicide, Durkheim might more easily
convince us of another. The great sociologist argued that
no one unhappiness could cause anyone to kill himself.
Looking at the nineteenth century, he persuasively
argued that suicide was part of a general intellectual
climate.[49]

According to Durkheim, the permissive environment
that Clover grew up in, the atmosphere that questioned
all institutions and traditional beliefs, including the idea
of professionalism, made the perfect climate for the self-
doubt that leads to suicide. A mind that questions everything, unless it is strong enough to bear the weight of its
ignorance, risks questioning itself and being engulfed by
its sense of ignorance. Henry Adams had perceived as
much when he wrote Gaskell that "perfect freedom" was
the most objectionable form of slavery. He went on to
refine the idea that man was not made for absolute freedom: "His mind when it has no daily chopped food set

before it, begins to eat itself, and to refuse to eat at all. The moral of which is that you must provide some regular occupation if you want to escape hypochondria. . . . Marriage is not enough."[50] Adams was not just speaking for man, but for woman as well, in fact for his entire class. But Adams knew, as clearly as Durkheim did, that human beings could not reject such freedom.

> When men, after having received their ready-made faith from tradition, claim the right to shape it for themselves, this is not because of the intrinsic desirability of free inquiry, for the latter involves as much sorrow as happiness. But it is because men henceforth need this liberty.[51]

Durkheim, in documenting the high rate of suicide among the better educated (a paradox that would have chastened the Hooper women), concluded that the suicidal tendency was greater in educated circles because of "the weakening of traditional beliefs" and the resultant state of "moral individualism." The other side of self-reliance might be the kind of "egoism" or "over-individuation" that necessarily left the individual entirely alone. The tiny ship lightly sparred, brave as it seemed, was doomed to sink by itself, for every sort of suicide, as Durkheim pointed out, was merely "the exaggerated or deflected form of a virtue."[52]

Clover had indeed lost every institutional connection—family, religion, community identity, political party, even organized voluntarism—that might have sustained her during a critical period of suffering. The letters of her mother and Aunt Carrie suggest that it was often their tightly-knit, ever-corresponding Transcendental group that kept them both going. Hard as she may have tried to establish such a compatible intellectual group, Clover never really succeeded. Her childlessness, moreover, would have made her even more susceptible to taking her own life, for no one seemed to need her. The reality of menopause, the end of her procreative life, might have also intensified her anguish in view of her intellectual alienation from any sustaining group of women. She never wrote as regularly to her sister as she had to her father.

Not only would Clover's education have been adequate enough to destroy her own identity with the traditional sources that supported women's vitality, but it also would have shaped her expectations about her society in an ironically destructive way. Her lifelong patriotism, which led her out of her own class and regional loyalties to explore the possibilities of American life, ultimately left her spiritually rootless. Its insistence on the richness, rather than on the cultural narrowness, of any one kind of life, as illustrated by her interest in the American Indian, underlined the fatal risks that Americans have always shared by being inclusive. Perhaps it was this adventuresome quality that tried to encompass so much of the variety of life—without any secure source of identity— that made Henry James keep defining Clover as quintessentially American. "The tragic element," Henry Adams had once written John Hay, "was bigger in America than ever on this earth before."[53]

There is no doubt, as her description of Cleveland's inauguration revealed, that Clover continued to share George Bancroft's vision of the dream of American progress. Such a vision, Durkheim claimed, would make her again more vulnerable to the idea of self-destruction: "As soon as men are inoculated with the precept that their duty is to progress, it is harder to make them accept resignation; so the number of the malcontent and disquieted is bound to increase. The entire morality of progress and perfection is thus inseparable from a certain amount of anomy."[54]

Durkheim's idea of alienation, "anomy," perhaps best characterized by Clover's final pathetic assertion that she was no longer "real," has haunted many sensitive human beings. The struggle to define life in social terms that leaves the individual with no sense of group identity but rather with a sense of emptiness must remain valid for all thinking human beings. The sociologist had not intended to condemn such anguished thought; on the contrary, he argued that it might truly produce the best kind of culture. Yet he understood its weaknesses:

> The hypercivilization which breeds the anomic tendency and the egoistic tendency also refines nervous systems, making them excessively delicate; through this very fact they are less capable of firm attachment to a definite object, more impatient of any sort of discipline, more accessible both to violent irritation and to exaggerated depression.[55]

That the intellectual world the Adamses inhabited along with the James family, James Russell Lowell, Clarence King, and John La Farge, was rife with mental instability is indisputable. But our "pursuit of happiness" culture has failed to dignify such suffering in social terms as Durkheim tried to do.[56] "Too cheerful a morality is a loose morality," he wrote; "It is appropriate only to decadent peoples." He saw intense individuals like Clover Adams in strangely romantic terms, as part of a sacrifice to social awareness and as essential as the myth of Prometheus to humankind's survival.

Durkheim finally insisted that a society in which "intellectual individualism could not be exaggerated"—as it was in nineteenth-century New England—"would be unable to shake off the yoke of tradition and renew its faiths," if such a time ever became necessary.[57] Curiously, Henry Adams read Durkheim's essay on *Suicide* when it appeared in 1897. As far as I know, Adams made no comment upon the text, but it would appear that his own celebration of individualism went along with this idea. The scientific determinism they both believed in did not prevent Adams from trying to renew his own faith.

Yet Henry Adams' cherished scientific compulsion must in the twentieth century lead in a more speculative direction. "In another generation," he wrote, "psychology, physiology and history will join in proving man to have as fixed and necessary a development as that of a tree; and almost as unconscious."[58] What should we make of the refined nervous systems Durkheim had noticed among the suicidal? Is it necessary also to look once again at hereditary factors for some greater understanding of the kind of depression Clover experienced? The age of sociobiology refuses to let us ignore the genetic tendencies that were, as Charles Rosenberg clarified, so real to Clover's own contemporaries. Most onlookers would not have felt, as she had, that the Guiteau assassination trial had dismissed the possibility of hereditary madness. A Puritanical insistence on moral responsibility had then outweighed all evidence for inherited mental instability. When Clover herself later expressed admiration and sympathy for a friend who was about to wrestle with the "hereditary traits" of a new family by marriage, we may be sure that she remained worried about the depression in her own background.[59]

Henry had told his none-too-stable brother Brooks that he was willing to take a risk by marrying into Clover's family. At that time, there was little effort made to hide the reality that he was indeed doing so. The family was more inbred than most; Clover's paternal grandfather Hooper "had married a distant cousin of the same name. . . . Her father and his brother had married sisters."[60] The biography of her brother Ned printed with the history of the Saturday Club made no attempt to disguise his early problems of withdrawal from society. Clover's Grandmother Sturgis not only retreated in a similar manner from her own family but also experienced different kinds of hallucinations. A printed obituary for Ellen Sturgis Hooper recorded the fact that she had conquered "the most difficult of all things, a constitutional tendency to depression." Even Aunt Carrie Sturgis, whose indomitable spirit gave so much to Clover, also described a period of suffering in her own life that drove her to Dr. Wesselhoeft's water-cure for relief: "Nothing else could have made me care whether I was dead or alive three days longer," Carrie wrote, "or rather I should have cared the wrong way."[61]

From several fragmented letters expressing a variety of

her fears and from the Harvard faculty notes that excused her husband for "domestic" reasons, we might deduce that Clover's brilliant sister Ellen, who was also childless, suffered intermittently from similar breakdowns. Whitman Gurney's 1852 Harvard class book honestly notes that the happiness of his marriage was "marred by periods of mental aberration on the part of Mrs. Gurney."[62] Francis Parkman commented that the compassionate Gurney, "one of the best men I ever knew," did for his wife "what perhaps no other man on earth could have done."[63] When Gurney died not long after Clover, Henry Adams anticipated Ellen's final breakdown: "His death," he wrote Gaskell, "makes us anxious . . . especially about his wife."[64] Ellen's decision to end her own terrible depression by throwing herself under a train caused one cousin to write that the family did not grieve as much at Ellen's being at rest as they had over the cloud which had "hung upon her for the last twelve months which perhaps could have been removed in no other way."[65] If Gurney's noted warmheartedness managed to keep Clover's sister alive, it is only fair to Henry Adams to conclude that such a happy marriage did not, however, prevent Ellen from experiencing the same kinds of anxiety that Clover felt.

Family papers reveal that one of Ned's daughters, by then the fourth generation, also suffered from a paralyzing melancholia. Although the repetition of cultural patterns in the environment remains real, it would seem unwise for any biographer now to attribute depressive tendencies wholly to environmental causes. Newer studies of depression appear to be going back to the nineteenth-century point of view about hereditary susceptibilities—albeit with a chemical, rather than a moral, bias.[66] We must once again, however, be wary of a tendency to use panaceas for complex emotional problems. If a biochemical solution to Clover's and Ellen's problems—the use of Lithium—might have saved their lives, it would not have provided them with any realistic means to emotional commitment, or any encouragement for the use of their intellectual potential.

Because the victims of melancholy in the Hooper clan were, for the most part, women, it becomes particularly hard to separate cultural from genetic factors. The fact that Clover's remarkable brother Ned, eventually succumbed to the same melancholic tendency at the age of sixty-two—when he may have felt his usefulness to Harvard coming to an end—makes the problem even more complex. Newspapers reported that he had accidentally fallen from the second story window of his Beacon Street home, yet he was taken to the McLean Hospital for the mentally ill to recuperate, not to nearby Massachusetts General Hospital. After he died of pneumonia at McLean, the family acknowledged that a lifetime of community service had left him in a state of exhaustion and nervous strain. The efforts of families to hide such truths have made it especially hard for scholars and scientists to ascertain what role genetics may have played in the shaping of cultural patterns. To put aside the idea of societal responsibility for the loss of such lives, however, might leave us as susceptible to shallowness as those societies Durkheim condemned for believing that unmixed joy was the normal state of human sensibility. Yet we must continue to struggle with the reality that every Hooper sibling in Clover Adams' generation attempted to destroy his or her own life; in the private achievement of death, the women proved themselves superior.

Henry Adams, who ironically took such pride in being a scientific historian and who liked to think of Jefferson and Madison as helpless grasshoppers gesticulating in the middle of the Mississippi River, would have been delighted to anticipate the cataloging of his own class in sociobiological terms. He might have enjoyed envisioning all his friends as "altruistic," like certain groups of insects, which are designed by nature to sacrifice their lives so that their entire race might eventually be improved.

Finally to conclude that there was an easy explanation for Clover Adams' suicide would be as shallow as to conclude that her life was a failure. Clover may have had more impact on people's ideas than any other Adams woman, with the possible exception of Abigail: she helped Henry Adams with his research and influenced his attitudes toward idealism; she encouraged her sister's involvement in the founding of Radcliffe College; she remained one of the most vivid characters in Henry James' irreverent imagination; and she provided a political salon for the most influential journalists and politicians of her time. The photographs she took, though few in number, left a record of many men and women who represented what was heroic in her own age, and the art she collected was meant to enrich America's awareness of its own possibilities as much as it underlined the European connections that help us understand our own worth. Finally, the many letters sent to her father became a lasting account by a free spirit of the intrigue and liveliness of the American political scene.

Clover remained active in her private domestic world as well. If having no children made her sad, she managed to direct much attention to her five nieces, for whom she wrote stories, nursed colic, built playhouses, and bought clothes, and to the dogs and horses that she cared for. She contributed regularly to a number of causes (a fact occasionally left out of the published letters, perhaps because her descendants did not adequately appreciate the reform traditions that helped shape her sensibilities), but it must be noted that after her work with the Sanitary Commission, her commitments to society were more desultory than commanding; in Washington, she found no organizations to engage her energy for reform. If Clover is to be seen as a failure, it must be in the same symbolic sense that Henry Adams used to describe Clarence King and himself as well—as one of the "best and brightest" of that generation whose talents and capabilities were so great that they were barely appreciated by the age in which they all lived.

# 10

# Immortality:
# From Emerson to Adams

*Let us treat the men and women well;*
*treat them as if they were real; perhaps they are.*
Ralph Waldo Emerson, "Experience"

*The manikin, therefore, has the same value as any other*
*geometrical figure of three or more dimensions, which is used*
*for the study of relation. For that purpose it cannot be spared;*
*it is the only measure of motion, of proportion,*
*of human condition; it must have the air of reality;*
*must be taken for real; must be treated as though it had life.*
*Who knows? Possibly it had.*
preface to *The Education of Henry Adams*

$C$larence King, as a geologist, was an expert on the evolution of the environment through massive upheavals. He taught that "moments of great catastrophy, thus translated into the language of life, become moments of creation when out of plastic organisms something new and nobler is called into being."[1] There can be no doubt that Henry Adams saw Clover's death, his personal catastrophe, in these terms; he felt he had somehow to justify her existence by making himself new and nobler.

It is easy to speculate that Henry must have felt guilty

about leaving his wife on the Sunday of her death at the time when she usually wrote to her father, or, that knowing she was depressed, he blamed himself for not hiding the cyanide she had been using in her photography work. He must have experienced again the overwhelming sorrow he had felt for his brilliant mother and sister, as he realized that Clover's life—in spite of her apparent self-reliance—had been equally dependent and as intellectually uncommitted as theirs had been. Close relatives of melancholy people must inevitably feel some measure of guilt at being relieved of their terrible burden, no matter what they have done to avert the final disaster of death. Clover's suicide note left no doubt, however, that Henry's behavior was "beyond all words tenderer and better than all of you even," a high compliment from one emotional Hooper to another. Yet Henry Adams may have been sensitive enough to perceive, as Freud suggested in *Mourning and Melancholia*, that "the woman who loudly pities her husband for being bound to such a poor creature as herself is really accusing her husband of being a poor creature in some sense or other." Clover's suicide would have suggested the unconscious pain of repeated rejection she felt as Henry retired to his study all day to write, or as he admired the lovely younger women who graced the Washington social scene at night. The obsessive nature of his subsequent actions, which included burning all her letters, destroying his own early diaries, avoiding mentioning his wife's name, and, finally, refusing to attend all weddings, suggests as much.[2] Perhaps as he realized that he had given too little value to the great emotional needs of life, Henry Adams, in spite of his honesty, saw one aspect of himself that he did not want to expose to posterity. His momentary anger at Clover for abandoning him to his rational, systematic self would finally surface only as he wrote his self-flagellating autobiography. Not mentioning her name at all could have been, on the part of the angelic-porcupine (as Saint-Gaudens pictured Henry Adams), simply a hostile gesture. Did Adams know that Clover's Grandfather Sturgis refused to mention his brilliant son's name after the boy had been killed by the boom on one of his own merchant ships? The old man later regretted having silenced his grief; he too came to realize that the celebration of feeling his wife and daughters demanded was essential to a richer humanity.

It seems clear that Henry felt uneasy about the obvious emotional hollows in his own background. What could be more poignant than Ellen Gurney's disclosure that he had not felt free to call on any member of his own family for support during the agonizing seven-month period of Clover's crisis. Would his family have reminded Henry that they had warned him about the dangers of this marriage? Perhaps Henry Adams also felt some guilt about the attention he had given the beautiful faces in Washington (Elizabeth Cameron had already begun to play a role in his life). He had once written that he and Clover were beginning to be bored with each other, as Clover had disclosed to her father that they were not as happy as in earlier days. There is little evidence, however, that his flirtations gave Clover any real reason to be jealous (not that an emotionally dependent woman needs real reasons), for Henry Adams—often to his regret—was a New Englander. Whatever momentary pleasures he found in admiring lovely women could not have long sustained his intellectual needs. The assertion he once made, that he had only met one woman he ever wanted to marry, and he married her, seems hard to argue against. Few of the pretty faces Henry admired would have been the intellectual match for him that Clover was. And frivolity was no more a part of his nature than it had been part of hers.

His immediate escape from the pain of mourning was writing—an escape that solidified into his "new and nobler" life. With all her perceptive literary talent, Clover would never have felt similarly encouraged to use her pen as an outlet for her emotions during her own period of grief. Henry urged the builders of the Richardson house to hurry with the new study so he could lose his pain in work. He would learn more about human possibilities finally from writing about himself.

Emerson had died in 1882, three years before Clover. The Concord sage who had meant so much to all the Hoopers was now a tradition—no longer a memory. Though Henry Adams may have looked with irony on many of the democratic philosopher's ideas, they nevertheless remained applicable still to his own behavior. Emerson had protested that "we do not make a world of our own, but fall into institutions already made, and have to accommodate ourselves to them to be useful at all, and this accommodation is," he said, "a loss of so much integrity and of course, of so much power."[3] It was just such accommodations that Henry Adams had always made for the sake of his fathers. In his new search after Clover's death for a different meaning for power he would once again feel Emerson's influence. But Adams turned the philosophy of self-reliance into a philosophy of self-consciousness. The yearning to dramatize the limitations of the analytic mind, which allies him to the most creative aspects of modernism, grew directly from the nourishment of the transcendental stream. It seems curious that the death of Emerson's own first wife had precipitated a similar change in the Concord philosopher's values, making all traditions and institutions less important to him. After Ellen Emerson died, her young husband gave up the ministry to become a critic of his culture in much the same way that Henry Adams gave up the "profession" of historian after Clover's death. Personal tragedy made both Emerson and Adams more aware of the need for human beings to redefine truth in terms of their own individual needs and to explore the values of a democratic society in search of consolation.

Although Henry Adams remarked in his *Education* that the universe seemed too "real" for him ever to have felt at home in Concord, he conceded that "he did not lack the wish to be Transcendental."[4] One perceptive critic has noted that "Concord . . . might have saved Adams a trip back to the twelfth century."[5] The truth was, however, that through Clover he had already spent more imaginative time in Concord than he might have chosen to admit. Her family associations with the Concord circle and the Transcendentalists were a matter of pride to her and continued to influence her ideas and the activities she pursued. Her indirect connections with such people as Margaret Fuller, Emerson, Hawthorne, George William Curtis, James Freeman Clarke, Samuel Gray Ward, and Catharine Sedgwick, as well as her direct connections with the Bancrofts, always meant more to Clover than any of the powerful political associations of the Adamses, or the "society rabble" of Washington.

Is it far-fetched to suggest that, when Henry turned his interest from the political history of his country to the values of the Middle Ages he was indulging in his own peculiar version of Transcendental Utopianism? Some historians would argue that the society he envisioned had no more realistic bearing on the twelfth century than the society at Brook Farm had on pre-Civil War America. Although he disguised his own susceptibility with characteristic irony, when Henry ended up comparing the Concord world with the Gothic, he suggested as much:

> Concord, in the dark days of 1856, glowed with pure light. Adams approached it in much the same spirit as he would have entered a Gothic Cathedral, for he well knew that the priests regarded him as only a worm. To the Concord Church all Adamses were minds of dust and emptiness, devoid of feeling, poetry or imagination; little higher than the common scourings of State Street; politicians of doubtful honesty; natures of narrow scope; and already, at eighteen years old, he concluded, Henry had begun to feel uncertainty about so many matters more important than Adamses.[6]

Such quotations suggest concretely that Henry Adams had become so closely identified with the values of his wife that he was able to look at himself with quite a different viewpoint from the one he grew up with— although it may be necessary to state again that such

identifications are often unconscious rather than deliberate. What may be more convincing, is that in absorbing
so much of Clover's way of looking at things, he never
had to give her up.[7]

To suggest that Henry Adams had not always shown
some interest in the feminine values to which he turned
with intensity after Clover's death, would be to ignore
the complexity of his character. Many distinguished literary critics, Robert Spiller, J. C. Levenson, Ferner Nuhn,
Elizabeth Stevenson, and Ernest Samuels have pointed
out how important the women in his life were to him. A
lengthy, unpublished doctoral dissertation "A Study of
Non-Rational Elements in the Works of Henry Adams as
Centralized in his Attitude Toward Women" emphasized
how extensively Adams was *not* the scientific historian he
pretended to be.[8] Like the Adamses' good friend Henry James, Henry Adams seemed always to sense that
because women were not primarily concerned with getting and spending, they were consistently more interesting than men; and more in touch with what mattered
most. "No woman had ever driven him wrong," he had
written, and "no man had ever driven him right."[9] The
new identity he forged after Clover's death was con-
structed out of a lifetime of experiences with women that
convinced him that feminine vitality was worth trying to
understand. When he gave up writing history and began
to travel, he already carried the values he expected to
find within himself.[10]

Before setting out for the Far East six months after Clover's death, Henry Adams commissioned Augustus Saint-
Gaudens, whose work Clover had so admired in New
York, to begin sculpting the distinguished memorial
monument which would grace their Rock Creek burial
place. It was fitting that Adams chose an American artist,
reaffirming the belief he and Clover shared in the richness of this country's talents. It was fitting also that
Saint-Gaudens used both male and female models in the
making of the statue designed to liberate the mind in
contemplation, rather than to confine it to any one system of beliefs.

No need exists to document the exotic life Henry Adams began to follow after Clover's suicide. Like Herman Melville's exploration of Mardi, Adams' search for a deeper reality led him to worlds so new he could barely communicate his response to them: "I am not the man to write Polynesian," he ruefully discovered, "my methods are all intellectual, analytic, and modern."[11]

He struggled to admire the dark-skinned women Clarence King had found so exciting, but ended up asserting reluctantly that sex, for him, began with the Aryan. If he acknowledged that one could not "ignore the foundations of society," he also confessed that he was "a bit aghast" when a young woman called his attention to a temple as "a remains of phallic worship."[12] Henry Adams' New England conscience was hard to put down, but, like Clover's Grandfather Sturgis, he made an honest effort to look at different kinds of societies on their own terms; and he concluded that there was much that was commendable, even superior in the most primitive cultures. He could finally write with conviction to Ned Hooper from Polynesia that "the manners and tempers of these people are a long way more civilised than my own."[13]

During these years of spiritual exile from America, Adams wrote and enlarged the *Memoirs of Marau Taaroa, Last Queen of Tahiti* and composed a poetic tribute, again suggestive of Emerson, to "Buddha and Brahma":

*Thought*
    *Travelling in constant circles, round and round*
*Must ever pass through endless contradictions,*
    *Returning on itself at last, till lost*
*In silence.*

But he finally decided upon a more traditionally western direction for emotional identity; Adams would go on to dedicate a "Prayer to the Virgin of Chartres," and to pay tribute to the Middle Ages in *Mont-Saint-Michel and Chartres*. "I have gone on talking," he wrote his former student, Henry Cabot Lodge, obliquely, "but it has been to myself and *to her*" (italics mine).[14]

All of Adams' final literary gestures become important for what they tell us about his efforts to redefine himself in non-rational, symbolic terms; he could not ignore the Transcendental connection. When he turned against his early historical work saying that there were "not nine pages in the nine volumes that now express anything of my interests or feelings," had he also rejected the American world that meant so much to Clover?[15] Or was he trying to restore to that world elements that were rightfully part of his intellectual background—that had been separated from it through the narrowing education he received. "The mind resorts to reason for want of training," he finally declared.[16] Egotistical as he was, Henry Adams nevertheless believed (as Walt Whiman did) that individuals were important chiefly for what they could reveal of the life of society as a whole. The interest of autobiography, he wrote, is "the only interest that lasts forever and holds its own in history."[17] His own autobiography would have had little significance if it had been simply a matter of personal historical record rather than a critique of the values of his culture.

Perhaps Adams opened Henry James' commissioned biography of William Wetmore Story with the thought of what Clover's comments might have been about writing such a tribute. In any case, he later wrote James about the book to comment on how much their entire circle of friends had been shaped by the limitations of their world:

> The painful truth is that all of my New England generation, counting the half-century, 1820–1870, were in actual fact only one mind and nature; the individual was a facet of Boston. We knew each other to the last nervous centre, and feared each other's knowledge. . . . There was hardly a difference even in depth, for Harvard College and Unitarianism kept us all shallow. We knew nothing—no! but really nothing! of the world. One cannot exaggerate the profundi-

ty of ignorance of Story in becoming a sculptor, or Sumner in becoming a statesman, or Emerson in becoming a philosopher. Story and Sumner, Emerson and Alcott, Lowell and Longfellow, Hillard, Winthrop, Motley, Prescott, and all the rest, were of the same mind,—and so, poor worm!—was I!

*Type bourgeois-bostonien!* A type quite as good as another, but more uniform. What you say of Story is at bottom exactly what you would say of Lowell, Motley and Sumner, barring degrees of egotism. You cannot help smiling at them, but you smile at us all equally. God knows that we knew our want of knowledge! the self-distrust became introspection—nervous self-consciousness-irritable dislike of America, and antipathy to Boston. *Auch ich war in Acadien geboren!*

So you have written not Story's life, but your own and mine,—pure autobiography,—the more keen for what is beneath implied, intelligible only to me, and half a dozen other people still living; . . . Improvised Europeans we were, and—Lord God!—how thin! . . . Long ago,—at least thirty years ago I discovered it, and have painfully held my tongue about it.[18]

At the time he wrote James, Henry Adams was preparing his own impressions of Boston through still another autobiography meant to extend beyond Boston to all America. Adams' comment that it was "at least thirty years ago" —exactly one year after his marriage—when he discovered how "thin" they all were, again indirectly suggests that his intimacy with Clover was the beginning of his real education. Henry James answered Henry Adams' lamentation calmly that there was a kind of inevitableness in his having made Adams squirm. He went on to conclude charitably that the fault might not have been in Story's life so much as in the art of the biographer, which was "somehow practically thinning." "I wanted to invest dull old Boston with a mellow, a golden glow," James argued, but "for those who know, like yourself, I only make it bleak—and weak!"[9]

The qualities of New England that finally came to represent its bleakness and weakness to Adams might have represented its strengths to others, even to Clover, who had learned to criticize William Wetmore Story in the same environment that shaped them both. To many of Adams' friends, Harvard still stood for critical moral values as well as for intellectual aridity; it also suggested the "golden glow" of civilized decency that Henry James wanted to remember, if never to live near. Henry Adams finally might have conceded that his own education, with all its flaws, had at least trained him to analyze and articulate its weaknesses. It also allowed him the degree of emotion necessary to criticize and judge America's failures at the same time that it provided him with the tools to turn his disappointments into art.

Yet Adams felt that the heritage of discipline so necessary to building a new civilization in the wilderness, had, after several generations, denied his own social group—"the men of aim"—vitality. He believed that the training they all received in survival stunted their feelings: "To stand alone is quite natural when one has no passions," Adams wrote, "still easier when one has no pains."[20] Like Emerson again, Adams also sensed that the exclusive ended up excluding himself: "No great man has existed who did not rely on the sense and heart of mankind as represented by the good sense of the people, as correcting the modes and over-refinements and class-prejudices of the lettered men of the world."[21] If Henry Adams did not succeed in throwing off the over-refinements and class-prejudices of the lettered men of the world he had hoped to leave behind when he left Cambridge, it was not because he did not attempt to do so. His strange silent dramatization of the missing years that clarified a different set of values for him was simply too reticent, too unassertive. Although he self-consciously and unconsciously tried to change himself, he realized "painfully" how his upbringing had limited even his capacity for willing change.

In the biography he would write in 1911, after the death of the young poet "Bay" Lodge, a few years after Henry James' tome on William Wetmore Story, Henry Adams continued to criticize his own civilization. "A poet, born in Boston, in 1873," he protested, "saw about him a society which commonly bred refined tastes, and often did refined work, but seldom betrayed strong emotions."[22] What Adams most despised in the shaping atmosphere that surrounded Lodge, was the utter indifference, the failure of commitment. Poetry could no longer be a "reaction against society, as in Emerson and the Concord School, or further away and more roughly in Walt Whitman."[23] The society without passions resented nothing and stood for nothing. The apathy that made Lodge helpless also numbed the more self-conscious Adams as he, like the imaginary Prufrock later managed to record his own symptoms. Lodge had "loved Walt Whitman to fanaticism," but could not draw even so much energy as Adams had from Whitman's democratic sources. The eighteenth-century poetry that Henry Adams' amazing grandfather John Quincy Adams wrote in such quantity, the poetry that his good friend John Hay published by the volume, ironically suggested only "the suppression of instinct and imagination" that Adams came to appreciate as characteristic of his time and place.[24] Most of all, it revealed the formal dominance of the European institutions that had trained them all. They were a limited group, he felt, dominated by traditions of formal conventional restraints that reached deeply into their private lives. Clover, although certainly not bohemian or consciously romantic, had nonetheless given him much insight into less conventional life styles. It was through her, not through his proudly American family, that Henry came to realize the American temperament that Lionel Trilling characterized as wishing to resist all conditioning and all actual society—the temperament that aspires to a life which will permit the spirit to make its own terms.[25] Although Adams had not cared for his wife's "reform" connections during the years of their marriage, it is obvious that by 1911 he had come to admire their capacity, especially Emerson's, for emotional commitment. To Adams, the "dry-lighted soul" Clover's mother had praised, partly because he was spared the excesses of their radical contemporaries, represented a healthy reaction against society. Such men were still needed to criticize institutions even if they would play no active political role.

Walt Whitman—the spiritual son of Emerson—loved to fanaticism by the genteel Lodge, read aloud by Henry James, honored by Henry Adams as the only American writer not afraid of sex, remained through his "cosmical artist mind" one of the rare nineteenth-century figures able to be simultaneously superior and democratic. In casting new literary forms to encompass all human beings within the single self, Whitman stood alone and exemplary. As a "man of letters," Henry Adams could not ignore the great solitary singer. In his own way, Adams too would use his *self* to extend his democratic identity, for his personal suffering enabled him briefly to see what life was like for most men. Soon after Clover's death, we recall, he wrote compassionately to his publisher, "What a vast fraternity it is,—that of 'Hearts that Ache.' For the last three months it has seemed to me as though all society were coming to me to drop its mask for a moment and initiate me into its mystery. How we do suffer."[26] Such feeling, he understood, could never be confined by class or social group, or contained within any progressive political philosophy. When he told Mrs. Ward that the saddest discovery of all was that he did not stand alone in his extremity of suffering, he seemed honestly enlightened: "My table was instantly covered with messages from men and women whose own hearts were still aching with the same wounds, and who received me, with a new burst of their own sorrows, into their sad fraternity. . . . My pain seemed lost in the immensity of human distress; and all these people were still carrying on their daily lives, as I must do. Certainly I could do what had proved possible for them."[27] As consolation to a friend whose daughter had just died, he noted, soon after, "I have learned that, in the mass of human distress, trials like yours and mine can be endured, since so many men and women do endure them."[28]

Many years later, his travels to the Far East over, Adams wrote objectively of his continued efforts to renew his own democratic identity with the groups of people who came to look at the Saint-Gaudens monument at Clover's grave. His disappointment overwhelmed him. The statue, he said, represented "the oldest idea known to human thought," yet the fact that it asked a question rather than provided an answer to the mystery of life and death seemed to antagonize people. Clover would not have been surprised to learn that Henry thought it was the clergy who saw in the sculpture only what they brought to it, who broke out "most passionately against the expression they felt in the figure of despair, of atheism, of denial."[29]

If Adams himself called the statue "the peace of God" and if he meant it to suggest the Nirvana that human beings may achieve after suffering, he had other thoughts about its paradoxical nature. In 1902, he wrote to Saint-Gaudens:

> Every now and then in certain lights, I see or think I see, an expression almost answering to defiance in the mouth and nostrils. You did not put it there nor did I.
>
> What puzzles me is whether the figure says this to me, or I say it to the figure. . . . I shall never know. I have gone on reading and thinking . . . without ever finding an answer to the question which is the absolute, the ultimate, the universal: Infinity or Finity.[30]

"A real artist would be very careful to give it no name that the public could turn with a limitation of its nature,"[31] Henry had guardedly written to Richard Watson Gilder, the editor who once wanted to publish Clover's photograph of George Bancroft. To another journalist, he reaffirmed his searching democratic optimism: "All considerable artists make a point of compelling the public to think for itself, and their rule is to require each observer to see what he can, and this will be what the artist meant."[32] Although for many years he never mentioned Clover's name to his friends, he went often to Rock Creek Cemetery. The statue continued to awaken his emotions as he contemplated the eternity he would share with Clover there. At one point, he wrote Saint-Gaudens that the feeling behind the statue reminded him of Michelangelo's slave, who also seemed to have achieved a kind of Nirvana in suffering. That the public would end up labeling the shrouded figure simply "Grief" is an irony that would not have escaped Henry Adams, who clearly preferred to remember Clover in all her spirited complexity.

Clover herself would have been greatly satisfied with Saint-Gaudens' work, but not merely for its American-made beauty. Idealist that she was, she would have particularly liked the idea that her spirit could extend from the scene to nourish and inspire others. One remarkable woman who had trouble defining her active identity often went to sit near the monument. Eleanor Roosevelt frequently visited Rock Creek to meditate, to think about her own role in society, and to try to come to terms with her rebellious spirit. The two women had more in common than capability and position, for encouraging a great husband would never be an adequate role for Eleanor Roosevelt either. She managed finally to achieve the kind of powerful independence that had to remain an illusion for Clover Adams. Without losing the capacity to identify with the powerless, Eleanor Roosevelt became, indeed, the most celebrated American woman of the twentieth century.

Yet *The Education of Henry Adams*, with its pointed omission, may remain the greatest monument to Clover Adams. As a criticism of our culture, it honored the vitality and imagination of all the women Henry Adams knew who did not want to imitate men and who stood for something more than technological progress. To Adams, the instinctive sensibilities that Clover represented surpassed anything a man could learn at Harvard. If Henry failed entirely to understand the irony of how important the thoroughness of his education would have been for these women, it was because he had come to see it as worthless for men. He would never realize that many bright women would always be grateful to "fail" on the same terms as he and Clarence King had done.

Adams thought that the unfeeling, scientific world, the product of his own kind of education, had little to commend it to either sex. The social class of women that Antoinette Blackwell had once described as "the disinterested pioneers in every needed enterprise: careful and conscientious investigators into many of the marvelous but open secrets of the universe" would soon be gone.[33] Henry Adams saw the women that he admired trying to find their way by "imitating" men and turning into "machine-made collectivist females." He believed that all the people who saw themselves as knowing guardians of humanistic values—himself included—must simply continue to play their social roles freely and bravely without "the awkward stage-fright of amateurs."[34] Walt Whitman had similarly once declared, "Play the old role, the role that is great or small according as one makes it!"[35]

In assessing the value of the lives that the members of his circle had led, Adams could comment only on what they had all attempted to achieve:

> He had no notion whether they served a useful purpose; he had worked in the dark, but so had most of his friends, even the artists, none of whom held any lofty opinions of their success in raising the standards of society, or felt profound respect for the methods or manners of their time, at home or abroad, but all of whom had tried, in a way, to hold the standard up.

When Henry concluded that "the effect had been, for the older generation, exhausting," he mentioned William

Morris Hunt, the artist who had also found suicide his solution to the problems of existence. In this instance, we cannot help wondering if Adams was thinking again of Clover.[36]

The Genteel Tradition, which—according to George Santayana—was afraid to acknowledge the reality of suffering, was not Clover Hooper Adams' tradition. Her feelings had always been as much a part of her own definition of standards as her deliberate unconventionality was. Both these qualities made her particularly vulnerable to the rigidity of her environment; yet they also made her much more vital than the safer, more conforming, feminine spirits around her. The kind of psychic disorder that finally led her to take her own life may be an intrinsic part of a culture in which freedom of choice, rather than conformity to tradition, remains the source of ideal strength. If Henry Adams was driven for the rest of his life to try to understand the sources of Clover's vitality, he was merely paying tribute to all that he had learned from his wife during their years together. Because of his efforts to evaluate himself by Clover's standards, he was eventually able to write *The Education of Henry Adams*, a book that thinking Americans will continue to honor for its unconventional, sceptical spirit.

"Prosperity and pound-cake are for very young gentlemen whom such things content," wrote Emerson in his essay "Aristocracy." Attempting to clarify the role that gifted people should play in a democratic society, Emerson insisted that "the noble mind is here to teach us that failure is part of success."[37] Henry Adams would have agreed. The elegant Saint-Gaudens monument where Clover and Henry Adams are now buried together remains accessible to the public in Rock Creek Park—a mystical reminder of the ongoing identity of success and failure in American life.

# Notes

I have used at least four different sources for the letters of Henry Adams: the published volumes of Worthington C. Ford; *Henry Adams and His Friends*, edited by Harold Dean Cater; the microfilm reels of the Adams Manuscript Trust, specifically reels 590–598; and miscellaneous Adams papers both at the Massachusetts Historical Society and in private collections. It seems wisest to list such letters simply by date and correspondent. Such an approach anticipates the Harvard University Press edition of Henry Adams' letters, which is being prepared by Ernest Samuels, J. C. Levenson, Jayne Samuels, Charles Vandersee, and Viola Hopkins Winner.

Clover Adams' letters have been drawn from three main sources: the Thoron edition of published letters; the Adams Manuscript Trust microfilms; and the miscellaneous manuscript collections of the Massachusetts Historical Society. The private papers of Faith Knapp and Mary Swann provided a great deal of background material concerning Clover Adams' life. Because these manuscript collections are not yet organized, I shall specify when they are used.

## Abbreviations

| | |
|---|---|
| AMT | Adams Manuscript Trust |
| BPL | Boston Public Library |
| *EHA* | Henry Adams, *The Education of Henry Adams*, ed. Ernest Samuels. 1907. Reprint edition. Boston, 1973. |
| ES, vol. I | Ernest Samuels, *The Young Henry Adams*. vol. 1 of *Henry Adams*. 3 vols. Cambridge, Mass., 1948. |
| ES, vol. II | Ernest Samuels, *Henry Adams: The Middle Years*. vol. 2 of *Henry Adams*. 3 vols. Cambridge, Mass., 1958. |
| ES, vol. III | Ernest Samuels, *Henry Adams: The Major Phase*. vol. 3 of *Henry Adams*. 3 vols. Cambridge, Mass., 1964. |
| HCL | Harvard College Library |
| Knapp | Knapp Papers, Cazenovia, New York |
| MHS | Massachusetts Historical Society |
| Swann | Swann Papers, Stockbridge, Mass. |

## Chapter 1

[1]Henry Adams, *The Education of Henry Adams*, ed. Ernest Samuels (Boston, 1973; orig. pub. 1907), p. 353.

[2]Henry Adams to Edwin L. Godkin, December 16, 1885.

[3]Henry Adams to Charles Milnes Gaskell, February 8, 1872.

[4]Adams, *EHA*, p. 384.

[5]Adams, *EHA*, p. 385.

[6]Ernest Samuels, *The Middle Years*, vol. 2 of *Henry Adams* (Cambridge, Mass., 1958), p. 303.

[7]Adams, *EHA*, p. 385.

[8]Henry Adams to Elizabeth Cameron, February 6, 1891.

[9]Hans Loewald, "Internalization, Separation, Mourning, and the Super-Ego," *Psychoanalytic Quarterly* 31 (October 1962): 493.

[10]Roy Schafer, *Aspects of Internalization* (New York, 1968), p. 150.

[11]Adams, *EHA*, p. 26.

[12]ES, vol. II, p. 256.

[13]Adams, *EHA*, p. 443.

[14]F. O. Matthiessen, *American Renaissance: Art and Expression in the Age of Emerson and Whitman* (New York, 1941), p. 630.

[15]ES, vol. II, pp. 25–26.

[16]Ralph Waldo Emerson, "History," *Essays, Poems, Lectures*, 12 vols., ed. J. E. Cabot (Boston, 1883), vol. 2, p. 12.

[17]Clover Adams to Dr. Robert William Hooper, May 14, 1882.

## Chapter 2

[1]Henry Adams, *EHA*, ed. Ernest Samuels (Boston, 1973; orig. pub. 1907), p. 353.

[2]Faculty Records, vol. 8, Harvard Archives.

[3]Thomas Hooper and Charles Pope, *Hooper Genealogy* (Salem, 1908).

[4]Katherine Simonds, "The Tragedy of Mrs. Henry Adams," *New England Quarterly* 9 (December 1936): 571.

[5]William Sturgis to Ellen Sturgis Hooper, April 10, 1848, Knapp.

[6]This letter was inserted in Swann Papers among many documents reflecting feminine concerns.

[7]Ralph Waldo Emerson, "Life and Letters in New England," *Essays, Poems, Lectures*, 12 vols., ed. J. E. Cabot (Boston, 1883), vol. 10, p. 325.

[8]Perry Miller, ed., *The Transcendentalists: An Anthology* (Cambridge, Mass., 1950), p. 402.

[9]Ernest Samuels, *The Young Henry Adams*, vol. 1 of *Henry Adams* (Cambridge, Mass., 1948), p. 297.

[10]Joseph J. Deiss, *The Roman Years of Margaret Fuller* (New York, 1969), p. 62.

[11]Perry Miller, ed., *Margaret Fuller: American Romantic* (New York, 1963), p. xxii.

[12]Margaret Fuller, *Memoirs of Margaret Fuller Ossoli*, 2 vols., ed. R. W. Emerson, W. H. Channing, and J. F. Clarke (New York, 1884), vol. 1, p. 325.

[13]Ernest Samuels, *The Middle Years*, vol. 2 of *Henry Adams* (Cambridge, Mass., 1958), p. 266.

[14]Mason Wade, *Margaret Fuller: Whetstone of Genius* (New York, 1940), p. 78; for a feminist interpretation of Fuller's life, see also Paula Blanchard, *Margaret Fuller: From Transcendentalism to Revolution* (New York, 1978).

[15]Emerson, "The Transcendentalist," *Essays*, vol. 1, p. 323.

[16]Arthur M. Schlesinger, Jr., *The Age of Jackson* (Boston, 1953), p. 381.

[17]Ellen Sturgis Hooper, *Poems* (privately printed, n.d.), BPL. All of the subsequent poetic excerpts are from the privately printed volume in the Treasure Room at the Boston Public Library. A few of the poems have titles, but there are no page numbers or dates.

[18]Ellen S. Hooper, to "The Bell," n.d., Treasure Room, BPL.

[19]Jacques Barzun, ed., *Selected Writings of John Jay Chapman* (New York, 1957), p. 172.

[20]Emerson, "The American Scholar," *Essays*, vol. 1, pp. 101–102.

[21]Barzun, *Selected Writings*, p. 180.

[22]Henry Adams to Oliver Wendell Holmes, Jr., January 4, 1885.

[23]Emerson, "The Transcendentalist," *Essays*, vol. 1, p. 325.

[24]R. P. Blackmur, *The Expense of Greatness* (New York, 1958), p. 249.

[25]Henry Lee Higginson, *Life and Letters* (Boston, 1921), p. 373.

[26]Adams, *EHA*, p. 27.

[27]Henry Adams to Charles Milnes Gaskell, June 28, 1872.

[28]Obituary Files, April 13, 1885, Harvard Archives.

[29]Staff of the Worchester Asylum to Dr. Robert William Hooper, March 3, 1881, Knapp.

[30]Charles Francis Adams, Diary, October 5, 1877, p. 33.

[31]Clippings, Harvard Archives.

[32]Included in Knapp Papers.

[33]Charles Francis Adams, Jr., *Memorabilia*, May 3, 1891, in Woodrow Wilson Papers, ed. John E. Little (Princeton, unpublished).

[34]ES, vol. II, p. 272.

[35]Ellen Gurney to Charles Eliot Norton, n.d., Gurney Papers, HCL.

[36]George Santayana, *The Genteel Tradition: Nine Essays by George Santayana*, ed. Douglas Wilson (Cambridge, Mass., 1967), p. 51.

[37]Samuel Gray Ward, March 5, 1831, in David Baldwin, "Puritan Aristocrat in the Age of Emerson: A Study of Samuel Gray Ward," unpub. Ph.D. diss. (University of Pennsylvania, 1961), p. 38.

# Chapter 3

[1]Edward Lurie, *Louis Agassiz: A Life in Science* (Chicago, 1960), p. 201.

[2]William Sturgis to a grandchild [?], December 26, 1859, Knapp.

[3]Lurie, *Louis Agassiz*, p. 141.

[4]Louise H. Tharp, *Adventurous Alliance* (Boston, 1959), p. 139.

[5]Henry Adams, *EHA*, ed. Ernest Samuels (Boston, 1973; orig. pub. 1907), p. 60.

[6]Ernest Samuels, *The Young Henry Adams*, vol. 1 of *Henry Adams* (Cambridge, Mass., 1948), p. 17.

[7]Lucy Allen Paton, *Elizabeth Cary Agassiz* (Cambridge, Mass., 1918), pp. 396–397.

[8]Lurie, *Louis Agassiz*, p. 140.

[9]Charles Eliot Norton, *Letters of Charles Eliot Norton*, 2 vols., ed. Sara Norton and Mark A. DeWolfe Howe (Boston, 1913), vol. 2, p. 4.

[10]Edward Waldo Forbes, "The Agassiz School," Cambridge Historical Society publication 35 (Cambridge, Mass., 1954), p. 40.

[11]See Dolores Hayden, *Seven American Utopias: The Architecture of Communitarian Socialism 1790–1975* (Cambridge, Mass., 1976), p. 28.

[12]Ward Thoron, ed., *Letters of Mrs. Henry Adams*, p. 472.

[13]*Ibid.*, p. 473.

[14]*Ibid.*

[15]Clover Adams to Dr. Robert William Hooper, December 28, 1879.

[16]Thoron, *Letters*, pp. 474–475.

[17]Ellen Emerson, Letters, 1855–1856, February 1856, Gregg Papers.

[18]Mason Wade, *Margaret Fuller: Whetstone of Genius* (New York, 1940), p. 74.

[19]Clover Adams to Ellen Gurney, January 25, 1884.

[20]Clover Adams to Dr. Robert William Hooper, February 18, 1883.

[21]Hugh Hawkins, *Between Harvard and America: The Educational Leadership of Charles W. Eliot* (New York, 1972), p. 195.

[22]*Ibid.*

[23]Paton, *Elizabeth Cary Agassiz*, p. 402.

[24]Arthur Gilman Papers, MHS.

[25]Elizabeth Cary Agassiz to Charles W. Eliot, June 30, 1903. See also Harvard Archives, March 25, 1893.

[26]Gilman Papers, MHS.

[27]Elizabeth Cary Agassiz to Charles W. Eliot, December 17, 1884, Gilman Papers, MHS.

[28]Ellen Gurney to Justin Winsor, May 24, 1887, Gurney Papers, Harvard Archives.

[29]All of these fragments are from the Gilman Papers, MHS.

[30]*Ibid.*

[31]Hawkins, *Harvard and America*, p. 196.

[32]Mary Maguire, "The Curtain-Raiser to the Founding of Radcliffe College," Cambridge Historical Society publication 36 (Cambridge, Mass., 1955), p. 38.

[33]Paton, *Elizabeth Cary Agassiz*, p. 234.

[34]ES, vol. I, pp. 8–9.

[35]Adams, *EHA*, p. 389.

[36]ES, vol. I, p. 9.

[37]Adams, *EHA*, p. 69.

[38]Henry Adams to Henry Cabot Lodge, September 28, 1915.

[39]Louise H. Tharp, *The Appletons of Beacon Hill* (New York, 1973), p. 298.

[40]Charles Eliot Norton, "The Work of the Sanitary Commission," *North American Review*, January 1867, pp. 150–151.

[41]Thoron, *Letters*, pp. 469, 10, 8.

[42]*Ibid.*, p. 471.

[43]*Ibid.*, p. 10.

# Chapter 4

[1]Clover Adams to Dr. Robert William Hooper, November 5, 1872.

[2]Charles Francis Adams, "Memoir of Abigail Smith Adams" in *The Letters of Mrs. Adams, The Wife of John Adams* (Boston, 1840), p. xxiv.

[3]Henry Adams to Charles Milnes Gaskell, October 5, 1869.

[4]Newton Arvin, ed., *The Selected Letters of Henry Adams* (New York, 1951), p. lix.

[5]Ernest Samuels, *The Young Henry Adams*, vol. 1 of *Henry Adams* (Cambridge, Mass., 1948), p. 42.

[6]Clover Adams to Dr. Robert William Hooper, December 2, 1877.

[7]Adams, "Memoir," p. 127.

[8]*Ibid.*, pp. 445–556.

[9]March 27, 1816, Adams Papers, HCL.

[10]Henry Adams, *EHA*, ed. Ernest Samuels (Boston, 1973; orig. pub. 1907), p. 19.

[11]ES, vol. I, p. 297.

[12]Adams, *EHA*, p. 16.

[13]*Ibid.*, p. 17.

[14]*Ibid.*, p. 18.

[15]AMT microfilm 269.

[16]*Ibid.*

[17]Adams Papers, HCL.

[18]*Ibid.*

[19]J. C. Levenson, *The Mind and Art of Henry Adams* (Cambridge, Mass., 1957), p. 193.

[20]AMT microfilm 269.

[21]Charles Francis Adams, *Letters of Mrs. Adams*, p. 144.

[22]Charles Francis Adams, Diary, June 30, 1873.

[23]Regina Morantz, "The Lady and Her Physician," and Barbara Sicherman, "Wear and Tear: Doctors, Patients, and the Rise of Neurasthenia," in *Clio's Consciousness Raised: New Perspectives on the History of Women*, ed. Mary Hartman and Lois Banner (New York, 1974).

[24]ES, vol. I, p. 93.

[25]Henry Adams to Charles Milnes Gaskell, March 6, 1871.

[26]Adams, *EHA*, p. 211.

[27]Clover Adams to Dr. Robert William Hooper, June 1, 1873.

[28]Mary Adams to Charles Francis Adams, January 5, 1872, AMT microfilm 590.

[29]Henry Adams to Charles Francis Adams, January 7, 1872, AMT microfilm 590.

[30]Henry Adams to Charles Francis Adams, January 14, 1872, AMT microfilm 590.

[31]Henry Adams to Charles Francis Adams, January 20, 1872, AMT microfilm 590.

[32]Henry Adams to Charles Milnes Gaskell, January 22, 1872.

[33]Charles Francis Adams, Diary, November 23, 1873.

[34]Henry Adams to Charles Milnes Gaskell, March 27, 1877.

[35]Abigail Brooks Adams to Charles Francis Adams, November 20, 1876 and December 13, 1876, AMT microfilm 595.

[36]Abigail Brooks Adams to Charles Francis Adams, April 7, 1877, AMT microfilm 595.

[37]Abigail Brooks Adams to Charles Francis Adams, April 10, 1877, AMT microfilm 595.

[38]Abigail Brooks Adams to Charles Francis Adams, December 13, 1876, AMT microfilm 595.

[39]Abigail Brooks Adams to Charles Francis Adams, April 10, 1877, AMT microfilm 595.

[40]Henry Adams to Charles Milnes Gaskell, January 21, 1872, AMT microfilm 595.

[41]Abigail Brooks Adams to Charles Francis Adams, November 28, 1876, AMT microfilm 595.

[42]Martin Duberman, *Charles Francis Adams, 1807–1886* (Stanford, 1968), p. 398.

[43]Adams, *EHA*, p. 85.

[44]Charles Francis Adams to Henry Adams, July 11, 1870, AMT microfilm 588.

[45]Adams, *EHA*, pp. 35, 288.

[46]A poem by Louisa Johnson, AMT microfilm 601.

[47]Abigail Brooks Adams to Charles Francis Adams, April 11, 1877, AMT microfilm 595.

[48]Edward C. Kirkland, *Charles Francis Adams, Jr., 1835–1915: The Patrician at Bay* (Cambridge, Mass., 1965), p. 4.

[49]Charles Francis Adams, Jr., *Memorabilia*, in Woodrow Wilson Papers, ed. John E. Little (Princeton) unpublished.

[50]Henry Adams to Brooks Adams, March 3, 1872.

[51]Clover Adams to Dr. Robert William Hooper, April 16, 1882. See also Dr. Abraham Myerson and Rosalie Boyle, "The Incidence of Manic-Depressive Disease in Certain Socially Prominent Families," *American Journal of Psychiatry* 98 (1941–1942): 11–21.

[52]Charles Francis Adams, Diary, May 20, 1879.

[53]Kirkland, *Patrician at Bay*, p. 56.

[54]Clover Adams to Ellen Gurney, September 5, 1872.

[55]Clover Adams to Dr. Robert William Hooper, January 1, 1873.

[56]Clover Adams to Dr. Robert William Hooper, January 24, 1873.

[57]James Truslow Adams, *Henry Adams* (New York, 1933), p. 145.

[58]Henry Adams to Charles Milnes Gaskell, May 30, 1872.

[59]Henry Adams to Charles Milnes Gaskell, April 27, 1872.

[60]James Truslow Adams, *Henry Adams*, p. 145.

[61]Mason Wade, *Margaret Fuller: Whetstone of Genius* (New York, 1940), p. 160.

# Chapter 5

[1]Henry Adams to Charles Milnes Gaskell, June 23, 1872.

[2]Henry Adams to Charles Francis Adams, Jr., February 7, 1860.

[3]Clover Adams to Anne Palmer, April 26, 1885, Adams Misc. MHS.

[4]Included in Knapp collection.

[5]Henry James to William James, March 8, 1870, *Letters of Henry James*, ed. Leon Edel (Cambridge, 1974), vol. 1, p. 208.

[6]Clover Adams to Dr. Robert William Hooper, December 5, 1880; also, the *Nation*, December 19, 1878, pp. 386–389; *North American Review*, January 1879, pp. 96–116.

[7]George Willis Cooke, "The Poetry of Ellen Sturgis Hooper," *Journal of Speculative Philosophy*, July 3, 1885.

[8]Ellen Sturgus Hooper to Dr. Robert William Hooper, n.d.; April 6, 1848; Knapp.

[9]These letters are found in both the Knapp and Swann collections of family papers.

[10]Ellen Sturgis Hooper, *Poems*, BPL.

[11]I am indebted to Mrs. Ropes Cabot, now living in the Samuel Hooper compound at Cotuit, for showing me where this was.

[12]E. H. to Ellen [?], 1853, Knapp. Grandfather Sturgis kept a spacious summer house in Woburn at Horn Pond.

[13]Clover Hooper to Ellen Hooper, July 24, 1856, Knapp.

[14]Henry Adams to George Cabot Lodge, April 9, 1903.

[15]Clover Hooper to Ellen Hooper, series of letters without dates, Knapp.

[16]Ralph Waldo Emerson, "Friendship," *Essays*, vol. 2, p. 203.

[17]Clover Hooper to Dr. Robert William Hooper, September 10, 1854, Knapp.

[18]Henry Adams to Abigail Brooks Adams, January 6, 1860, re: Louisa: "Children might give her employment and busy her in that way, but even this would never make her happy. . . . I'm satisfied of one thing and that is that she is not a person for America, for she has there no field and doesn't even herself know what she wants."

[19]Richard D. Birdsall, *Berkshire County: A Cultural History* (New Haven, 1959), p. 333.

[20]*Ibid.*, pp. 332–333.

[21]Nathaniel Hawthorne to Carrie Sturgis Tappan, July 13, 1845, Knapp: "Do come to our Eden (as Sophia persists in calling it)—and which, at least, will be more like Eden if I leave an angel to guard it during our own expulsion." Sophia concluded, "For a person who likes 'marble talk' as my husband told me the other day, I think the above flight quite uncommon."

[22]Clover Hooper to Dr. Robert William Hooper, August 1, 1861 and August 7 [1861], Knapp.

²³Clover Hooper to Anne Hooper, March 9, 1862, Knapp.

²⁴Ellen Hooper to Alice Hooper, August 20, 1863, Knapp.

²⁵Clover Hooper to Dr. Robert William Hooper, August 13, 1862, Knapp.

²⁶Letter to the editors of *The Boston Daily Advertiser*, July 21, 1863; Francis Parkman, *Letters of Francis Parkman*, 2 vols., ed. Wilbur R. Jacobs (Norman, Okla., 1960), vol. 1, p. 166.

²⁷Oliver Wendell Holmes, Jr., "Memorial Day," speech delivered at Keene, N.H., 1884, from Max Lerner, ed., *The Mind and Faith of Justice Holmes* (New York, 1943), p. 10.

²⁸Clover Hooper to Anne Hooper, May 8, 1861, Knapp.

²⁹Clover Hooper to Dr. Robert William Hooper, December 5, 1862, Knapp.

³⁰Clover Hooper to Ned Hooper, July 8, 1862, Knapp.

³¹Willie Lee Rose, *Rehearsal for Reconstruction: The Port Royal Experiment* (New York, 1964), p. 258. This book provides brilliant insight into the historical significance of the Beaufort experiment.

³²Clover Hooper to Dr. Robert William Hooper, December 5, 1862, Knapp.

³³Clover Hooper to Dr. Robert William Hooper, September 5, 1880.

³⁴Clover Adams to Anne Palmer, October 28, 1881.

³⁵Alice Hooper to Samuel Hooper, October 17, 1864, Knapp.

³⁶Alice Hooper to Samuel Hooper, December 19, 1864, Knapp.

³⁷Clover Adams to Dr. Robert William Hooper, December 3, 1882.

³⁸Oliver Wendell Holmes, Jr., "Parts of the Unimaginable Whole" and "Harvard College in the War," Max Lerner, ed., *The Mind and Faith of Justice Holmes: His Speeches, Essays, Letters and Judicial Opinions* (New York, 1945), pp. 17–18, 26.

³⁹"Commemoration Ode, July 21, 1865," in James Russell Lowell, *The Poetical Works of James Russell Lowell*, 4 vols. (Boston, 1868), vol. 4, pp. 28–30.

⁴⁰Alice Hooper to her mother, August 6, 1865, Knapp.

⁴¹"Parkman's Dark Years: Letters to Mary Dwight Parkman," *Harvard Library Bulletin* 4 (1950): 53–54.

⁴²Ernest Samuels, *The Middle Years*, vol. 2 of *Henry Adams* (Cambridge, Mass., 1958), p. 47 (letters now missing from HCL).

⁴³Mary E. D. Parkman, "Report," *Journal of Social Science* (1871), p. 158 (Boston Athenaeum). See also, William Leach, *True Love and Perfect Union: The Feminist Reform of Sex and Society* (New York, 1980).

⁴⁴Clover Adams to Edwin L. Godkin, December 25, 1879, HCL.

⁴⁵Clover Hooper to Anne Hooper, May 8, 1861, Knapp.

⁴⁶Henry Adams, *EHA*, ed. Ernest Samuels (Boston, 1973; orig. pub. 1907), p. 214.

⁴⁷Clover Hooper to Ellen Hooper, Marblehead, 1853, Knapp.

⁴⁸Clover Hooper to Ellen Hooper, July 24, 1856, Knapp.

⁴⁹Clover Hooper to Eleanor Whiteside (Shattuck), March 5, 1871, Shattuck Papers, MHS.

⁵⁰Henry Adams to Charles Milnes Gaskell, August 21, 1878.

⁵¹Catherine L. Albanese, *Corresponding Motion: Transcendental Religion and the New America* (Philadelphia, 1977), p. 101.

⁵²Trumbull Stickney, *The Poems of Trumbull Stickney*, ed. Amberys Whittle (New York, 1966), pp. xlii–xliii.

[53]Katherine Simonds, "The Tragedy of Mrs. Henry Adams," *New England Quarterly* 9 (December 1936): 570.

[54]Wade, *Margaret Fuller* (New York, 1940), p. 80.

[55]Henry Adams to Charles Milnes Gaskell, March 26, 1872 and May 30, 1872.

[56]This is described as a "child's note" accompanying bequest on the night of January 6, 1857, Knapp.

[57]Henry Adams to Charles Milnes Gaskell, January 13, 1870.

[58]Henry Adams to Charles Milnes Gaskell, March 26, 1872, and June 23, 1872.

[59]Henry Adams' review, "Howells' *Their Wedding Journey*," *North American Review* (April 1872): 444–445, unsigned.

[60]Charles Francis Adams, Diary, December 14, 1873.

[61]Clover Hooper to Eleanor Whiteside (Shattuck), March 8, 1872, Shattuck Papers, MHS.

[62]Henry Adams to Charles Milnes Gaskell, April 27, 1872.

[63]Clover Hooper to Ellen Gurney, March 5, 1872.

# Chapter 6

[1]Ralph Waldo Emerson to Carrie Sturgis Tappan, October 13, 1857, in Ralph Waldo Emerson, *Letters of Ralph Waldo Emerson*, 6 vols., ed. Ralph Rusk (New York, 1939), vol. 5, p. 86.

[2]Ralph Waldo Emerson, "Aristocracy," *Essays, Poems, Lectures*, 12 vols., ed. J. E. Cabot (Boston, 1883), vol. 10, p. 42.

[3]Charles Francis Adams to Henry Adams, July 11, 1870.

[4]Ernest Samuels, *The Young Henry Adams*, vol. 1 of *Henry Adams* (Cambridge, Mass., 1948), p. 275.

[5]Henry Adams to Charles Milnes Gaskell, October 25, 1870.

[6]ES, vol. I, 275.

[7]Henry Adams to Charles Milnes Gaskell, November 19, 1870.

[8]Fanny Hooper to Lillian Clarke, June 1868, Swann.

[9]Paul Buck, "Harvard Attitudes toward Radcliffe in the Early Years," (Boston, 1962), MHS.

[10]Mark A. DeWolfe Howe, *Later Years of the Saturday Club, 1870–1920* (Boston, 1927), p. 444.

[11]Henry Adams to C. W. Eliot, November 13, 1886, Harvard Archives.

[12]Kenneth S. Lynn, *William Dean Howells: An American Life* (New York, 1970), p. 209.

[13]This is included with the Knapp Papers.

[14]Lynn, *William Dean Howells*, p. 208.

[15]Clover Adams to Dr. Robert William Hooper, June 28, 1872.

[16]Clover Adams to Dr. Robert William Hooper, October 9, 1872; October 20, 1872.

[17]Fanny Hooper to Lillian Clarke, October 9, 1872, Swann.

[18]Henry Adams to Charles Milnes Gaskell, March 27, 1871.

[19]Richard C. Vitzthum, *The American Compromise: Theme and Method in the Histories of Parkman, Bancroft, and Adams* (Norman, Okla., 1936), p. 150.

[20]This correspondence is included in the Homans Papers at the MHS.

[21]Elizabeth Davis Bancroft, *Letters from England, 1846–1849* (New York, 1904), p. 32.

[22]Clover Adams to Dr. Robert William Hooper, June 29, 1873 and January 14, 1883.

[23]Henry James praised Alice's passionate "radicalism" and maintained that she would have been a "political force" had she been well enough to live in the world; he labeled her an "Irishwoman." F. O. Matthiessen, *The James Family: A Group Biography* (New York, 1964), p. 285. See also Jean Strouse, *Alice James: A Biography* (Boston, 1980).

[24]Henry Adams to Clover Adams, April 9, 1885.

[25]Henry Adams to H. Grigsby, October 9, 1877.

[26]Bernard Bergonzi, "The Ideology of Being English," *The Situation of the Novel* (London, 1970).

[27]Clover Adams to Dr. Robert William Hooper, June 29, 1873.

[28]Clover Adams to Dr. Robert William Hooper, June 18, 1873.

[29]*Ibid.*

[30]Clover Adams to Anne Palmer, December 16, 1884, Adams Papers, MHS.

[31]Clover Adams to Dr. Robert William Hooper, March 22, 1873.

[32]Clover Adams to Dr. Robert William Hooper, June 1, 1873.

[33]See Ernest Samuels, *Bernard Berenson: The Making of a Connoisseur* (Cambridge, Mass., 1979).

[34]See Jane W. Hipolito, "The Secret World of Henry Adams," unpub. Ph.D. diss. (UCLA, 1968).

[35]Henry Adams to Charles Milnes Gaskell, November 21, 1879.

[36]Clover Adams to Theodore Dwight, January 30, 1882, Adams Misc., MHS.

[37]Clover Adams to Dr. Robert William Hooper, October 27, 1872.

[38]Clover Adams to Dr. Robert William Hooper, April 20, 1873.

[39]*Ibid.*

[40]Clover Adams to Dr. Robert William Hooper, May 14, 1873.

[41]Harold Dean Cater, ed., *Henry Adams and His Friends* (Boston, 1947), introduction.

[42]Clover Adams to Dr. Robert William Hooper, December 5, 1872; January 3, 1873; November 17, 1872; and February 16, 1873.

[43]Henry Parkman to his mother, March 14, 1872, HCL.

[44]Henry Adams to Henry Cabot Lodge, January 2, 1873.

[45]Clover Adams to Dr. Robert William Hooper, February 16, 1873.

[46]Ralph L. Rusk, *The Life of Ralph Waldo Emerson* (New York, 1949), p. 467.

[47]*Ibid.* p. 468.

[48]Anna Barker Ward to Ellen Sturgis Hooper, August 15, 1848, Swann.

[49]Henry Adams to Anna Barker Ward, December 22, 1885.

[50]Richard D. Birdsall, *Berkshire County: A Cultural History* (New Haven, 1959), p. 325.

[51]*Ibid.*

[52]Rusk, *Life of Emerson*, p. xxvi.

[53]Birdsall, *Berkshire County*, p. 327.

[54]*Ibid.*, p. 328.

[55]Henry Adams to Anna Barker Ward, December 22, 1885.

[56]Ralph Waldo Emerson, *Letters to a Friend, 1838–1853*, ed. C. E. Norton (Boston, 1899), p. 16.

[57]Charles Eliot Norton, *The Letters of Charles Eliot Norton with a Biographical Comment*, 2 vols., Sara Norton and Mark A. DeWolfe Howe (Boston, 1913), vol. 2, pp. 243, 300, 316.

[58]Ellen Gurney to Samuel Gray Ward, February 24, 1886, Swann.

[59]Clover Adams to Dr. Robert William Hooper, March 11, 1873 and July 23, 1873.

[60]Henry Adams to Charles Milnes Gaskell, October 26, 1873 and June 22, 1874.

[61]William James, *North American Review*, October 1869, p. 558.

[62]*Ibid.*, p. 563.

[63]*Ibid.*, p. 565.

[64]Henry Adams to Charles Francis Adams, Jr., February 13, 1863.

[65]Ellen Sturgis Hooper to Carrie Sturgis Tappan, n.d., Knapp.

[66]Carrie Sturgis Tappan to Ralph Waldo Emerson, November 8, 1868, Knapp.

[67]Carrie Sturgis Tappan to Ralph Waldo Emerson, October 9, 1872, Knapp.

[68]Henry Adams to Robert Cunliffe, August 18, 1874.

[69]Ellen Sturgis Hooper to Susan Sturgis, n.d., Swann.

[70]Ednah Dow Cheney, *Reminiscences* (Boston, 1902), p. 168.

[71]Jacques Barzun, ed., *Selected Writings of John Jay Chapman* (New York, 1957), p. 168.

[72]Clover Adams to Dr. Robert William Hooper, November 30, 1879.

[73]John Hay, *Letters and Extracts from a Diary*, 3 vols. (privately printed, 1908), vol. 2, p. 235.

[74]Ernest Samuels, *The Middle Years*, vol. 2 of *Henry Adams* (Cambridge, Mass., 1958), p. 261.

[75]Henry Adams to George Cabot Lodge, April 27, 1903.

[76]"Perils of American Women," in Nancy F. Cott, ed., *Root of Bitterness* (New York, 1972), p. 292.

[77]Henry Adams, "Dr. Clarke's 'Sex in Education,'" *North American Review*, January 1874, pp. 141–142.

[78]*Ibid.*, p. 152.

[79]*Ibid.*, p. 144.

[80]*Ibid.*, p. 142.

[81]"Clarke's 'Building of a Brain,'" *North American Review*, January 1875, p. 188.

[82]Carrie Sturgis Tappan to Ellen Sturgis Hooper, n.d., Swann.

[83]Mark A. DeWolfe Howe, "The Tale of Tanglewood," *Yale Review*, Winter, 1943, p. 330.

[84]See William H. Jordy, *Henry Adams: Scientific Historian* (New Haven, 1952).

[85]Henry Adams to Henry Cabot Lodge, May 26, 1875.

[86]Henry Adams to Robert Cunliffe, August 31, 1875.

[87]Henry Adams to Charles Milnes Gaskell, February 15, 1875.

[88]Clover Hooper to Elihu Vedder, December 8, 1866, Vedder Papers, Archives of American Art, Smithsonian Institution (reel no. 516). I am grateful to Mr. Henry La Farge for calling this letter to my attention.

# Chapter 7

[1]Ralph Waldo Emerson, "Man the Reformer," *Essays, Poems, Lectures*, 12 vols., ed. J. E. Cabot, (Boston, 1883), vol. 1, p. 236.

[2]Ernest Samuels, *The Young Henry Adams*, vol. 1 of *Henry Adams* (Cambridge, Mass., 1948), p. 298.

[3]Henry Adams to Charles Milnes Gaskell, February 13, 1874.

[4]Henry Adams to Charles Milnes Gaskell, November 28, 1878.

[5]Copied with the papers of Dr. Robert William Hooper, n.d., Knapp.

[6]Clover Adams to Dr. Robert William Hooper, December 23, 1877.

[7]Clover Adams to Dr. Robert William Hooper, December 16, 1877.

[8]Henry Adams to Charles Milnes Gaskell, August 22, 1877.

[9]Henry Adams, October 29, 1881: "I have but one offspring, and am nearly forty-four while it is nothing but an embryo." August 7, 1881: "I am now straining my weary muucles to put four bulky volumes into this tired world." October 8, 1882: "My *John Randolph* is just coming into the world, naked, helpless, and beggarly, yet the poor wretches must live forever and curse their father"; he called it his "brat." On December 3, 1882, he spoke of being "accouché of his small volume"; and on October 30, 1887, he said: "As I am seasick every time I see a proof, the sense of its being a baby becomes overpowering."

[10]Henry Adams to Charles Milnes Gaskell, August 22, 1877.

[11]Ellen Sturgis Hooper to Carrie Sturgis, n.d., Swann.

[12]Clover Adams to Dr. Robert William Hooper, December 30, 1877.

[13]Ellen Sturgis Hooper, *Poems* (privately printed, n.d.), BPL.

[14]Clover Adams to Dr. Robert William Hooper, January 6, 1878.

[15]Clover Adams to Dr. Robert William Hooper, December 23, 1877.

[16]*Ibid.*

[17]Clover Adams to Dr. Robert William Hooper, February 24, 1878.

[18]Clover Adams to Dr. Robert William Hooper, January 6, 1878.

[19]John Hay to Henry Adams, January 22, 1883. See also William Leach, *True Love and Perfect Union: The Feminist Reform of Sex and Society* (New York, 1980), p. 282.

[20]Clover Adams to Dr. Robert William Hooper, December 16, 1877.

[21]Josephine Shaw Lowell, *Public Relief and Private Charity* (New York, 1884), p. 111. See also Eleanor Flexner, *Century of Struggle: The Woman's Rights Movement in the United States*, rev. ed. (Cambridge, Mass., 1975), pp. 211–214.

[22]Hooper, *Poems*, BPL.

[23]Clover Adams to Dr. Robert William Hooper, December 9, 1877.

[24]Clover Adams to Dr. Robert William Hooper, November 17, 1877.

[25]Clover Adams to Dr. Robert William Hooper, December 29, 1878.

[26]Clover Adams to Dr. Robert William Hooper, February 24, 1878.

[27]Clover Adams to Dr. Robert William Hooper, May 11, 1879.

[28]F. O. Matthiessen, *American Renaissance: Art and Expression in the Age of Emerson and Whitman* (New York, 1941), p. 336.

[29]Clover Adams to Dr. Robert William Hooper, November 18, 1877.

[30]Clover Adams to Anne Palmer, May 18, 1879, Adams Papers, MHS; Clover Adams to Dr. Robert William Hooper, April 20, 1879.

[31]Henry Adams to Charles Milnes Gaskell, May 30, 1878.

[32]Clover Adams to Dr. Robert William Hooper, March 7, 1880 and June 29, 1879.

[33]Clover Adams to Dr. Robert William Hooper, March 28, 1880.

[34]Clover Adams to Dr. Robert William Hooper, May 30, 1880.

[35]Clover Adams to Dr. Robert William Hooper, May 9, 1880.

[36]Henry Adams to Charles Milnes Gaskell, February 10, 1881.

[37]Henry Adams to Charles Francis Adams, Jr., May 17, 1860.

[38]Clover Adams to Dr. Robert William Hooper, July 6, 1879.

[39]Clover Adams to Dr. Robert William Hooper, June 15, 1879.

[40]Ned Hooper to James McNeill Whistler, n.d., Knapp.

[41]Clover Adams to Dr. Robert William Hooper, July 13, 1879.

[42]Mrs. Frank E. Harris, superintendent of the Adams National Historic Site at Quincy, believed this to be the case.

[43]Clover Adams to Dr. Robert William Hooper, August 8, 1880.

[44]Clover Adams to Dr. Robert William Hooper, September 5, 1879.

[45]Jean Rhys, "Illusions," *Tigers Are Better Looking* (New York, 1976), p. 166.

[46]Clover Adams to Dr. Robert William Hooper, July 25, 1880; July 24, 1880; and June 22, 1879.

[47]Clover Adams to Dr. Robert William Hooper, April 4, 1880.

[48]Margaret Fuller, January 18, 1847, in *Memoirs of Margaret Fuller Ossoli*, ed. R. W. Emerson, W. H. Channing, and J. F. Clarke (Boston, 1899).

[49]Clover Adams to Dr. Robert William Hooper, May 9, 1880.

[50]Clover Adams to Dr. Robert William Hooper, February 27, 1880.

[51]Clover Adams to Dr. Robert William Hooper, November 11, 1883.

[52]Clover Adams to Dr. Robert William Hooper, May 24, 1880.

[53]Clover Adams to Dr. Robert William Hooper, July 18, 1880.

[54]Henry James, June 27, 1879 and October 11, 1879 in Leon Edel, ed., *The Letters of Henry James*, 2 vols. (Cambridge, Mass., 1974), vol. 2.

[55]Clover Adams to Dr. Robert William Hooper, August 31, 1879; Clover Adams to Dr. Robert William Hooper, May 23, 1880.

[56]Henry James, September 14, 1879 in Edel, *Letters*, vol. 2.

[57]Clover Adams to Dr. Robert William Hooper, August 31, 1879.

[58]Clover Adams to Dr. Robert William Hooper, October 18, 1880.

[59]Clover Adams to Dr. Robert William Hooper, September 21, 1879 and February 22, 1880.

[60]Clover Adams to Dr. Robert William Hooper, August 11, 1880.

[61]Clover Adams to Dr. Robert William Hooper, October 19, 1879.

[62]Clover Adams to Dr. Robert William Hooper, December 14, 1879 and June 6, 1880.

[63]Clover Adams to Dr. Robert William Hooper, June 6, 1880 and February 15, 1880.

[64]Clover Adams to Dr. Robert William Hooper, February 8, 1880 and July 11, 1880.

[65]Clover Adams to Dr. Robert William Hooper, August 18, 1880.

[66]Henry James, September 20, 1880 in Edel, *Letters*, vol. 2.

# Chapter 8

[1]Clover Adams to Dr. Robert William Hooper, August 1, 1880.

[2]I am indebted to Polly Kaufman of the Boston School System for this information.

[3]Worthington C. Ford to Louisa Thoron, January 11, 1937, Knapp. See references cited in Henry Nash Smith, "Emerson's Problem of Vocation: A Note on the American Scholar," *New England Quarterly* 12 (1939): n. 31.

[4]Henry Adams to Charles Milnes Gaskell, July 9, 1881: "I am working ten hours a day to get myself on the shelf"; January 29, 1882: "I write for five hours a day."

[5]Henry Adams to John Hay, October 31, 1883.

[6]Henry Adams, *History of the United States during the Administration of Jefferson and Madison*, abe. ed., vol. 1, ed. G. Dangerfield and O. M. Scruggs (Englewood Cliffs, N.J., 1968), ch. 6.

[7]Henry Adams to John Hays, June 8, 1882.

[8]Henry Adams to Charles Milnes Gaskell, October 18, 1871.

[9]Henry Adams to Charles Milnes Gaskell, October 31, 1875.

[10]Ernest Samuels, *The Middle Years*, vol. 2 of *Henry Adams* (Cambridge, Mass., 1958), p. 270.

[11]Clover Adams to Dr. Robert William Hooper, February 5, 1882.

[12]Clover Adams to Dr. Robert William Hooper, April 15, 1883.

[13]George Santayana, "The Intellectual Temper of the Age," *Winds of Doctrine* (New York, 1913), p. 19.

[14]Henry Adams to Clover Adams, April 2, 1885.

[15]Clover Adams to Dr. Robert William Hooper, January 16, 1881 and November 28, 1880.

[16]Henry Adams to Charles Milnes Gaskell, April 30, 1882.

[17]Clover Adams to Dr. Robert William Hooper, May 29, 1881.

[18]Charles Eliot Norton, *The Letters of Charles Eliot Norton with a Biographical Comment*, 2 vols., ed. Sara Norton and Mark A. DeWolfe Howe (Boston, 1913), vol. 1, p. 8.

[19]Charles Francis Adams's diary, December 15, 1877 in Martin Duberman, *Charles Francis Adams, 1807–1886* (Stanford, 1968).

[20]Thomas Woolner to Clover Adams, June 12, 1881, Adams Editorial Office Papers, MHS.

[21]The collection was catalogued by Theodore Dwight, Henry Adams' secretary and companion, and may be found in Knapp.

[22]Clover Adams to Thomas Woolner, June 12, 1881, Adams Editorial Office Papers, MHS.

[23]Thomas Woolner to Clover Adams, June 13, 1881, Adams Editorial Office Papers, MHS.

[24]Clover Adams to Dr. Robert William Hooper, January 31, 1882.

[25]Henry Adams to Robert Cunliffe, November 12, 1882.

[26]Henry Adams to Charles Milnes Gaskell, September 21, 1884.

[27]Thurman Wilkins, *Clarence King* (New York, 1958), p. 309.

[28]Clarence King, *Memoirs* (New York, 1904), p. 125.

[29]Henry Adams to Charles Milnes Gaskell, April 30, 1882.

[30]Clover Adams to Dr. Robert William Hooper, February 23, 1881.

[31]Clover Adams to Dr. Robert William Hooper, January 1, 1882 and September 21, 1882.

[32]Clover Adams to Dr. Robert William Hooper, May 8, 1882.

[33]Clover Adams to Dr. Robert William Hooper, June 13, 1882.

[34]Clover Adams to Dr. Robert William Hooper, February 18, 1883.

[35]Clover Adams to Dr. Robert William Hooper, November 6, 1881.

[36]Charles E. Rosenberg, *The Trial of the Assassin Guiteau: Psychiatry and the Law in the Gilded Age* (Chicago, 1968), p. 168.

[37]Clover Adams to Dr. Robert William Hooper, December 11, 1881.

[38]Leon Edel, ed., *The Letters of Henry James*, 2 vols. (Cambridge, Mass., 1974), vol. 1, p. 335.

[39]Henry James to Clover Adams, November 6, 1881, Adams papers, MHS.

[40]Henry James to Sir John Clark, January 8, [1882], in Edel, *Letters*, vol. 2, p. 366.

[41]Leon Edel, *Henry James: The Middle Years, 1882–1895* (Philadelphia, 1962), p. 30.

[42]Clover Adams to Dr. Robert William Hooper, January 8, 1882.

[43]ES, vol. II, p. 168.

[44]Henry James to Grace Norton, January 8, 1882.

[45]Henry James, *Portrait of a Lady* (New York, 1881), vol. II, p. 198.

[46]Ezra Pound, "Henry James," *The Literary Essays*, ed. T. S. Eliot (London, 1954), p. 296.

[47]James, *Portrait of a Lady*, p. 200. Vol. II.

[48]ES, vol. II, p. 168.

[49]Clover Adams to Dr. Robert William Hooper, May 14, 1882.

[50]Clover Adams to Dr. Robert William Hooper, March 12, 1882.

[51]Clover Adams to Dr. Robert William Hooper, April 3, 1881.

[52]Clover Adams to Dr. Robert William Hooper, May 4, 1885.

[53]Henry Adams, *Democracy and Esther*, ed. Ernest Samuels (New York, 1961), p. 71.

[54]Clover Adams to Dr. Robert William Hooper, December 2, 1883.

[55]Henry Adams to Charles Milnes Gaskell, February 8, 1885.

[56]Henry Adams to Elizabeth Cameron, December 7, 1884.

[57]Henry Adams to John Hay, March 4, 1883.

[58]Ernest Samuels, *Bernard Berenson: The Making of a Connoisseur* (Cambridge, Mass., 1979), p. 65. See addendum on page 279.

[59]Henry Adams to Charles Milnes Gaskell, January 21, 1883.

[60]Henry Adams to Charles Milnes Gaskell, April 30, 1882.

[61]Henry Adams to Henry Cabot Lodge, November 15, 1881.

[62]Henry Adams to Charles Milnes Gaskell, November 8, 1885.

[63]James, *Portrait of a Lady*, vol. II, p. 199.

[64]F. O. Matthiessen, *The James Family: A Group Biography* (New York, 1948), p. 634.

[65]Henry Adams to Henry Cabot Lodge, October 29, 1881.

[66]Adams, *Democracy and Esther*, p. 273.

[67]*Ibid.*, p. 247.

[68]*Ibid.*, p. 366.

[69]Robert Taft, *Photography and the American Scene: A Social History, 1839–1899* (New York, 1938), p. 204.

[70]Clover Adams to Dr. Robert William Hooper, December 31, 1883.

[71]Whitman Gurney to Charles Eliot Norton, January 18, 1874.

[72]See David Levin, *History as Romantic Art: Bancroft, Prescott, Motley, and Parkman* (Stanford, 1959).

[73]Clover Adams to Dr. Robert William Hooper, February 24, 1884.

[74]Clover Adams to Dr. Robert William Hooper, December 2, 1883.

[75]John Hay to Richard Watson Gilder, December 29, 1883, in John Hay, *Letters and Extracts from a Diary*, 3 vols., selected by Henry Adams (privately printed, 1908), vol. 2, p. 86.

[76]Henry Adams to John Hay, January 6, 1884.

[77]Clover Adams to Dr. Robert William Hooper, January 6, 1884.

[78]Henry Adams to John Hay, August 28, 1883.

[79]J. C. Levenson, *The Mind and Art of Henry Adams* (Cambridge, Mass., 1957), p. 10. It may be worth noting that all the Adams archivists have honored Henry's opinions; no attempt to collect and publish Clover's photographs has ever been made.

[80]Clover Adams to Dr. Robert William Hooper, April 8, 1883.

[81]See Eleanor Flexner, *Century of Struggle: The Woman's Rights Movement in the United States*, rev. ed. (Cambridge, Mass., 1975), pp. 212–214; Clover Adams to Anne Palmer, April 21, 1883; Clover Adams to Dr. Robert William Hooper, April 22, 1883.

[82]Clover Adams to Dr. Robert William Hooper, May 25, 1884.

[83]Clover Adams to Dr. Robert William Hooper, May 15, 1881.

[84]ES, vol. II, p. 241.

[85]Adams, *Democracy and Esther*, p. 228.

[86]Ralph Waldo Emerson, "Aristocracy," *Essays, Poems, Lectures*, 12 vols., ed. J. E. Cabot (Boston, 1883), vol. 10, p. 47.

[87]Clover Adams to Dr. Robert William Hooper, April 6, 1884; February 10, 1884; April 2, 1884; and April 21, 1883.

[88]Clover Adams to Dr. Robert William Hooper, December 16, 1883.

[89]Clover Adams to Dr. Robert William Hooper, January 8, 1882; December 24, 1882; and April 29, 1883.

[90]Clover Adams to Dr. Robert William Hooper, February 19, 1882.

[91]Walt Whitman, "When Lilacs Last in the Dooryard Bloom'd," *Leaves of Grass* (New York, 1944), p. 376.

[92]Clover Adams to Dr. Robert William Hooper, April 20, 1884.

[93]Clover Adams to Dr. Robert William Hooper, January 11, 1884.

[94]Clover Adams to Dr. Robert William Hooper, March 30, 1884.

[95]Henry Hobson Richardson to Henry Adams, June 7, 1885.
[96]Henry Adams to Theodore Dwight, September 26, 1885.
[97]Henry Hobson Richardson to Henry Adams, September 27, 1885.
[98]Henry Adams to John Hay, January 18, 1883.
[99]Henry Hobson Richardson to Henry Adams, July 6, 1885.

# Chapter 9

[1]Henry Adams, *Democracy and Esther*, ed. Ernest Samuels (New York, 1961), p. 348.
[2]See Millicent Bell, "Adams' *Esther*: The Morality of Taste," *New England Quarterly* (June 1962).
[3]Adams, *Democracy and Esther*, p. 364, 368.
[4]Ralph Waldo Emerson, "Divinity School Address," *Essays, Poems, Lectures*, 12 vols., ed. J. E. Cabot (Boston, 1883), vol. 1, p. 138.
[5]Mark A. DeWolfe Howe, The Tale of Tanglewood," *Yale Review*, Winter, 1943.
[6]Clover Adams to Dr. Robert William Hooper, July 26, 1883.
[7]For examples of the impact of nineteenth-century religion on different kinds of feminine temperaments, see Ann Douglas, *The Feminization of American Culture* (New York, 1977); Kathryn Kish Sklar, *Catherine Beecher: A Study in American Domesticity* (New Haven, 1973); Richard B. Sewall, *The Life of Emily Dickinson*, 2 vols. (New York, 1974).
[8]Clover Adams to Dr. Robert William Hooper, February 17, 1884.
[9]Clover Adams to Dr. Robert William Hooper, February 21, 1883 and December 9, 1883.
[10]Ernest Samuels, *The Middle Years*, vol. 2 in *Henry Adams* (Cambridge, Mass., 1958), p. 226.
[11]Henry Adams to William James, July 27, 1882.
[12]Clover Adams to Dr. Robert William Hooper, May 6, 1883.
[13]Henry Adams to Oliver Wendell Holmes, January 4, 1885.
[14]Ellen Sturgis Hooper, *Poems*, BPL.
[15]William James to Henry Adams, June 29, 1901, Knapp.
[16]Adams, *Democracy and Esther*, p. 296.
[17]*Ibid.*, p. 33.
[18]Charles Francis Adams, Jr., to his wife, April 28, 1873 and May 3, 1873.
[19]Charles Francis Adams to Henry Adams, January 29, 1878.
[20]Henry Adams to John Hay, April 12, 1885.
[21]Sigmund Freud, "Mourning and Melancholia," *Collected Papers of Sigmund Freud*, vol. 4, trans. Joan Riviere (New York, 1959), p. 161.
[22]*Ibid.*, p. 158.
[23]Adams, *Democracy and Esther*, p. 288.
[24]Louis Zukofsky, "Henry Adams: A Criticism in Autobiography," *Prepositions* (New York, 1967), p. 113.
[25]Clover Adams to Dr. Robert William Hooper, March 5, 1885.

[26]Clover Adams to Dr. Robert William Hooper, April 9, 1882; Clover Adams to Anne Palmer, April 26, 1885, Adams Papers, MHS.

[27]Henry Adams to Charles Milnes Gaskell, May 10, 1885.

[28]Henry Adams to Charles Milnes Gaskell, August 30, 1885.

[29]Ellen Gurney to Mrs. J. E. Cabot, January 1, 1886, Swann.

[30]For a list of distinguished Greek suicides, see A. Alvarez, *The Savage God: A Study of Suicide* (London, 1971), p. 61.

[31]Henry Adams to Charles Milnes Gaskell, August 31, 1875.

[32]Henry Adams, *EHA*, ed. Ernest Samuels (Boston, 1973; orig. pub. 1907), p. 445.

[33]John Hay to Henry Adams, December 9, 1885; ES, vol. II, p. 282.

[34]Leon Edel, *Henry James*, 5 vols. (New York, 1953–1972), vol. 3, p. 166.

[35]Henry James, "The Modern Warning," *Complete Tales of Henry James*, 12 vols., ed. Leon Edel (Philadelphia, 1963), vol. 7, pp. 50, 57.

[36]*Ibid.*, p. 75.

[37]See L. G. Siggins, "Mourning: A Critical Survey of the Literature," *International Journal of Psychoanalysis* 47 (1966); Edwin S. Shneidman, ed., *Essays in Self-Destruction* (New York, 1967); Humberto Nagera, "Children's Reactions to the Death of Important Objects," *Psychoanalytic Study of the Child* 25 (New York, 1970); Herbert Hendin, *Suicide and Scandinavia: A Psychoanalytic Study of Culture and Character* (New York, 1964).

[38]Ellen Sturgis Hooper to Carrie Sturgis, n.d., Swann. The involvement of many upper-class women in Abolitionist activity must also be seen as symbolically self-liberating. After the Civil War many more women turned their energies toward women's rights with greater assurance: "Margaret Fuller (1810–1850): Her Work as an Art Critic," Adele M. Holcomb and Corlette R. Walker, in *Women as Interpreters of the Visual Arts, 1820–1979*, ed. Claire R. Sherman (Westport, Conn., 1981), p. 142.

[39]Nathaniel Hawthorne, *The Blithedale Romance*, ed. G. P. Lathrop (Boston, 1883), p. 573.

[40]ES, vol. II, p. 139.

[41]Adams, *Democracy and Esther*, p. 230.

[42]Carrie Sturgis Tappan to her mother, n.d., Knapp, and August 26, 1881, Swann.

[43]Elizabeth Peabody to Carrie Sturgis Tappan, February 12, 1837, Knapp.

[44]Ellen Sturgis Hooper to Carrie Sturgis Tappan, n.d., 1840, Swann.

[45]Adams, *Democracy and Esther*, p. 223.

[46]Henry James to William James, March 29, 1870 in Leon Edel, ed., *The Letters of Henry James*, 2 vols. (Cambridge, Mass., 1974), vol. 1, p. 223.

[47]Clover Adams to Dr. Robert William Hooper, November 18, 1883.

[48]Edward Waldo Emerson, *The Early Years of the Saturday Club* (Boston, 1918).

[49]Emile Durkheim, *Suicide: A Study in Sociology*, ed. George Simpson (New York, 1951).

[50]Henry Adams to Charles Milnes Gaskell, February 6, 1876.

[51]Durkheim, *Suicide*, p. 158.

[52]*Ibid.*, p. 240.

[53]See Nancy F. Cott, *The Bonds of Womanhood: "Woman's Sphere" in New Eng-*

*land, 1780–1835* (New Haven, 1977) for early examples of women's networks; Henry Adams to John Hay, March 4, 1883.

[54]Durkheim, *Suicide*, p. 364.

[55]*Ibid.*, p. 323.

[56]See the writings of Van Wyck Brooks, which reflect the angry tone of the disappointed idealist.

[57]Durkheim, *Suicide*, pp. 364–365.

[58]Henry Adams to Francis Parkman, December 21, 1884.

[59]Clover Adams to Anne Palmer, April 26, 1885, Adams Misc., MHS.

[60]Katherine Simonds, "The Tragedy of Mrs. Henry Adams," *New England Quarterly* 9 (December 1936): 570.

[61]Quoted by Ephraim Peabody to Mrs. Swain, November 6, 1848, Knapp. Copy also in Swann; Carrie Sturgis to Ellen Sturgis Hooper, n.d., Swann.

[62]Harvard Class of 1852, Harvard Archives.

[63]Francis Parkman to Edwin L. Godkin, *Letters of Francis Parkman*, 2 vols., ed. Wilbur R. Jacobs (Norman, Okla., 1960), vol. 2, p. 217.

[64]Henry Adams to Charles Milnes Gaskell, December 12, 1886.

[65]Ellen [Lothrop] to [?] Brimmer, December 11, 1887, Knapp.

[66]See R. J. Cadoret and J. Dorzob, "Depressive Disease: A Genetic Study," *Archives of General Psychiatry* 24 (1971); R. J. Cadoret and G. Winokur, G., "Genetic Studies of Affective Disorders," in *The Nature and Treatment of Depression*, ed. F. F. Flach and S. C. Draghi (1975); J. Price, "The Genetics of Depressive Behavior," in *Recent Developments in Affective Disorders*, ed. A. Coppen and A. Walk, *British Journal of Psychiatry*—Special Publication No. 2 (1968) or the more comprehensive texts: Solomon Snyder, ed., *Biochemistry and Behavior* (Cambridge, 1976); G. Winokur, P. J. Clayton, and T. Reich, *Manic Depressive Illness* (St. Louis, 1969). I am indebted to Dr. Joseph Lipinski of the Mailman Center for Psychiatric Research, McLean Hospital, Belmont, Mass. for these references.

# Chapter 10

[1]William H. Goetzmann, *Exploration and Empire: The Explorer and the Scientist in the Winning of the American West* (New York, 1966), p. 465.

[2]Sigmund Freud, "Mourning and Melancholia," *Collected Papers of Sigmund Freud*, vol. 4, tr. Joan Riviere (New York, 1917), p. 158. See also Freud's *Totem and Taboo* (New York, 1918), p. 80: "Obsessive reproaches are in a certain sense justified and therefore are immune to refutation or objections. Not that the mourner has really been careless, as the obsessive reproach asserts; but still there was something in her [him], a wish of which she herself [he himself] was aware which was not displeased with the fact that death came, and which would have brought it about sooner had it been strong enough. The reproach now reacts against this unconscious wish after the death of the beloved person. Such hostility hidden in the unconscious behind tender love exists in almost all

cases of intensive emotional allegiance to a particular person, indeed it represents the classic case, the prototype of the ambivalence of human emotions."

[3]Ralph L. Rusk, *The Life of Ralph Waldo Emerson* (New York, 1949), pp. 159–160.

[4]Henry Adams, *EHA*, ed. Ernest Samuels (Boston, 1973; orig. pub. 1907), p. 63.

[5]Ferner Nuhn, *The Wind Blew from the East: A Study in the Orientation of American Culture* (Port Washington, N.Y., 1967; orig. pub. 1940), p. 191.

[6]Adams, *EHA*, p. 62.

[7]See Roy Schafer, *Aspects of Internalization* (New York, 1968), p. 144: "The process of identifying one spirit with another is unconscious, though it may also have prominent and significant conscious components; in this process the subject modifies his motives and behavior patterns, and the self-representations corresponding to them, in such a way as to experience being like, the same as, and merged with one or more representations of that object; through identification, the subject both represents as his own one or more regulatory influences or characteristics that have become important to him and continue his tie to the object."

[8]Sister M. Aquinas Healy, "A Study of Non-Rational Elements in the Work of Henry Adams as Centralized in His Attitude Toward Women," unpub. Ph.D. thesis (University of Wisconsin, 1956).

[9]Adams, *EHA*, p. 85.

[10]Schafer, *Aspects*, p. 147: "Identifications cannot be created out of nothing. They involve selective reorganization of already existing wishes, behavior capacities, viewpoints and emphases—and quite possibly earlier identifications too. . . . It is the reorganization itself (and the accompanying fantasy of continued but revised object relation) that is the novelty in identification. And since this reorganization selectively opens up and closes down certain lines of action, learning, and development, it paves a particular route toward new experience, activity and capacity."

[11]J. C. Levenson, *The Mind and Art of Henry Adams* (Boston, 1957), p. 216.

[12]Henry Adams to Charles Milnes Gaskell, August 22, 1886.

[13]Henry Adams to Ellen Hooper, December 27, 1890.

[14]Henry Adams to Henry Cabot Lodge, September 28, 1915.

[15]Levenson, *Mind and Art* p. 217.

[16]Adams, *EHA*, p. 370.

[17]Henry Adams to C. W. Eliot, November 13, 1886.

[18]Henry Adams to Henry James, November 18, 1903.

[19]Henry James to Henry Adams, November 19, 1903 in Leon Edel, ed., *The Letters of Henry James*, 2 vols. (Cambridge, Mass., 1974), vol. 2.

[20]Adams, *EHA*, p. 56.

[21]Ralph Waldo Emerson, "Aristocracy," *Essays, Poems, Lectures*, 12 vols., ed. J. E. Cabot (Boston, 1883), vol. 10, p. 65.

[22]Edmund Wilson, "The Life of George Cabot Lodge," in *The Shock of Recognition: The Development of Literature in the United States Recorded by the Men Who Made It*, 2 vols. (New York, 1943), vol. 2, p. 749.

[23]*Ibid.*, p. 751.

[24]*Ibid.*, pp. 751, 823.

[25]Tony Tanner, ed., "The Fearful Self: Henry James's *Portrait of a Lady*," *Henry James: Modern Judgments* (London, 1968), ed. T. Tanner (ref. to Lionel Trilling's essay on W. D. Howells in *The Opposing Self*), p. 152.

[26]Henry Adams to Henry Holt, March 8, 1886.

[27]Henry Adams to Anna Barker Ward, December 22, 1885.

[28]Henry Adams to T. F. Bayard, January 20, 1886.

[29]Adams, *EHA*, p. 329.

[30]Henry Adams to Augustus Saint-Gaudens, April 30, 1902, Knapp.

[31]Henry Adams to Richard Watson Gilder, October 14, 1896.

[32]Henry Adams to Edwin L. Godkin, December 20, 1894.

[33]A. B. Blackwell, "On Marriage and Work," in Nancy Cott, ed., *The Roots of Bitterness* (New York, 1972), p. 354.

[34]Henry Adams to Whitelaw Reid, February 15, 1909.

[35]Walt Whitman, "Crossing Brooklyn Ferry," *Leaves of Grass*, p. 185.

[36]Adams, *EHA*, p. 315.

[37]Emerson, "Aristocracy," *Essays*, pp. 59–60.

Addendum to n. 58, chapter 8 (p. 273): After Clover's death, Clarence King married an African American under an assumed name and John Hay had a notorious affair not mentioned in earlier books on "the five of hearts."

# Bibliography

The books and articles listed below contributed to my understanding of the issues and problems discussed in the text. For a more comprehensive specific bibliography of Henry Adams, consult Ernest Samuels' three-volume biography, or the two bibliographical articles on Henry Adams by Charles Vandersee, which have appeared in *American Literary Realism, 1910–1970* (Summer, 1969; Winter, 1975). A condensed introduction to the six volumes of Henry Adams' letters, also by Charles Vandersee, appeared in "Henry Adams: Archives and Microfilm," *Resources for American Literary Study* (Spring, 1979).

## The Adams Family

Aaron, Daniel. "Henry Adams: The Public and Private View." *Hudson Review* 5 (Winter, 1953).

Adams, Charles Francis. *Familiar Letters of John Adams and His Wife Abigail Adams, during the Revolution.* Cambridge, Mass., 1876.

———. "Memoir of Abigail Smith Adams." In *The Letters of Mrs. Adams, The Wife of John Adams.* Boston, 1840.

Adams, Charles Francis, Jr. *An Autobiography.* Boston, 1916.

———. *Memorabilia.* In Woodrow Wilson Papers, Princeton, ed. John E. Little. unpub.

Adams, Henry. "Buddha and Brahma." *Yale Review* 5 (October 1915).

———. "Clarke's Building of a Brain." *North American Review* 120 (January 1875).

———. *The Degradation of the Democratic Dogma.* New York, 1969.

———. *Democracy and Esther,* ed. Ernest Samuels. New York, 1961.

———. "Dr. Clarke's 'Sex in Education'." *North American Review* 118 (January 1874).

————. *The Education of Henry Adams*, ed. Ernest Samuels. 1907. Reprint. Boston, 1973.

————. *History of the United States During the Administrations of Jefferson and Madison*, Abr. and ed. G. Dangerfield and O. M. Scruggs. Englewood Cliffs, N.J., 1968.

————. *Letters of Henry Adams, 1858–1891; 1892–1918.* ed. Worthington C. Ford. 2 vols. Boston, 1930; 1938.

————. *Letters to a Niece and Prayer to the Virgin of Chartres*, ed. Mabel La Farge. Boston, 1920.

————. *The Life of George Cabot Lodge.* Boston, 1911.

————. *Memoirs of Marau Taaroa, Last Queen of Tahiti.* Privately printed, 1893.

————. *Mont-Saint-Michel and Chartres.* Boston, 1905.

————. "Primitive Rights of Women." In *Historical Essays.* New York, 1891.

————. *The Selected Letters of Henry Adams*, ed. Newton Arvin. New York, 1951.

————. "William Dean Howells' *Their Wedding Journey*." *North American Review* 114 (April 1872).

Adams, James Truslow. *Henry Adams.* New York, 1933.

Adams, Louisa Catherine. *The Adventures of a Nobody.* In Adams Papers, Adams Manuscript Trust microfilm 269. July, 1840.

————. Miscellaneous poetry. In Adams Papers, Adams Manuscript Trust microfilm 601.

*The Adams Memorial*, Eastern National Park and Monument Association, Saint-Gaudens National Historic Site. Cornish, N.H., 1970.

Anderson, Thornton. *Brooks Adams: Constructive Conservative.* Ithaca, 1951.

Baym, M. I. *The French Education of Henry Adams.* New York, 1951.

Bell, Millicent. "Adams' *Esther*: The Morality of Taste." *New England Quarterly* 35 (June 1962).

Beringause, Arthur F. *Brooks Adams.* New York, 1955.

Blackmur, Richard P. *The Expense of Greatness.* 1940. Reprint. New York, 1958.

————. *Henry Adams*, ed. Veronica Makowsky. New York, 1980.

————. *A Primer of Ignorance*, ed. Joseph Frank. New York, 1940.

Blunt, Hugh F. "The Mal-Education of Henry Adams." *Catholic World* 14 (April 1937).

Butterfield, Lyman H. "The Papers of the Adams Family." *Proceedings of the Massachusetts Historical Society (1953–1957).* Cambridge, Mass., 1971.

————, ed. *The Book of Abigail and John: Selected Letters of the Adams Family, 1762–1784.* Cambridge, Mass., 1975.

Cater, Harold Dean, ed. *Henry Adams and His Friends.* Boston, 1947.

Conder, John. *A Formula of His Own: Henry Adams's Literary Experiment.* Chicago, 1970.

Cox, James M. "Autobiography and America." *Virginia Quarterly Review* 47 (Spring, 1971).

Duberman, Martin. *Charles Francis Adams, 1807–1886.* Stanford, 1968.

————. *James Russell Lowell.* Boston, 1966.

Dusinberre, William. *Henry Adams: The Myth of Failure.* Charlottesville, N.C., 1980.

Harbert, Earl N. *The Force So Much Closer To Home: Henry Adams and The Adams Family.* New York, 1977.

Healy, Sister M. Aquinas. "A Study of Non-Rational Elements in the Works of

Henry Adams as Centralized in His Attitude toward Women." Unpub. Ph.D. thesis, University of Wisconsin, 1956.

Hipolito, Jane. "The Secret World of Henry Adams." Unpub. Ph.D. thesis, UCLA, 1968.

Homans, Abigail. *Education by Uncles*. Boston, 1966.

Jordy, William H. *Henry Adams: Scientific Historian*. New Haven, 1952.

Kirkland, Edward C. *Charles Francis Adams, Jr., 1835–1915: The Patrician at Bay*. Cambridge, Mass., 1965.

Levenson, J. C. "Henry Adams and the Culture of Science." *Studies in American Culture: Dominant Ideas and Images*, ed. Joseph J. Kwiat and Mary C. Turpie. Minneapolis, 1960.

————. *The Mind and Art of Henry Adams*. Cambridge, Mass., 1957.

Lyon, Melvin. *Symbol and Idea in Henry Adams*. Lincoln, Neb., 1970.

Mane, Robert. *Henry Adams on the Road to Chartres*. Cambridge, Mass., 1971.

Mumford, Lewis. "Apology to Henry Adams." *Virginia Quarterly* 38 (Spring, 1962).

Rowe, John Carlos. *Henry Adams and Henry James: The Emergence of a Modern Consciousness*. Ithaca, 1976.

Samuels, Ernest. "Henry Adams and the Gossip Mills." In *Essays in American and English Literature Presented to Bruce McElderry, Jr.*, ed. Max Schulz. Athens, Ohio, 1968.

————. *The Young Henry Adams*. vol. 1 of *Henry Adams*. 3 vols. Cambridge, Mass., 1948.

————. *The Middle Years*. vol. 2 of *Henry Adams*. 3 vols. Cambridge, Mass., 1958.

————. *The Major Phase*. vol. 3 of *Henry Adams*. 3 vols. Cambridge, Mass., 1964.

Scheyer, Ernst. *The Circle of Henry Adams: Art and Artists*. Detroit, 1970.

Simonds, Katherine. "The Tragedy of Mrs. Henry Adams." *New England Quarterly* 9 (December 1936).

Spiller, Robert. *The Oblique Light*. New York, 1948.

————, et al. *Literary History of the United States*. New York, 1946.

Stevenson, Elizabeth. *A Henry Adams Reader*. New York, 1958.

————. *Henry Adams: A Biography*. New York, 1956.

Thoron, Ward, ed. *The Letters of Mrs. Henry Adams: 1865–1883*. Boston, 1936.

Vandersee, Charles. "The Hamlet in Henry Adams." *Shakespeare Survey* 24. Cambridge, Eng., 1971.

————. "The Pursuit of Culture in Adams' *Democracy*." *American Quarterly* 19 (Summer, 1967).

Wagner, Vern. *The Suspension of Henry Adams: A Study of Manner and Matter*. Detroit, 1969.

Zukofsky, Louis. "Henry Adams: A Criticism in Autobiography." *Prepositions*. New York, 1967.

# General Intellectual Background

Aaron, Daniel. *The Unwritten War: American Writers and the Civil War*. New York, 1973.

Ahlstrom, Sydney E. *A Religious History of the American People*. New Haven, 1972.

Albanese, Catherine L. *Corresponding Motion: Transcendental Religion and the New America*. Philadelphia, 1972.

Andrews, Edward Deming. *The People Called Shakers: A Search for the Perfect Society*. New York, 1953.

Armstrong, William M., ed. *Sisyphus in Sodom: The Gilded Age Letters of E. L. Godkin*. Albany, 1974.

Ballowe, James C. "The Last Puritan and the Failure of American Culture." *American Quarterly* 18 (Summer, 1966).

Bercovitch, Sacvan. "How the Puritans Won the American Revolution." *Massachusetts Review* 17 (Winter, 1976).

Bergonzi, Berhard. *The Situation of the Novel*. London, 1970.

Berthoff, Warner. *The Ferment of Realism: American Literature, 1884–1919*. New York, 1965.

Bewley, Marius. *The Complex Fate: Hawthorne, Henry James, and Some American Writers*. London, 1954.

Boller, Paul F., Jr. *American Transcendentalism, 1830–1860: An Intellectual Inquiry*. New York, 1974.

Bradford, Gamaliel. *Damaged Souls: Discredited Figures in American History*. Boston, 1923.

———. *Portraits of American Women*. New York, 1919.

Brown, Francis A. *Harvard University in the War of 1861–1865: A Record of Service*. Cambridge, Mass., 1886.

Callcott, George H. *History in the United States, 1800–1860: Its Practice and Purpose*. Baltimore, 1970.

Cameron, Julia M. *Victorian Photographs of Famous Men and Fair Women*, ed. Tristram Powell. Boston, 1973.

Carlyle, Jane Welsh. *I Too Am Here: Selected Letters*, ed. Alan and Mary McQueen Simpson. Cambridge, Mass., 1972.

Chase, Richard. *The American Novel and Its Tradition*. Garden City, N.Y., 1957.

Clark, Kenneth. *The Romantic Rebellion: Romantic Versus Classic Art*. New York, 1973.

Conrad, Susan. *Perish the Thought: Intellectual Women in Romantic America*. New York, 1976.

Craven, Wayne. *Sculpture in America*. New York, 1968.

Davidoff, Leonore. *The Best Circles: Women and Society in Victorian England*. London, 1973.

Dobson, John. *Politics in the Gilded Age: A New Perspective on Reform*. New York, 1972.

Douglas, Ann. *The Feminization of American Culture*. New York, 1977.

Feidelson, Charles, Jr. *Symbolism and American Literature*. Chicago, 1953.

Fiedler, Leslie H. *Love and Death in the American Novel*. rev. ed. New York, 1966.

Flexner, Eleanor. *Century of Struggle: The Woman's Rights Movement in the United States*. rev. ed. Cambridge, Mass., 1975.

Fredrickson, George M. *The Inner Civil War: Northern Intellectuals and the Crisis of the Union*. New York, 1965.

285

BIBLIOGRAPHY

Frothingham, Octavius B. *Transcendentalism in New England: A History*. New York, 1959.

Goetzmann, William H. *Exploration and Empire: The Explorer and the Scientist in the Winning of the American West*. New York, 1966.

Goodman, Paul. "Ethics and Enterprise: The Values of the Boston Elite, 1800–1860." *American Quarterly* 28 (Fall, 1966).

Guttmann, Allan. *The Conservative Tradition in America*. New York, 1967.

Hayden, Dolores. *Seven American Utopias: The Architecture of Communitarian Socialism, 1790–1975*. Cambridge, Mass., 1976.

Hofstadter, Richard. *Social Darwinism in American Thought, 1860–1915*. Philadelphia, 1945.

Howe, Daniel Walker, ed. "Victorian Culture in America." *American Quarterly* 27 (December 1975).

Jones, Howard M. *The Age of Energy: Varieties of American Experience, 1865–1915*. New York, 1971.

Kaplan, Harold. *Democratic Humanism and American Literature*. Chicago, 1972.

Lash, Joseph P. *Eleanor and Franklin*. New York, 1971.

Leach, William. *True Love and Perfect Union: The Feminist Reform of Sex and Society*. New York, 1980.

Leech, Margaret. *Reveille in Washington: 1860–1865*. New York, 1941.

Levin, David. *History as Romantic Art: Bancroft, Prescott, Motley, and Parkman*. New York, 1959.

Lewis, R. W. B. *The American Adam: Innocence, Tragedy and Tradition in the Nineteenth Century*. Chicago, 1955.

Martin, Jay. *Harvests of Change: American Literature, 1865–1914*. Englewood Cliffs, N.J., 1967.

Marx, Leo. *The Machine in the Garden: Technology and the Pastoral Ideal in America*. New York, 1964.

Matthiessen, F. O., ed. *The American Novels and Stories of Henry James*. New York, 1964.

———. *American Renaissance: Art and Expression in the Age of Emerson and Whitman*. New York, 1941.

———, and Kenneth Murdock, eds., *The Notebooks of Henry James*. New York, 1947.

———. *The James Family: A Group Biography*. New York, 1947.

Maxwell, William. *Lincoln's Fifth Wheel: The Political History of the U.S. Sanitary Commission*. New York, 1956.

Miller, D. T. *Jacksonian Aristocracy: Class and Democracy in New York, 1830–1860*. New York, 1967.

Miller, Perry, ed. *American Thought: Civil War to World War One*. New York, 1954.

———. *Errand into the Wilderness*. Cambridge, Mass., 1956.

———, ed. *Margaret Fuller: American Romantic*. New York, 1963.

———. *Nature's Nation*. Cambridge, Mass., 1967.

———, ed. *The Transcendentalists: An Anthology*. Cambridge, Mass., 1950.

Nuhn, Ferner. *The Wind Blew from the East: A Study in the Orientation of American Culture*. 1940. Reprint. Port Washington, N.Y., 1967.

Peabody, Elizabeth, ed. *Aesthetic Papers*. Boston, 1849.

Peckham, Morse. *Victorian Revolutionaries: Speculations on Some Heroes of a Culture Crisis.* New York, 1970.

Poirier, Richard. *A World Elsewhere: The Place of Style in American Literature.* New York, 1966.

Raleigh, John H. *Matthew Arnold and American Culture.* Berkeley, 1961.

Rose, Willie Lee *Rehearsal for Reconstruction: The Port Royal Experiment.* New York, 1964.

Rosenberg, Charles E. "The Bitter Fruit: Hereditary Disease and Social Thought in Nineteenth-Century America." *Perspectives in American History* 8. Cambridge, Mass., 1974.

———. *The Trial of the Assassin Guiteau: Psychiatry and the Law in the Gilded Age.* Chicago, 1968.

Ruskin, John. *Beauty and Nature.* New York, 1858.

Santayana, George. *The Genteel Tradition: Nine Essays by George Santayana,* ed. Douglas L. Wilson. Cambridge, Mass., 1967.

———. *The Last Puritan: A Memoir in the Form of a Novel.* New York, 1936.

———. *Winds of Doctrine.* New York, 1913.

Schlesinger, Arthur M., Jr., *The Age of Jackson.* Boston, 1953.

Sewall, Richard B. *The Life of Emily Dickinson.* 2 vols. New York, 1974.

Shea, Daniel B., Jr. *Spiritual Autobiography in Early America.* Princeton, 1968.

Sherman, Claire R. with Adele Holcomb, ed. *Women As Interpreters of the Visual Arts, 1820–1979.* Westport, Conn., 1981.

Sklar, Kathryn Kish. *Catherine Beecher: A Study in American Domesticity.* New Haven, 1973.

Solomon, Barbara M. *Ancestors and Immigrants.* Cambridge, Mass., 1956.

Sontag, Susan. *Illness As Metaphor.* New York, 1978.

Spacks, Patricia Meyer. *The Female Imagination.* Cambridge, Mass., 1975.

Stannard, David, ed. "Death in America." *American Quarterly* 26 (December 1974)

Steegman, John. *Victorian Taste: A Study of the Arts and Architecture from 1830 to 1870.* Cambridge, Mass., 1971.

Stein, Roger. *John Ruskin and Aesthetic Thought in America, 1840–1900.* Cambridge, Mass., 1967.

Stone, Albert E. "Autobiography and American Culture." *American Studies* 11, no. 2 (Winter, 1972).

Sussman, Herbert L. *Victorians and the Machine: Literary Response to Technology.* Cambridge, Mass., 1968.

Taft, Lorado. *History of American Sculpture.* New York, 1903.

Taft, Robert. *Photography and the American Scene: A Social History, 1839–1889.* New York, 1938.

Tharp, Louise Hall. "The Appletons of Beacon Hill." New York, 1973.

Tompkins, Calvin. *Merchants and Masterpieces: The Story of the Metropolitan Museum of Art.* New York, 1973.

Trachtenberg, Alan, ed. *Democratic Vistas, 1860–1880.* New York, 1970.

Trilling, Lionel. *Freud and the Crisis of Our Culture.* Boston, 1955.

Warren, Austin. *The New England Conscience.* Ann Arbor, Mich., 1966.

Wilson, Edmund. "Notes on Gentile Pro-Semitism: New England's 'Good Jew.'" *Commentary,* vol. 22, no. 4 (October 1956).

———. *Patriotic Gore: Studies in the Literature of the American Civil War*. New York, 1962.

———, ed. *The Shock of Recognition: The Development of Literature in the United States Recorded by the Men Who Made It*. 2 vols. New York, 1943.

———. *The Triple Thinkers: Twelve Essays on Literary Subjects*. New York, 1963.

Woody, Thomas. *A History of Women's Education in the United States*. 2 vols. New York, 1929.

# Friends and Influences

Baldwin, David. "Puritan Aristocrat in the Age of Emerson: A Study of Samuel Gray Ward." Unpub. Ph.D. thesis, University of Pennsylvania, 1961.

Bancroft, Elizabeth Davif. *Letters from England, 1846–1849*. New York, 1904.

Bartlett, Irving H. *Wendell Phillips: Brahmin Radical*. Boston, 1961.

Barzun, Jacques, ed. *Selected Writings of John Jay Chapman*. New York, 1957.

Birdsall, Richard D. *Berkshire County: A Cultural History*. New Haven, 1959.

Blanchard, Paula. *Margaret Fuller: From Transcendentalist to Revolutionary*. New York, 1978.

Brooks, Van Wyck. *The Dream of Arcadia: American Writers and Artists in Italy, 1760–1915*. New York, 1958.

———. *Fenellosa and His Circle*. New York, 1962.

———. *The Life of Emerson*. New York, 1932.

———. *New England Indian Summer, 1865–1915*. New York, 1940.

———. *Opinions of Oliver Allston*. New York, 1941.

Buitenhuis, Peter. *The Grasping Imagination: A Study of the American Writings of Henry James*. Toronto, 1970.

Burr, Anna R. *S. Weir Mitchell: His Life and Letters*. New York, 1929.

Carter, Morris. *Isabella Stewart Gardner and Fenway Court*. Boston, 1925.

Chanler, Mrs. Winthrop. *Autumn in the Valley*. Boston, 1936.

———. *Roman Spring*. Boston, 1934.

Chapman, John J. *Memories and Milestones*. New York, 1915.

Cheney, Ednah Dow. *Reminiscences*. Boston, 1902.

Chevigny, Bell Gale. "Growing Out of New England: The Emergence of Margaret Fuller's Radicalism." *Women's Studies*, vol. 5, no. 1 (1977). Queens College.

———. *The Woman and the Myth: Margaret Fuller's Life and Writings*. Old Westbury, Conn., 1976.

Cortissoz, Royal. *John La Farge, a Memoir and a Study*. Boston, 1911.

Dannett, Sylvia G. *Noble Women of the North*. New York, 1959.

Deiss, Joseph J. *The Roman Years of Margaret Fuller*. New York, 1969.

Edel, Leon, ed. *The Letters of Henry James*. 2 vols. Cambridge, Mass., 1974.

———. *Henry James*. 5 vols. New York, 1953–1972.

Elliott, Maud Howe. *Uncle Sam Ward and His Circle*. New York, 1938.

Emerson, Edward Waldo. *The Early Years of the Saturday Club*. Boston, 1918.

Emerson, Ralph Waldo. *Essays, Poems, Lectures*, ed. J. E. Cabot. 12 vols. Boston, 1883.

——. *Journals*, ed. and annot. E. W. Emerson and W. E. Forbes. 10 vols. Boston, 1909.

——. *Letters of Ralph Waldo Emerson*, ed. Ralph Rusk. 6 vols. New York, 1939.

——. *Letters to a Friend, 1838–1853*, ed. C. E. Norton. Boston, 1899.

——. *Parnassus*, ed. an Anthology of Favorite Poems. Boston, 1874.

Fuller, Margaret. *Memoirs of Margaret Fuller Ossoli*, ed. R. W. Emerson, W. H. Channing, and J. F. Clarke. Boston, 1852.

Friedlaender, Marc. "H. H. Richardson, Henry Adams, and John Hay." *Journal of the Society of Architectural Historians* 29 (October 1970).

Gray, John Chipman, and John Codman Ropes. *War Letters, 1862–1865*. Boston, 1927.

Hawkins, Hugh. *Between Harvard and America: The Educational Leadership of Charles W. Eliot*. New York, 1972.

Hawthorne, Nathaniel. *Passages from American Notebooks*, ed. G. P. Lathrop. Boston, 1883.

——. *The Blithedale Romance*, ed. G. P. Lathrop. Boston, 1883.

Hay, John. *Letters and Extracts from a Diary*. 3 vols. Privately printed, 1908.

Higginson, Henry Lee. *Life and Letters*. Boston, 1921.

Higginson, Thomas Wentworth. *Army Life in a Black Regiment*. 1869. Reprint. New York, 1962.

——. *Letters and Journals of Thomas Wentworth Higginson: 1846–1906*, ed. Mary T. Higginson. Boston, 1921.

——. *Margaret Fuller Ossoli*. Boston, 1884.

——. *Part of a Man's Life*. 1905. Reprint. Port Washington, N.Y., 1971.

Hitchcock, Henry Russell. *The Architecture of H. H. Richardson and His Times*. New York, 1937.

Holmes, Oliver Wendell, Jr. *Touched with Fire: Civil War Letters and Diary of Oliver Wendell Holmes, 1861–1864*, ed. Mark A. DeWolfe Howe. New York, 1969.

Hooper, Ellen Sturgis. *Poems*. Privately printed, n.d.

Hovey, R. B. *John Jay Chapman: An American Mind*. New York, 1959.

Howe, Mark A. DeWolfe. *John Jay Chapman and His Letters*. Boston, 1937.

——, ed. *Later Years of the Saturday Club, 1870–1920*. Boston, 1927.

——. *Life and Letters of George Bancroft*. New York, 1908.

——. "The Tale of Tanglewood." *Yale Review* 32 (Winter, 1943).

James, Henry. *The American Scene*. New York, 1967.

——. *The Complete Tales of Henry James*, ed. Leon Edel. 12 vols. Philadelphia, 1964.

——. *The Golden Bowl*. New York, 1905.

——. *Portrait of a Lady*. New York, 1881.

——. *The Speech and Manners of American Women*, ed. E. S. Riggs. Lancaster, Pa., 1973.

——. *William Wetmore Story and His Friends*. 2 vols. Boston, 1903.

James, William. *Letters*, ed. Henry James. Boston, 1920.

King, Clarence. *Memoirs*. New York, 1904.

La Farge, John. *An Artist's Letters from Japan*. New York, 1897.

Lerner, Max, ed. *The Mind and Faith of Justice Holmes: His Speeches, Essays, Letters and Judicial Opinions.* New York, 1943.

Lodge, Henry C. *Early Memories.* New York, 1913.

Loring, Charles G. *Memoir of the Honorable William Sturgis.* Boston, n.d.

Lowell, James Russell. *The Poetical Works of James Russell Lowell.* 4 vols. Boston, 1868.

Lowell, Josephine Shaw. *Public Relief and Private Charity.* New York, 1884.

Lurie, Edward. *Louis Agassiz: A Life in Science.* Chicago, 1960.

Lynn, Kenneth S. *William Dean Howells: An American Life.* New York, 1971.

Massey, Mary E. *Bonnet Brigades.* New York, 1966.

Nightingale, Barbara (Lady Stephen). *Emily Davis and Girton College.* London, 1927.

Norton, Charles Eliot. *The Letters of Charles Eliot Norton with Biographical Comment,* ed. Sara Norton and Mark A. DeWolfe Howe. 2 vols. Boston, 1913.

Nye, Russell. *George Bancroft: Brahmin Rebel.* New York, 1944.

Parkman, Francis. *Letters of Francis Parkman,* ed. Wilbur R. Jacobs. 2 vols. Norman, Okla., 1960.

————. "Parkman's Dark Years: Letters to Mary Dwight Parkman." *Harvard Library Bulletin* 4 (1950).

Paton, Lucy Allen. *Elizabeth Cary Agassiz.* Cambridge, Mass., 1918.

Pearson, Elizabeth W., ed. *Letters from Port Royal, 1862–1868.* New York, 1969.

Perry, Ralph Barton. *The Thought and Character of William James.* 2 vols. Boston, 1935.

Porte, Joel. *Representative Man: Ralph Waldo Emerson in his Time.* New York, 1979.

Pumpelly, Raphael. *Reminiscences.* New York, 1918.

Rusk, Ralph L. *The Life of Ralph Waldo Emerson.* New York, 1949.

Saint-Gaudens, Homer. *The Reminiscences of Augustus Saint-Gaudens.* New York, 1913.

Samuels, Ernest. *Bernard Berenson: The Making of a Connoisseur.* Cambridge, Mass., 1979.

Sayre, R. F. *The Examined Self: Benjamin Franklin, Henry Adams, Henry James.* Princeton, 1964.

Smith, Henry Nash. "Emerson's Problem of Vocation: A Note on the American Scholar." *New England Quarterly* 12 (March 1939).

Stafford, William T. *James's Daisy Miller: The Story, the Play, the Critics.* New York, 1963.

Stewart, William R., ed. *The Philanthropic Work of Josephine Shaw Lowell.* New York, 1911.

Stickney, Trumbull. *The Poems of Trumbull Stickney,* ed. Amberys Whittle. New York, 1966.

Strouse, Jean. *Alice James: A Biography.* Boston, 1980.

Sturgis, William. "The Northwest Fur Trade and the Indians of the Oregon Country, 1788–1820." In *Old South Leaflets,* no. 219 (Massachusetts Historical Society).

Swift, Lindsay. *Brook Farm: Its Members, Scholars, and Visitors.* Secaucus, N.J., 1973.

Tanner, Tony, ed. *Henry James: Modern Judgments*. London, 1968.

Tharp, Louise H. *Adventurous Alliance*. Boston, 1959.

———. *The Appletons of Beacon Hill*. New York, 1973.

———. *The Peabody Sisters of Salem*. Boston, 1950.

———. *Saint-Gaudens and the Gilded Era*. Boston, 1969.

Thayer, William R. *The Life and Letters of John Hay*. 2 vols. New York, 1908.

Vanderbilt, Kermit. *Charles Eliot Norton: Apostle of Culture in a Democracy*. Cambridge, Mass., 1959.

Vedder, Elihu. Papers. Archives of American Art, microfilm 516 (1866). Smithsonian Institution.

Vitzthum, Richard C. *The American Compromise: Theme and Method in the Histories of Parkman, Bancroft, and Adams*. Norman, Okla., 1936.

Wade, Mason. *Margaret Fuller: Whetstone of Genius*. New York, 1940.

Waern, Cecilia. *John La Farge*. London, 1896.

Whitehill, Walter M. *The Boston Public Library: A Centennial History*. Cambridge, Mass., 1956.

Whitman, Walt. *Leaves of Grass*. New York, 1944.

Wilkins, Thurman. *Clarence King*. New York, 1938.

Winner, Viola Hopkins. *Henry James and the Visual Arts*. Charlottesville, N.C., 1970.

Yeazell, Ruth Bernard. *The Death and Letters of Alice James*. Berkeley, 1980.

# Non-Rational Influences

Alvarez, A. *The Savage God: A Study of Suicide*. London, 1971.

Appignanesi, Lisa. *Femininity and the Creative Imagination: A Study of Henry James, Robert Musil, and Marcel Proust*. New York, 1973.

Beard, Mary. *Woman as Force in History*. New York, 1940.

Beck, Aaron T. *Depression: Clinical, Experimental and Theoretical Aspects*. New York, 1970.

Bowlby, John. *Separation: Anxiety and Anger*. Vol. 2 of Psychology of Attachment and Loss Series. London, 1973.

———. "Pathological Mourning and Childhood Mourning." *Journal of American Psychiatric Association* 11 (1963).

Buck, Paul. "Harvard Attitudes Toward Radcliffe in the Early Years." Massachusetts Historical Society Publication (Boston, 1962).

Caplan, Ruth B., and Gerald Caplan. *Psychiatry and Community in Nineteenth-Century America*. New York, 1969.

Cott, Nancy F. *The Bonds of Womanhood: "Woman's Sphere" in New England, 1780–1835*. New Haven, 1977.

———, ed. *Root of Bitterness*. New York, 1972.

Dain, Norman. *Concepts of Insanity in the United States, 1789–1865*. New Brunswick, N.J., 1964.

Degler, Carl. *At Odds: Women and the Family in America from the Revolution to the Present*. New York, 1980.

Deutsch, Helene. *The Psychology of Women.* 3 vols. New York, 1944.

Douglas, Jack D. *Social Meanings of Suicide.* Princeton, 1967.

Durkheim, Emile. *Suicide: A Study in Sociology,* ed. George Simpson. New York, 1951.

Fieve, Ronald. *Moodswing: The Third Revolution in Psychiatry.* New York, 1975.

Finley, Ruth. *Lady of Godey's.* Philadelphia, 1931.

Forbes, Edward Waldo. "The Agassiz School." Cambridge Historical Society Publication. Cambridge, Mass., vol. 35, October 1954.

Freud, Sigmund. *The Basic Writings of Sigmund Freud.* New York, 1938.

———. *Civilization and Its Discontents,* ed. and tr. James Strachey. New York, 1962.

———. *Creativity and the Unconscious: Papers on the Psychology of Art, Literature, Love, Religion.* New York, 1958.

———. "Mourning and Melancholia." In vol. 4 of *Collected Papers of Sigmund Freud,* 5 vols. tr. Joan Riviere. New York, 1917.

———. *Totem and Taboo.* Tr. A. A. Brill. New York, 1918.

Gibbs, Jack P., and Walter T. Martin. *Status Integration and Suicide: A Sociological Study.* Eugene, Ore., 1964.

Grob, Gerald N. *The State and the Mentally Ill: A History of Worcester State Hospital in Massachusetts, 1830–1920.* Chapel Hill, N.C., 1965.

Hendin, Herbert. *Black Suicide.* New York, 1969.

———. *Suicide and Scandinavia: A Psychoanalytic Study of Culture and Character.* New York, 1964.

Hooper, Thomas, and Charles H. Pope. *Hooper Genealogy.* Salem, 1908.

Janeway, Elizabeth. *Man's World, Woman's Place: A Study in Social Mythology.* New York, 1971.

Lerner, Gerda. *The Majority Finds Its Past: Placing Women in American History.* New York, 1974.

Lifton, Robert J., and Erik Erikson, eds. *Explorations in Psychohistory: The Wellfleet Papers.* New York, 1974.

———. *History and Human Survival.* New York, 1961.

Loewald, Hans. "Internalization, Separation, Mourning, and the Super-Ego." *Psychoanalytic Quarterly* 31 (October 1962).

McCaughey, Robert A. "The Transformation of American Adademic Life: Harvard University, 1821–1892." *Perspectives in American History* 8. (Cambridge, Mass., 1974).

Maguire, Mary. "A Curtain-Raiser to the Founding of Radcliffe College." Cambridge Historical Society Publication. Cambridge, Mass. vol. 36, April 1955.

Masaryk, Thomas G. *Suicide and the Meaning of Civilization,* tr. William B. Weist and Robert G. Batson. Chicago, 1970.

Mazlish, Bruce, ed. *Psychoanalysis and History.* Englewood Cliffs, N.J., 1963.

Menninger, Karl A. *Man Against Himself.* New York, 1938.

Mill, John Stuart. *Essays on Sex Equality,* ed. Alice S. Rossi. Chicago, 1970.

Miller, Jean Baker, ed. *Psychoanalysis and Women.* Harmondsworth, Eng., 1973.

Miller, Jill Barbara Menes. "Children's Reactions to the Death of a Parent: A Review of the Psychoanalytic Literature." *Journal of the American Psychoanalytic Association* 19 (October 1971).

Morantz, Regina. "The Lady and Her Physician." In *Clio's Consciousness Raised:*

*New Perspectives on the History of Women*, ed. Lois Banner and Mary Hartman. New York, 1974.

Morison, Samuel Eliot. *Three Centuries of Harvard, 1636–1936*. Cambridge, Mass., 1936.

Myerson, Dr. Abraham, and Rosalie Boyle. "The Incidence of Manic-Depressive Disease in Certain Socially Prominent Families." *American Journal of Psychiatry* 98 (1941–1942).

Nagera, Humberto. "Children's Reactions to the Death of Important Objects." *Psychoanalytic Study of the Child* 25 (July 1970).

O'Neill, William L. *Everyone Was Brave: The Rise and Fall of Feminism in America*. Chicago, 1969.

Parkman, Francis. "The Woman Question." *North American Review* 129 (October 1879).

———. "The Woman's Question Again." *North American Review* 130 (January 1880).

Pollock, George H. "Childhood Parent and Sibling Loss in Adult Patients." *Archives of General Psychiatry* 7 (New York, 1962).

Pollock, G. H., B. Malzberg and R. G. Fuller. *Hereditary and Environmental Factors in the Causation of Manic-Depressive Psychoses and Dementia Praecox*. Utica, N.Y., 1939.

Pomeroy, Sarah. *Little-Known Sisters of Well-Known Men*. Boston, 1912.

Putnam, Emily James. *The Lady: Studies of Certain Significant Phases of Her History*. New York, 1910.

Rahv, Philip. "The Heiress of All the Ages." In *Image and Idea*. New York, 1957.

Roosevelt, Eleanor. *Autobiography of Eleanor Roosevelt*. New York, 1961.

Rhys, Jean. *Tigers Are Better Looking*. New York, 1976.

Rothman, David J. *The Discovery of the Asylum: Social Order and Disorder in the New Republic*. Boston, 1971.

Sartre, Jean-Paul. *Anti-Semite and Jew*. New York, 1948.

Schafer, Roy. *Aspects of Internalization*. New York, 1968.

Shneidman, Edwin S., ed. *Essays in Self-Destruction*. New York, 1967.

Sicherman, Barbara. "Wear and Tear: Doctors, Patients, and the Rise of Neurasthenia." In *Clio's Consciousness Raised: New Perspectives on the History of Women*, ed. Lois Banner and Mary Hartman. New York, 1974.

Siggins, L. "Mourning: A Critical Survey of the Literature." *International Journal of Psychoanalysis* 47 (1966).

Smith-Rosenberg, Carroll. "The Female World of Love and Ritual: Relations between Women in Nineteenth-Century America." In *Signs* I, no. 1. (Chicago, 1975).

Stengel, Erwin. *Suicide and Attempted Suicide*. London, 1964.

Sturgis, Roger Foxton. *Edward Sturgis and His Descendants*. Boston, 1914.

Veevers, J. E. "Parenthood and Suicide: An Examination of a Neglected Variable." *6th International Association for Suicide Prevention Proceedings*. Los Angeles, 1972.

Verbrugge, Martha. "Woman and Medicine in Nineteenth-Century America." *Signs* I, no. 4. (Chicago, 1976).

Vicinus, Martha, ed. *Suffer and Be Still: Women in the Victorian Age*. Bloomington, Ind., 1972.

Von Andics, Margarethe. *Suicide and the Meaning of Life.* London, 1947.

Warner, Marina. *Alone of All Her Sex: The Myth and the Cult of the Virgin Mary.* New York, 1976.

Welter, Barbara. "The Cult of True Womanhood, 1820–1860." *American Quarterly* 18 (Summer, 1966).

———, ed. *The Woman Question in American History.* Hinsdale, Ill., 1973.

Wilson, E. O. *Sociobiology.* Cambridge, Mass., 1975.

———. *The Insect Societies.* Cambridge, Mass., 1971.


## Bibliographical Supplement to the Paperback Edition

Adams, Henry. *The Letters of Henry Adams, 1858–1918,* ed. J. C. Levenson et al. 6 vols. Cambridge, Mass., 1982–1988.

Chalfant, Edward. *Both Sides of the Ocean.* Vol. 1 of *A Biography of Henry Adams.* Hamden, Conn., 1982.

———. *Better in Darkness.* Vol. 2 of *A Biography of Henry Adams, His Second Life, 1862–1891.* Hamden, Conn., 1994.

Contosta, David R., and Robert Muccigrosso, eds. *Henry Adams and His World.* Philadelphia, 1993.

Dawidoff, Robert. *The Genteel Tradition and the Sacred Rage: High Culture vs. Democracy in Adams, James, and Santayana.* Chapel Hill, N.C., 1992.

Jacobson, Joanne. *Authority and Alliance in the Letters of Henry Adams.* Madison, Wisc., 1992.

James, Henry, and Henry Adams. *The Correspondence of Henry James and Henry Adams, 1877–1914,* ed. George Monteiro. Baton Rouge, La., 1992.

Nagel, Paul C. *The Adams Women: Abigail and Louisa Adams, Their Sisters and Daughters.* New York, 1987.

———. *Descent from Glory: Four Generations of the John Adams Family.* New York, 1983.

O'Toole, Patricia. *The Five of Hearts: An Intimate Portrait of Henry Adams and His Friends, 1880–1918.* New York, 1990.

Secrest, Meryle. *Being Bernard Berenson.* New York, 1979.

# A Selective Genealogy of the Three Families of Marian (Clover) Hooper Adams

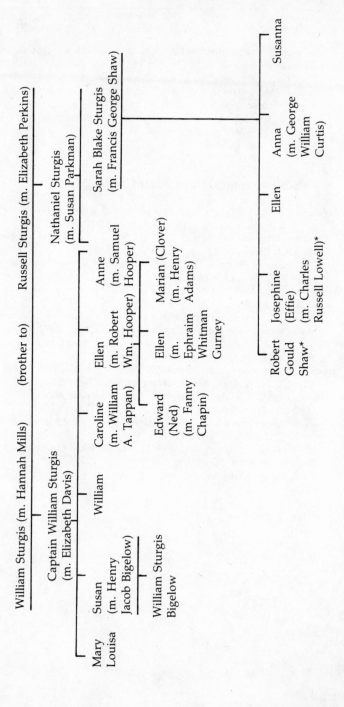

STURGIS

William Sturgis (m. Hannah Mills)    (brother to)    Russell Sturgis (m. Elizabeth Perkins)

Captain William Sturgis
(m. Elizabeth Davis)

Nathaniel Sturgis
(m. Susan Parkman)

Sarah Blake Sturgis
(m. Francis George Shaw)

Mary Louisa

Susan
(m. Henry Jacob Bigelow)

William

Caroline
(m. William A. Tappan)

Ellen
(m. Robert Wm. Hooper)

Anne
(m. Samuel Hooper)

Robert Gould Shaw*

Josephine (Effie)
(m. Charles Russell Lowell)*

Ellen

Anna
(m. George William Curtis)

Susanna

William Sturgis Bigelow

Edward (Ned)
(m. Fanny Chapin)

Ellen
(m. Ephraim Whitman Gurney)

Marian (Clover)
(m. Henry Adams)

HOOPER

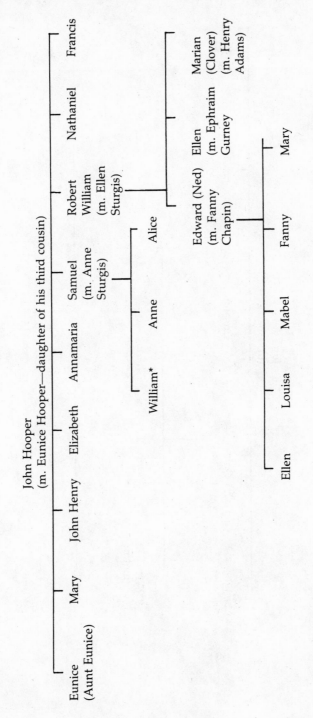

John Hooper
(m. Eunice Hooper—daughter of his third cousin)

Eunice
(Aunt Eunice)

Mary

John Henry

Elizabeth

Annamaria

Samuel
(m. Anne
Sturgis)

William*

Anne

Alice

Robert
William
(m. Ellen
Sturgis)

Nathaniel

Francis

Edward (Ned)
(m. Fanny
Chapin)

Ellen
(m. Ephraim
Gurney)

Marian
(Clover)
(m. Henry
Adams)

Ellen

Louisa

Mabel

Fanny

Mary

*Killed in the Civil War

ADAMS

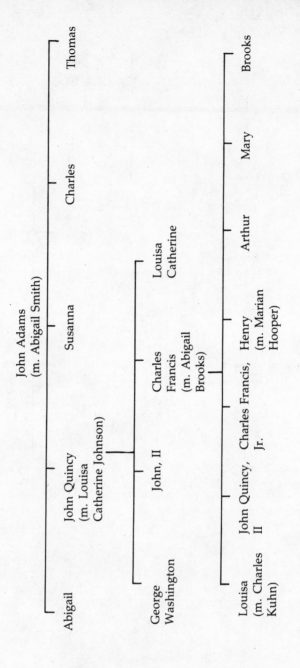

John Adams
(m. Abigail Smith)

Abigail — John Quincy (m. Louisa Catherine Johnson) — Susanna — Charles — Thomas

George Washington — John, II — Charles Francis (m. Abigail Brooks) — Louisa Catherine

Louisa (m. Charles Kuhn) — John Quincy, II — Charles Francis, Jr. — Henry (m. Marian Hooper) — Arthur — Mary — Brooks

# Index